# THE REAWAKENING OF THE ARAB WORLD

# The Reawakening of the Arab World

Challenge and Change in the Aftermath of the Arab Spring

Samir Amin

MONTHLY REVIEW PRESS
*New York*

Copyright © Samir Amin 2012, 2016
All rights reserved.

A portion of this book was originally published by Pambazuka Press under the title of *The People's Spring: the Future of the Arab Revolution* (2012).

Library of Congress Cataloging-in-Publication Data:
Names: Amin, Samir, author.
Title: The reawakening of the Arab world : Challenge and Change in the Aftermath of the Arab Spring
  / by Samir Amin.
Other titles: People's spring
Identifiers: LCCN 2015044225 | ISBN 9781583675977 (pbk.) | ISBN 9781583675984 (hardcover) | ISBN 9781583675991 (ebk. trade) | ISBN 9781583676004 (ebk. institutional)
Subjects: LCSH: Arab countries—Politics and government—21st century. | Arab Spring, 2010- | Democracy—Arab countries. | Nationalism—Arab countries. | Arab countries—Foreign relations—United States. | United States—Foreign relations--Arab countries.
Classification: LCC JQ1850.A91 A55 2016 | DDC 909/.097492708312—dc23
LC record available at http://lccn.loc.gov/2015044225

Monthly Review Press
146 West 29th Street, Suite 6W
New York, New York 10001

monthlyreview.org

5 4 3 2 1

# Contents

Introduction to the English Edition – An Afterword on
the Long-Term Prospects of the Arab World     6

Introduction to the French Edition     18

1　An Arab Springtime?     21

2　The Geostrategic Plan of the U.S. in Trouble     45

3.　The Middle East as the Hub of the Ancient World System     84

4　The Decline: The Mameluke State, the Miscarriage of the Nahda, and Political Islam     124

5　The Leap Forward: The Bandung Era and Arab Popular Nationalisms     141

6　The Drift of the National Popular Project towards 'Re-Compradorising'     168

Conclusion: A Formidable Challenge     229

Index     233

# Introduction to the English Edition
# —An Afterword on the *Reawakening of the Arab World*

I would like to comment on the important events that have taken place since I sent the original French edition of this book to the publisher in May 2011.

## Why the so-called Arab spring?

The uprising of Arab peoples as of early 2011 was not unexpected, at least by many Arab activists, if not by the Western powers.

During the Bandung and non-alignment period (1955–80), the Arab countries were in the forefront of the struggles of the peoples, the nations and the states of the South for a better future and a less unequal global system. Algeria's National Liberation Front (FLN) and Boumediene, Nasser's Egypt, the Baath regimes in Iraq and Syria, and the South Yemen Republic shared common characteristics. These were not 'democratic' regimes according to Western criteria (they were one-party systems), nor even according to our criteria, which imply positive empowerment of the people. But they were nevertheless legitimate in the eyes of their peoples for their actual achievements – mass education, health and other public services, industrialisation and guarantees of employment, upward social mobility – all of which were associated with independent initiatives and anti-imperialist postures. They were therefore continuously and fiercely fought by the Western powers, in particular through Israel's repeated aggressions.

These regimes achieved whatever they could within a short time frame, say 20 years, and thereafter ran out of steam, as a result of their internal limits and contradictions. This, coinciding with the breakdown of Soviet power, facilitated the imperialist neoliberal offensive. The ruling circles, in order to remain in office, chose to retreat and submit to the demands of neoliberal globalisation. The result was a fast degradation of social conditions and the loss within a few years of all that which had been achieved in the era of the national popular state, to the benefit of the popular and middle classes, with poverty and mass unemployment being the normal result of the neoliberal policies that were pursued. That created the objective conditions for the revolts. It is curious to note that some of the most vocal supporters of the 'democratic revolutions', calling on the West to come to their rescue, are some of the former leaders who supported the neoliberal alignment with enthusiasm.

The revolts were therefore not unexpected and many indicators pointed in their direction, for example the strike of the Tunisian miners (Gafsa), the Egyptian mass strikes of 2007–08, the growing resistance of small peasants to their accelerated expropriation by the rich peasants and the protest of the new middle class organisations such as Kefaya. I would also point to similar processes in Bahrain, which were savagely crushed by the army of Saudi Arabia (without the least protest from the West), and in Yemen where al Qaida was 'introduced' in order to neutralise the 'menace' coming from the progressive forces, which were particularly strong in the South.

This chapter was concluded by the elections in Tunisia and Egypt.

## The electoral victories of political Islam in Egypt and Tunisia

The electoral victory of the Muslim Brothers and the Salafists in Egypt (January 2012) came as little surprise. The degradation produced by contemporary capitalist globalisation has brought about a breathtaking expansion of so-called 'informal' activities which, in Egypt, provide the means of survival of more than half the population (60 per cent, according to the statistics). The Muslim Brothers are in a strong position to take advantage of this degradation and to perpetuate it. Their simple ideology gives a legitimacy to this primitive bazaar economy. The fabulous amounts of money put at their disposal (by the Gulf countries) enable them to carry out effective actions: financial advances to the informal economy and charity work (healthcare centres and others). This is how the Brothers have insinuated themselves into society and rendered it dependent on them. But this success would have been difficult if it had not responded perfectly to the objectives of the Gulf countries, Washington and Israel. These three intimate allies share the same concern: to dismantle the recovery of

Egypt. A strong Egypt, standing on its own feet, would mean the end of the triple hegemony of the Gulf (submission to the discourse on the Islamisation of society), of the United States (a compradorised and impoverished Egypt that remains in their fold) and of Israel (a powerless Egypt that leaves Palestine alone).

The planned aborting of the Egyptian revolution would thus guarantee the continuation of the system that has been in place since Sadat, based on the alliance between the army command and political Islam. Any change in the sharing out of the benefits of this alliance to the benefit of the Brothers may, however, prove difficult.

The Constituent Assembly that issued from the elections of October 2011 in Tunisia will be dominated by a right-wing bloc, bringing together Ennahda, the Islamist party and numerous reactionary cadres who used to be part of the Ben Ali regime and who are still in place, infiltrated into the 'new parties' under the name of 'Bourguibism'. They all share the same unconditional support for the market economy – such as it is – in other words, a system of dependent and subaltern capitalism. France and the United States want nothing more: 'If we want things to stay as they are, things will have to change' (from Lampedusa's *The Leopard*).'

Nevertheless there are two changes on the agenda. The positive one is that it will be a democracy that is political but not social (that is, a low-intensity democracy), which will tolerate different opinions, have more respect for 'human rights' and put an end to the horrors of the preceding regime. The negative one is that there will probably be a regression as far as women are concerned.

In other words, it will be a return to a multiparty Bourguibism with Islamic colouring. The plan of the Western powers, which is based on the strength of the reactionary comprador bloc, is to end this transition that should be short (which the movement has accepted without calculating the consequences) so as not to give time for the social struggles to organise themselves, thus allowing the reactionary bloc to claim exclusive legitimacy through proper elections. The Tunisian movement has not been very interested in the economic policy of the deposed regime, concentrating its criticism on the corruption of the president and his family. Many of the protesters, even on the left, do not question the basic orientations of the development model that

Bourguiba and Ben Ali have implemented. The result was therefore foreseeable.

However, the same causes sometimes produce the same effects. What will the popular classes in Egypt and Tunisia think and do when they see their social conditions inexorably deteriorate, with all the unemployment and precariousness that this entails, not to mention probable further deteriorations intensified by the general crisis of the capitalist world? It is too soon to say, but one cannot ignore the fact that only a rapid consolidation of a radical left, going well beyond the demand for proper elections, can enable a return to the struggle for change that is worthy of the name. It is the responsibility of this radical left to formulate a strategy for the democratisation of the society which will go much further than the simple holding of proper elections and associate this democratisation with social progress. This would mean abandoning the present development model and reinforcing initiatives for an international stance that is independent and openly anti-imperialist. It is not the imperialist monopolies and their international servants (the World Bank, the International Monetary Fund, the World Trade Organisation) that will help the countries to climb out of their ditch. It is by turning towards new partners in the South that this can become less difficult.

None of the fundamental questions seem to concern the main political players. It all seems as if the final objective of the revolution had been to proceed rapidly to elections – as if the exclusive source of the legitimacy of power lay in the ballot boxes. But there is a higher legitimacy – that of struggle. These two forms of legitimacy will face some serious confrontations in the future.

## A word about the Salafism (salafiyya)

Salafism came to complement an obscurantist advocacy by Rachid Reda and the Muslim Brotherhood. It openly rejects the idea of liberty (and therefore democracy) as it contradicts, in their view, the nature of the human being, who is created as a slave (note the word used by the Salafis) to serve the creator-master in the way that a slave is required to serve their master. Of course, this doctrine does not explain how we come to establish the actual demands of this master-creator in the modern world. Does he accept or reject the increase in wages, for example? This opens the way for a religious, Iranian-style rule (*wilayat al-faqih*), through the dictatorship of the clerics, who declared themselves *ulema,* who monopolise this knowledge.

The Salafis are the enemies of modernity because modernity is grounded on the right to human creativity in dealing with earthly matters and questions concerning human society. And creativity requires freedom and free critical thought, which is rejected by the Salafis. What then about Salafi leaders who say that they belong to the modern world because they teach their students about computers and business management (and this by resorting to the mediocre kind of American pamphlets distributed by USAID)? These statements are not only a farce; they also show that the real master here is the prevailing capitalist imperialism that needs servants who practise this art and nothing more.

The Muslim Brotherhood and the Salafis operate in conjunction and divide the tasks between them. The Muslim Brotherhood needed a 'certificate' of democracy, which Obama gave them, and to win that had to separate themselves from the 'extremists', the Salafis.

## Are internal reforms possible in Algeria?

Algeria and Egypt were, in the Arab world, the two avant-garde countries in the first 'awakening of the South', the Bandung era of non-alignment and the victorious affirmation of post-colonial nationalism. This was because of their authentic, progressive and important economic and social achievements and it should have ushered in a promising future. But then these two countries got bogged down and finally accepted their 'return to the fold' of the states and societies dominated by imperialism.

The Algerian model gave clear signs of being more coherent, which explains why it has been able to resist further deterioration. For this reason the Algerian governing class remains composite yet divided, split between the national aspirations still held by some and the rallying to compradorisation of others (sometimes these two conflicting elements combine in the same individuals). In Egypt, on the other hand, the dominant class has become, after Sadat and then

Mubarak, a comprador bourgeoisie that no longer has any national aspirations.

There are two major reasons for this difference. The war for liberation in Algeria naturally brought about a social and ideological radicalisation. But in Egypt, Nasserism developed towards the end of the period of growth, initiated by the revolution of 1919, which became radical in 1946. The ambiguous coup d'état of 1952 occurred in response to the impasse of the movement.

The colonisation of Algeria wrought major destruction of the society, and the new Algeria that emerged after the victory of independence had nothing in common with the pre-colonial epochs. It became a plebeian society, with a strong aspiration to equality. The strength of this aspiration was not to be found anywhere else in the Arab world, either in the Maghreb or in the Mashreq. In contrast, modern Egypt was built up from the beginning (starting with Mohamed Ali) by its aristocracy, which gradually became an aristocratic bourgeoisie (or a capitalist aristocracy). These differences led to another one, clearly important, concerning the future of political Islam. As Hocine Belalloufi shows in *La démocratie en Algérie: réforme ou revolution?* (forthcoming), Algerian political Islam (the FIS) had revealed its hideous face and was put to rout. This certainly does not mean that the question is definitively shelved. But this is very different to the situation in Egypt, which has seen a solid convergence between the power of the comprador bourgeoisie and the political Islam of the Muslim Brothers.

The different possible responses to the current challenges stem from these differences between the two countries. It seems to me that Algeria is better placed (or less badly placed) to respond to these challenges, at least in the short term. Economic, political and social reforms controlled from inside seem to me to still have some chance in Algeria. In contrast, in Egypt the confrontation between the movement and the anti-revolutionary reactionary bloc must, inexorably, become more acute.

Algeria and Egypt are two prime examples of societies that until now have been powerless to deal with the challenge. They are two countries that would be possible candidates for 'emergence'. The main responsibility for failure can certainly be put down to the governing classes and the existing power systems. But the role of society, its intellectuals and the militants in the movements in struggle, must also be seriously examined.

Is the same hope of a peaceful democratic evolution possible in Morocco? I doubt that the Moroccan people will continue to subscribe to an archaic dogma that does not dissociate the monarchy (of the divine right: *amir el mouminine*) from the nation. This is doubtless the reason why the Moroccans do not understand the Sahrawi question: the proud nomads of the Sahara have another conception of Islam, which prohibits them from kneeling to anyone else but Allah, even if he be the king.

## The Syrian disaster

The US were surprised by the Tunisian and Egyptian popular revolts. They now plan to pre-empt possible similar movements by initiating armed revolts of small groups supported by them. This strategy was tested with success in Libya (now a disintegrated country) and, as I write, in Syria. The reader can refer here to my papers on Libya (2011a) and Somalia (2011b) in Pambazuka News.

The Syrian Baathist regime belonged in the past to the cluster of national popular experiences (though not democratic) in the style of Nasserism and other experiences in the era of Bandung. And when the limits of possible, actual achievements within this framework became apparent, Hafez el Assad turned to a project that sought to combine the preservation of nationalist patriotism that is oppositional to colonialism on the one hand and, on the other hand, to benefit from the right-conservative concessions reflected in the 'openness' (liberalisation) which was similar to the route taken by Nasser following the defeat of 1967.

The subsequent history of this project became apparent. In Egypt, it led immediately after the death of Nasser in 1970 to surrender without reservation to the demands of the reactionary axis consisting of the United States, the Gulf and Israel. In Syria, this liberalisation led to the same results as it had in other countries, that is, to the serious, rapid deterioration of social conditions for poorer classes, which eroded the legitimacy of the regime. In the current developments, the Syrian regime has confronted protests with repression, and nothing else. The

Muslim Brotherhood took advantage of the opportunity to cast itself as the 'opposition'. Thus a coherent plan crystallised under the leadership of imperialism and its allies, which sought not to rid the Syrian people of a dictator, but to destroy the Syrian state in a manner modelled on the United States' work in Iraq and Libya.

This is where the profound relationship of the tripartite interests is apparent: (1) for the US, the goal is the breaking up of the Iran–Syria–Hezbollah alliance, which is an obstacle to the US entrenching its control over the region; (2) for Israel, the goal is to have Syria fragmented into sectarian mini-states; and (3) for the Gulf Arab states, the goal is the entrenching of a Sunni dictatorship in the Wahhabi style, although this dictatorship will be established on the massacres and criminal elimination of Alawis, Druze and Christians. Turkey plays an active role, along with the US (never forget that Turkey is a NATO member) in the implementation of that plan. In its Hatay province, Turkey has established camps for the recruitment and training of killers (so-called Muslims) who are infiltrated into Syria (see Kimyongur 2011).

In the face of this possible, dangerous fate, the Assad regime remains apparently unable to respond with the only effective policy, which is to engage in genuine reforms and negotiations. This is the only way to strengthen a democratic front, components of which are present despite the efforts being made to mute its voice. This wide movement has resisted joining the so-called liberation front, manipulated by the foreign powers, but simultaneously does not support the regime and the strategy of simply opposing state terrorism to the 'Islamic/Salafi' terrorism.

## The geostrategy of imperialism and the question of democracy

What I have wanted to show in this book is that depoliticisation has been decisive in allowing political Islam to come to the fore. This depoliticisation is certainly not confined to Nasserite Egypt. It has been the dominant practice in all the national popular experiences in the first awakening of the South and even in the historical socialisms after the first phase of revolutionary fervour had passed. The common denominator has been the suppression of democratic practice (which I do not reduce to the holding of multiparty elections), in other words the lack of respect for the diversity of opinions and political proposals and, possibly, their organisation. Politicisation requires democracy. And democracy cannot exist except when liberty is given to the 'adversaries'. In all cases its suppression, which is thus at the origin of depoliticisation, is responsible for the subsequent disaster. This may take the form of nostalgia for the past (religious or otherwise), or the adoption of 'consumerism' and the false individualism encouraged by the Western media, as was the case for the peoples of Eastern Europe and the former USSR. It was also the case, not only within the middle classes (possible beneficiaries of development) but equally within the popular classes who, lacking alternatives, aspire to benefit from it, even on a very small scale (which is perfectly understandable and legitimate).

In the case of Muslim societies, this depoliticisation is the principal form of the apparent 'return' of Islam. The articulation linking the power of reactionary political Islam, comprador submission and impoverishment through the informal bazaar economy is not specific to Egypt. It is already to be found in most Arab and Muslim societies, as far as Pakistan and beyond. The same articulation operates in Iran: the triumph of its bazaar economy was clearly, right from the start, the main result of the 'Khomeini revolution'. This same articulation of Islamic power and the bazaar market economy has devastated Somalia, which has now disappeared from the map of existing nations (Amin 2011b).

The strategy of contemporary imperialism for the region (the 'great Middle East') does not aim at all at establishing some form of democracy. It aims at destroying the countries and societies through the support of so-called Islamic regimes which guarantee the continuation of a 'lumpen development' (to use the words of my late friend A.G. Frank), that is, a process of continuous pauperisation. Eventual 'high rates of growth', praised by the World Bank, are meaningless, being based on the plunder of natural resources, associated with fast-growing inequality in the distribution of income and pauperisation for the majorities.

Iraq provides the model for the region. The dictatorship of Saddam Hussein has been replaced by no less than three (perhaps more) terror regimes, in the name of religion (Sunni and Shia) and of ethnicity (the Kurds), which are associated with the systematic destruction of the infrastructures and industries and the planned assassination of tens of thousands of the elite citizens, in particular engineers and scientists, as well as the destruction of the education system (which was not bad in the time of Saddam) so that it is reduced to the teaching of religion and business. These are also the aims for Syria.

The next target is Iran, under the pretext of its nuclear development, using to that effect Israel, which is unable to do the job without the active involvement of US forces. Iran, whatever one may think of its regime (associating the rule of Islam and the market economy) does constitute an obstacle to the deployment of US military control over the region, so this country must be destroyed.

The final real target of contemporary imperialism is containment and thereafter the rolling back by pre-emptive war of the most dangerous emerging countries (China first). Add here Russia, which, if it succeeds in modernising its army, can put an end to the exclusive military power of the US.

That implies the total subordination of all other countries of the South with a view to ensuring exclusive access to the natural resources of the whole planet by the societies of the Triad (US, Europe and Japan), their plunder and waste. It implies therefore further lumpen development, further pauperisation and more terrorist regimes. Contemporary capitalism has nothing else to offer.

What, therefore, could happen if this political Islam takes power in Egypt and elsewhere?

We are swamped by reassuring discourses about this, which are incredibly naïve – whether sincere or false. 'It's fate, our societies are impregnated by Islam. This has been ignored and it is now imposing itself', some say, as if the success of political Islam was not due to the depoliticisation and the social degradation that is deliberately ignored. 'It is not so dangerous; its success is only temporary and the failure of political Islam in power will lead to loss of support among the public.' This is what Washington pretends to believe, as do the opinions fabricated by the dominant media and the cohorts of Arab intellectuals, either through opportunism or lack of lucidity.

No, this is not true. Reactionary political Islam's exercise in power may last, say, 50 years. And while it helps to sink the societies that it subjugates each day into insignificance on the world chessboard, the others will continue their advance. At the end of this sad 'transition' these countries will find themselves at the bottom in the world classification.

The question of democratic politicisation is, in the Arab world as elsewhere, the central theme of the challenge. Our era is not one of democratic advances but, on the contrary, of regression in this field. The extreme concentration in the capital of the generalised monopolies permits, indeed demands, the unconditional and total submission of political power to its orders. The accentuation of presidential powers seems to be highly individualised but in fact it is integrally subordinated to servicing the financial plutocracy. This is the form taken by the drift that is annihilating the defunct bourgeois democracy (which was once reinforced by the conquests of the workers), replacing it by a democratic farce.

In the peripheries, the embryos of democracy, where they exist, go hand in hand with a social regression that is still more violent than in the centres of the system and they are thus losing their credibility. The retreat of democracy is synonymous with depoliticisation. Democracy implies the arrival on the scene of citizens capable of formulating alternative projects for society and not just envisaging *alternance* (alternation, with no change) through meaningless elections. As citizens who have creative imagination have disappeared, they are being replaced by depoliticised individuals who are passive spectators of the political scene, consumers modelled by the system, who (wrongly) believe that they are free individuals.

Progress towards the democratisation of societies and the repoliticisation of the peoples are indissoluble. But how to start? The movement can begin from one or the other of these two poles. Nothing can substitute the detailed analysis of actual situations, in Algeria and in Egypt, as in Greece, China, Congo, Bolivia, France or Germany. If there are no visible advances in this direction, the world will be caught up (as already it shows signs of doing) in the chaos caused by the implosion of the system. In that case, the worst is to be feared.

## References

Amin, Samir (2011a) 'Libya could break up like Somalia', Pambazuka, 7 September, http://www.pambazuka.org/en/category/features/76091, accessed 27 April 2012

Amin, Samir (2011b) 'Is there a solution to the problems of Somalia?', Pambazuka News, 17 February, http://www.pambazuka.org/en/category/features/70973, accessed 27 April 2012

Belalloufi, Hocine (forthcoming) *La démocratie en Algérie: réforme ou revolution?*

Kimyongur, Bahar (2011) *Syriana, la conquète continue*, Charleroi, Couleur Livre

# Introduction to the French Edition

The year 2011 opened with a series of shattering explosions of anger on the part of the Arab peoples. But will this Arab 'spring' be capable of finding solutions to the challenges facing the democratic forces in Egypt and other Arab countries? The arguments for positive or negative responses to this question are equally powerful and convincing.

The Arab world (and beyond it, the Muslim world in general) had managed, long ago, to impose itself as an active protagonist in shaping the ancient, pre-modern globalisation. But it was unable to avoid decline and it succumbed to the assaults of modern capitalist globalisation, despite repeated, serious attempts in the 19th century, and then in the 20th century, to emerge from its status as a periphery dominated by the imperialism of the Western powers.

If the challenge is to be met it is necessary to abandon, once and for all, backward-looking illusions, that is, the whole perspective of the 'Islamisation of society and politics'. This does not mean rallying to the shoddy goods of Westernisation, which can be perfectly compatible with the 'Islamisation' in process, but rather a liberation of the inventive capacities of the Arab peoples (oriented towards inventing the future and not harking back to the past). This is necessary if they are going to become active agents in shaping their future with and at the side of other peoples struggling against dominant capitalism/imperialism.

In order to reflect and act, it is necessary to return to a critical reading of the past and present of the Arab world. When did it become 'the Arab world'? I'll respond to this question in the introduction to chapter 2.

The first chapter of this book sets out an interpretation of the explosions of 2011, while the following four chapters retrace the long evolution of the place of the Arab world in the world systems of yesterday and today, in the framework of 'global history'.

These four chapters are organised around four main concepts: the hub, the decline, the leap forward, the drift. These correspond to the historical succession of the place and role of the Arab world in the ancient tributary systems of the world, then in the successive phases of the development of the globalised capitalist system. There is some overlapping because a few of the old characteristics have continued over time, sometimes up to the present day.

These thoughts have been developed in a good number of my former writings, some of them dedicated to countries in the Arab world (Egypt, the Maghreb, Syria and Iraq, the 'Arab nation'), others being about more general issues arising from the nature of the 'global' systems concerned. I have retained only the essential aspects of the question for this presentation. The more curious can read further about these developments, as indicated in the bibliography.

The world system up until 1500 was only concerned with the eastern hemisphere of the planet (Eurasia and Africa), which developed in (reciprocal) ignorance of the 'pre-Colombian' worlds. But from 1500 the system concerned the whole planet, integrated in the development of the new globalised capitalism.

The 'springs' of the Arab peoples, like those that the peoples of Latin America have been experiencing over the last two decades, are what I call the second awakening of the peoples of the South. The first awakening occurred in the 20th century until it came up against the counter-offensive of neoliberal capitalism/imperialism. The second has taken various forms, from explosions against the autocracies that accompanied the spread of neoliberalism to a questioning of the international order by the 'emergent' countries. These 'springs' thus coincide with the 'autumn of capitalism': the decline of the capitalism of the generalised, globalised and financialised monopolies. The movements aim, like those of the preceding century, at regaining the independence of the peoples and states of the peripheries of the system, to recover their initiative in transforming the world. They are, therefore, above all anti-imperialist movements and hence potentially anti-capitalist.

If the present movements succeed in converging with the workers in the imperialist centres in another necessary awakening, there could be an authentic socialist perspective at the level of the whole of humanity. But this is in no way bound to happen as a 'historical necessity'. The decline of capitalism can open the way to a long transition towards socialism – or it can conduct humanity into generalised barbarism. Such a terrifying prospect can be brought about by a combination of the project for the military control of the planet by the armed forces of the United States and their subordinate allies in NATO, which is already under way, the decline of democracy in the countries of the imperialist centre and the nostalgic refusal of democracy in the countries of the South in revolt (which take the form of illusions by religious 'fundamentalists' as proposed by Islam, Hinduism and Buddhism).

The struggle for secular democratisation is therefore decisive at the present time, opposing the prospect of an emancipation of peoples to that of generalised barbarism.

# 1

# An Arab Springtime?

The year 2011 began with a series of shattering, wrathful explosions from the Arab peoples. Was this springtime the inception of a second awakening of the Arab world? Or will these revolts bog down and finally prove abortive – as was the case with the first episode of that awakening, which was evoked in my book *The Awakening of the South (L'éveil du Sud)*? If the first hypothesis is confirmed, the forward movement of the Arab world will necessarily become part of the movement to go beyond imperialist capitalism on the world scale. Failure would maintain the Arab world in its current status as a submissive periphery, prohibiting its elevation to the rank of an active participant in shaping the world. It is always dangerous to generalise about the 'Arab world', thereby ignoring the diversity of objective conditions characterising each country of that world. So I will concentrate the following reflections on Egypt, which is easily recognised as playing and having always played a major role in the general evolution of its region.

Egypt was the first country in the periphery of globalised capitalism that tried to 'emerge'. Even at the start of the 19th century, well before Japan and China, the Viceroy Mohamed Ali had conceived and undertaken a programme of renovation for Egypt and its near neighbours in the Arab Mashreq (Mashreq means 'East', i.e., eastern North Africa and the Levant). That vigorous experiment took up two-thirds of the 19th century and only belatedly ran out of breath in the 1870s, during the second half of the reign of Khedive Ismail. The analysis of its failure cannot ignore the violence of the foreign aggression by Great Britain, the foremost power of industrial capitalism during that period. Three times, in the naval campaign of 1840 and then by taking control of the khedive's finances during the 1870s, and then finally by military occupation in 1882, England fiercely pursued its objective: to make sure that a modern Egypt would fail to emerge. Certainly, the Egyptian project was subject to the limitations of its time since it manifestly envisaged emergence within and through capitalism, unlike Egypt's second attempt at emergence – which we will discuss further on. That project's own social contradictions, like its underlying political, cultural, and ideological presuppositions, undoubtedly had their share of responsibility for its failure. The fact remains that without imperialist aggression those contradictions would probably have been overcome, as they were in Japan. Beaten, emergent Egypt was forced to undergo nearly 40 years (1880–1920) as a servile periphery, whose institutions were refashioned in service to that period's model of capitalist/imperialist accumulation. That imposed retrogression struck, over and beyond its productive system, the country's political and social institutions. It operated systematically to reinforce all the reactionary and medievalistic cultural and ideological conceptions that were useful for keeping the country in its subordinate position.

The Egyptian nation – its people, its elites – never accepted that position. This stubborn refusal in turn gave rise to a second wave of rising movements which unfolded during the next half-century (1919–67). Indeed, I see that period as a continuous series of struggles and major forward movements. It had a triple objective: democracy, national independence and social progress. These three objectives – however limited and sometimes confused were their formulations – were inseparable one from the other, an inseparability identical to the expression of the effects of modern Egypt's integration into the globalised capitalist/imperialist system of that period. In this reading, the chapter (1955–67) of Nasserist systematisation is nothing but the final chapter of that long series of advancing struggles, which began with the revolution of 1919–20.

The first moment of that half-century of rising emancipatory struggles in Egypt had emphasised – with the formation of the Wafd in 1919 – political modernisation through adoption (in 1923) of a bourgeois form of constitutional democracy (limited monarchy) and the reconquest of independence. The form of democracy envisaged allowed progressive secularisation – if not secularism in the radical sense of that term – whose symbol was the flag linking cross and crescent (a flag that reappeared in the demonstrations of January and February 2011). 'Normal' elections then allowed, without the least problem, not merely for Copts (native Egyptian Christians) to be elected by Muslim majorities but for those very Copts to hold high positions in the state.

The British put their full power, supported actively by the reactionary bloc comprising the monarchy, the great landlords and the rich peasants, into undoing the democratic progress made by Egypt under Wafdist leadership. In the 1930s the dictatorship of Sedki Pasha, abolishing the democratic 1923 constitution, clashed with the student movement then spearheading the democratic anti-imperialist struggles. It was not by chance that, to counter this threat, the British embassy and the royal palace actively supported the formation in 1927 of the Muslim Brotherhood, inspired by 'Islamist' thought in its most backward 'Salafist' variant of Wahhabism as formulated by Rachid Reda – the most reactionary version, antidemocratic and against social progress, of the newborn 'political Islam'.

The conquest of Ethiopia undertaken by Mussolini, with world war looming, forced London to make some concessions to the democratic forces. In 1936 the Wafd, having learned its lesson, was allowed to return to power and a new Anglo-Egyptian treaty was signed. The Second World War necessarily constituted a sort of parenthesis. But a rising tide of struggles, resumed as early as 21 February 1946 with the formation of the worker–student bloc, reinforced in its radicalisation by the entry on stage of the communists and of the working-class movement. Once again the Egyptian reactionaries, supported by London, responded with violence and to this end mobilised the Muslim Brotherhood behind a second dictatorship by Sedki Pasha – without, however, being able to silence the protest movement. Elections had to be held in 1950 and the Wafd returned to power. Its repudiation of the 1936 treaty and the inception of guerrilla actions in the Suez Canal Zone were defeated only by setting fire to Cairo (January 1952), an operation in which the Muslim Brotherhood was deeply involved.

A first coup d'état in 1952 by the Free Officers, and above all a second coup in 1954 by which Nasser took control, was taken by some to 'crown' the continual flow of struggles and by others to put it to an end. Rejecting the view of the Egyptian awakening advanced above, Nasserism put forth an ideological discourse that wiped out the whole history of the years from 1919 to 1952 in order to push the start of the Egyptian revolution to July 1952. At that time many among the communists had denounced this discourse and analysed the coups d'état of 1952 and 1954 as aimed at putting an end to the radicalisation of the democratic movement. They were not wrong, since Nasserism only took the shape of an anti-imperialist project after the Bandung Conference of April 1955. Nasserism then contributed all it had to give: a resolutely anti-imperialist international posture (in association with the Pan-Arab and Pan-African movements) and some progressive (but not socialist) social reforms. The whole thing was done from above, not only without democracy (the popular masses being denied any right to organise by and for themselves) but even by abolishing any form of political life. This was an invitation to political Islam to fill the vacuum thus created. In only ten short years (1955–65) the Nasserist project used up its progressive potential. Its exhaustion offered imperialism, henceforward led by the United States, the chance to break the movement by mobilising to that end its regional military instrument: Israel. The 1967 defeat marked the end of the tide that had flowed for half a century. Its reflux was initiated by Nasser himself, who chose the path of concessions to the right (the *infitah* or 'opening', an opening to capitalist globalisation, of course) rather than the radicalisation called for by, among others, the student movement (which held the stage briefly in 1970, shortly before and then after the death of Nasser). His successor, Sadat, intensified and extended the rightward turn and integrated the Muslim Brotherhood into his new autocratic system. Mubarak continued along the same path.

The following period of retreat lasted, in its turn, almost another half century. Egypt, submissive to the demands of globalised liberalism and to US strategy, simply ceased to exist as an active factor in regional or global politics. In its region the major US allies – Saudi Arabia and Israel – occupied the foreground. Israel was then able to pursue the course of expanding its colonisation of occupied Palestine with the tacit complicity of Egypt and the Gulf countries.

Under Nasser Egypt had set up an economic and social system that, though subject to criticism, was at least coherent. Nasser wagered on industrialisation as the way out of the colonial international specialisation which was confining the country in the role of cotton exporter. His system maintained a division of incomes that favoured the expanding middle classes without impoverishing the popular masses. Sadat and Mubarak dismantled the Egyptian productive system, putting in its place a completely incoherent system based exclusively on the profitability of firms most of which were mere subcontractors for the imperialist monopolies. Supposed high rates of economic growth, much praised for thirty years by the World Bank, were completely meaningless. Egyptian growth was extremely vulnerable. Moreover, such growth was accompanied by an incredible rise in inequality and by unemployment afflicting the majority of the country's youth. This was an explosive situation. It exploded.

The apparent 'stability of the regime', boasted of by successive US officials like Hillary Clinton, was based on a monstrous police apparatus counting 1,200,000 men (the army numbering a mere 500,000), free to carry out daily acts of criminal abuse. The imperialist powers claimed that this regime was protecting Egypt from the threat of Islamism. This was nothing but a clumsy lie. In reality the regime had perfectly integrated reactionary political Islam (on the Wahhabite model of the Gulf) into its power structure by giving it control of education, the courts and the major media (especially television). The sole permitted public speech was that of the Salafist mosques, allowing the Islamists, to boot, to pretend to make up 'the opposition'. The cynical duplicity of the US establishment's speeches (Obama no less than Bush) was perfectly adapted to its aims. The de facto support for political Islam destroyed the capacity of Egyptian society to confront the challenges of the modern world (bringing about a catastrophic decline in education and research), while by occasionally denouncing its 'abuses' (like assassinations of Copts) Washington could legitimise its military interventions as actions in its self-styled 'war against terrorism'. The regime could still appear 'tolerable' as long as it had the safety valve provided by mass emigration of poor and middle-class workers to the oil-producing countries. The exhaustion of that system (Asian immigrants replacing those from Arabic countries) brought with it the rebirth of opposition movements. The workers' strikes in 2007 (the strongest strikes on the African continent in the past 50 years), the stubborn resistance of small farmers threatened with expropriation by agrarian capital, and the formation of democratic protest groups among the middle classes (like the Kefaya and April 6 movements) foretold the inevitable explosion – expected by Egyptians but startling to foreign observers. And thus began a new phase in the tide of emancipation struggles, whose directions and opportunities for development we are now called on to analyse.

## The components of the democratic movement

The Egyptian revolution now underway shows that it possible to foresee an end to the neoliberal system, shaken in all its political, economic, and social dimensions. This gigantic movement of the Egyptian people links three active components: youth 'repoliticised' by their own will in 'modern' forms that they themselves have invented; the forces of the radical left; and the forces of the democratic middle classes. Youth (about one million activists) spearheaded the movement. They were immediately joined by the radical left and the democratic middle classes. The Muslim Brotherhood, whose leaders had called for a boycott of the demonstrations during their first four days (sure, as they were, that the demonstrators would be routed by the repressive apparatus) only accepted the movement belatedly once its appeal, heard by the entire Egyptian people, was producing gigantic mobilisations of 15 million demonstrators.

The youth and the radical left sought in common three objectives: restoration of democracy (ending the police/military regime), the undertaking of a new economic and social policy favourable to the popular masses (breaking with the submission to demands of globalised liberalism), and an independent foreign policy (breaking with the submission to the requirements of US hegemony and the extension of US military control over the whole planet). The democratic revolution for which they call is a democratic social and anti-imperialist revolution. Although the youth movement is diversified in its social composition and in its political and ideological expressions, it places itself as a whole 'on the left'. Its strong and spontaneous expressions of sympathy with the radical left testify to that.

The middle classes as a whole rally around only the democratic objective, without necessarily objecting thoroughly to the 'market' (such as it is) or to Egypt's international alignment. Not to be neglected is the role of a group of bloggers who take part, consciously or not, in a veritable conspiracy organised by the CIA. Its animators are usually young people from the wealthy classes, extremely 'Americanised', who nevertheless present themselves as opponents of the established dictatorships. The theme of democracy, in the version required for its manipulation by Washington, is uppermost in their discourse on the net. That fact makes them active participants in the chain of counter-revolutions, orchestrated by Washington, disguised as 'democratic revolutions' on the model of the East European 'color revolutions'. But it would be wrong to think that this conspiracy is behind the popular revolts. What the CIA is seeking is to reverse the direction of the movement, to distance its activists from their aim of progressive social transformation and to shunt them onto different tracks. The scheme will have a good chance of succeeding if the movement fails to bring together its diverse components, identify common strategic objectives, and invent effective forms of organisation and action. Examples of such failure are well known – look at Indonesia and the Philippines. It is worthy of note that those bloggers – writing in English rather than Arabic(!) – setting out to defend 'American-style democracy' in Egypt often present arguments serving to legitimise the Muslim Brotherhood.

The call for demonstrations enunciated by the three active components of the movement was quickly heeded by the whole Egyptian people. Repression, extremely violent during the first days (more than a thousand deaths), did not discourage those youths and their allies (who at no time, unlike in some other places, called on the Western powers for any help). Their courage was decisive in drawing 15 million Egyptians from all the districts of big and small cities, and even villages, into demonstrations of protest lasting days (and sometimes nights) on end. Their overwhelming political victory had as its effect that fear switched sides. Obama and Hillary Clinton discovered that they had to dump Mubarak, whom they had hitherto supported, while the army leaders ended their silence and refused to take over the task of repression – thus protecting their image – and wound up deposing Mubarak and several of his more important henchmen.

The generalisation of the movement among the whole Egyptian people represents in itself a positive challenge. For this people, like any other, are far from making up a homogeneous bloc. Some of its major components are without any doubt a source of strength for the perspective of radicalisation. The 5-million strong working class's entry into the battle could be decisive. The combative workers, through numerous strikes, have advanced further in constructing the organisations they began in 2007. There are already more than 50 independent unions. The stubborn resistance of small farmers against the expropriations permitted by abolition of the agrarian reform laws (the Muslim Brotherhood cast its votes in parliament in favour of that vicious legislation on the pretext that private property was 'sacred' to Islam and that the agrarian reform had been inspired by the Devil, a communist!) is another radicalising factor for the movement. What is more, a vast mass of the poor took active part in the demonstrations of February 2011 and often participate in neighbourhood popular committees 'in defence of the revolution'. The beards, the veils, the dress styles of these poor folk might give the impression that in its depths Egyptian society is Islamic, even that it is mobilised by the Muslim Brotherhood. In reality, they erupted onto the stage and the leaders of that organisation had no choice but to go along. A race is thus underway: who – the Brotherhood and its (Salafist) Islamist associates or the democratic alliance – will succeed in forming effective alliances with the still-confused masses and even to (a term I reject) 'get them under discipline'?

Conspicuous progress in constructing the united front of workers and democratic forces is happening in Egypt. In April 2011 five socialist-oriented parties (the Egyptian Socialist Party, the Popular Democratic Alliance – made up of a majority of the membership of the former loyal-left Tagammu party – the Democratic Labour Party, the 'Trotskyist' Socialist Revolutionary Party, and the Egyptian Communist Party, which had been a component of Tagammu) established an Alliance of Socialist Forces through which they committed themselves to carry out their struggles in common. In parallel, a National Council (Maglis Watany) was established by all the active political and social forces of the movement (the socialist-oriented parties, the diverse democratic parties, the independent unions, the peasant organisations, the networks of young people and numerous social associations). The council has about 150 members, the Muslim Brotherhood and the right-wing parties refusing to participate and thus reaffirming their well-known opposition to continuation of the revolutionary movement.

# An Arab Springtime?

## Confronting the democratic movement: the reactionary bloc

Just as in past periods of rising struggle, the democratic social and anti-imperialist movement in Egypt is up against a powerful reactionary bloc. This bloc can perhaps be identified in terms of its social composition (its component classes, of course) but it is just as important to define it in terms of its means of political intervention and the ideological discourse serving its politics.

In social terms, the reactionary bloc is led by the Egyptian bourgeoisie taken as a whole. The forms of dependent accumulation operative over the past 40 years brought about the rise of a rich bourgeoisie, the sole beneficiary of the scandalous inequality accompanying the globalised liberal model. They are some tens of thousands, not of 'innovating entrepreneurs' as the World Bank likes to call them but of millionaires and billionaires all owing their fortunes to collusion with the political apparatus (corruption being an organic part of their system). This is a comprador bourgeoisie (in the political language current in Egypt the people term them 'corrupt parasites'). They make up the active support for Egypt's placement in contemporary imperialist globalisation as an unconditional ally of the United States. Within its ranks this bourgeoisie counts numerous military and police generals, 'civilians' with connections to the state and to the dominant National Democratic Party created by Sadat and Mubarak, and religious personalities – the whole leadership of the Muslim Brotherhood and the leading sheikhs of the Al Azhar University are all of them billionaires.

Certainly there still exists a bourgeoisie of active small and medium entrepreneurs. But they are the victims of the racketeering system put in place by the comprador bourgeoisie, usually reduced to the status of subordinate subcontractors for the local monopolists, themselves mere transmission belts for the foreign monopolies. In the construction industry this system is the general rule: the 'greats' snap up the state contracts and then subcontract the work to the 'smalls'. That authentically entrepreneurial bourgeoisie is in sympathy with the democratic movement.

The rural side of the reactionary bloc has no less importance. It is made up of rich peasants who were the main beneficiaries of Nasser's agrarian reform, replacing the former class of wealthy landlords. The agricultural cooperatives set up by the Nasser regime included both rich and poor peasants and so they mainly worked for the benefit of the rich. But the regime also had measures to limit possible abuse of the poor peasants. Once those measures had been abandoned by Sadat and Mubarak, on the advice of the World Bank, the rural rich went to work to hasten the elimination of the poor peasants. In modern Egypt the rural rich have always constituted a reactionary class, now more so than ever. They are likewise the main sponsors of conservative Islam in the countryside and, through their close (often family) relationships with the officials of the state and religious apparatuses (in Egypt the Al Azhar University has a status equivalent to an organised Muslim 'church') they dominate rural social life. What is more, a large part of the urban middle classes (especially the army and police officers but likewise the technocrats and medical/legal professionals) stem directly from the rural rich.

This reactionary bloc has strong political instruments in its service: the military and police forces, the state institutions, the privileged National Democratic Party (a de facto single party), the religious apparatus (Al Azhar), and the factions of political Islam (the Muslim Brotherhood and the Salafists). The military assistance (amounting to some $1.5 billion annually) extended by the US to the Egyptian Army never went toward the country's defensive capacity. On the contrary, its effect was dangerously destructive through the systematic corruption that, with the greatest cynicism, was not merely known and tolerated but actively promoted. That 'aid' allowed the highest ranks to take over for themselves some important parts of the Egyptian comprador economy, to the point that 'Army Incorporated' (*Sharika al geish*) became a commonplace term. The high command, which made itself responsible for directing the transition, is thus not at all neutral despite its effort to appear so by distancing itself from the acts of repression. The 'civilian' government chosen by and obedient to it, made up largely of the less conspicuous men from the former regime, has taken a series of completely reactionary measures aimed at blocking any radicalisation of the movement. Among those measures are a vicious anti-strike law (on the pretext of economic revival), and a law placing severe restrictions on the formation of political parties, aimed at confining the electoral game to the tendencies of political Islam (especially the Muslim Brotherhood), which are already well organised thanks to their systematic support by the former regime. Nevertheless, despite all that, the attitude of the army remains, at bottom, unforeseeable. In spite of the corruption of its cadres (the rank and file are conscripts, the officers professionals) nationalist sentiment has still not disappeared entirely. Moreover, the army resents having in practice lost most of its power to the police.

In these circumstances, and because the movement has forcefully expressed its will to exclude the army from political leadership of the country, it is very likely that the high command will seek in the future to remain behind the scenes rather than to present its own candidates in the elections – including the presidential one, the date of which is still not fixed. Though it is clear that the police apparatus has remained intact (their prosecution is not contemplated) like the state apparatus in general (the new rulers all being veteran regime figures), the National Democratic Party vanished in the tempest and its legal dissolution has been ordered. But we can be certain that the Egyptian bourgeoisie will make sure that its party is reborn under a different label or labels.

## Political Islam

The Muslim Brotherhood makes up the only political force whose existence was not merely tolerated but actively promoted by the former regime. As mentioned above, Sadat and Mubarak turned over to them control of education, the courts and television. The Muslim Brotherhood have never been and can never be 'moderate', let alone 'democratic'. Their leader – the *murchid* (Arabic word for 'guide' – Führer) is self-appointed and its organisation is based on the principle of disciplined execution of the leaders' orders without any sort of discussion. Its top leadership is made up entirely of extremely wealthy men (thanks, in part, to financing by Saudi Arabia – which is to say, by Washington), its secondary leadership of men from the obscurantist layers of the middle classes, its rank and file by lower-class people recruited through the charitable services run by the Brotherhood (likewise financed by the Saudis), while its enforcement arm is made up of militias (the *baltaguis*) recruited among the criminal element.

The Muslim Brotherhood are committed to a market-based economic system of complete external dependence. They are in reality a component of the comprador bourgeoisie. They have taken their stand against large strikes by the working class and against the struggles of poor peasants to hold onto their lands. So the Muslim Brotherhood are 'moderate' only in the double sense that they refuse to present any sort of economic and social programme, thus in fact accepting without question reactionary neoliberal policies, and that they are submissive de facto to the enforcement of US control over the region and the world. They are thus useful allies for Washington (and does the US have a better ally than their patron, the Saudis?), which now vouches for their 'democratic credentials'. Nevertheless, the US cannot admit that its strategic aim is to establish Islamic regimes in the region. It needs to maintain the pretence that 'we are afraid of this'. In this way it legitimises its 'permanent war against terrorism', which in reality has quite different objectives: military control over the whole planet in order to guarantee that the US–Europe–Japan Triad retains exclusive access to its resources. Another benefit of this duplicity is that it allows the Triad to mobilise the 'Islamophobic' aspects of public opinion. Europe, as is well known, has no strategy of its own in the region and is content from day-to-day to go along with the decisions of Washington. More than ever it is necessary to point out clearly this true duplicity in US strategy, which has quite effectively manipulated its deceived public's opinions. The US (with Europe going along) fears more than anything a really democratic Egypt that would certainly turn its back on its alignments with economic liberalism and with the aggressive strategy of NATO and the US. The US will do all it can to prevent a democratic Egypt, and to that end will give full support (hypocritically disguised) to the false Muslim Brotherhood alternative, which has been shown to be only a minority within the movement of the Egyptian people for real change.

The collusion between the imperialist powers and political Islam is, of course, neither new nor particular to Egypt. The Muslim Brotherhood, from its foundation in 1927 up to the present, has always been a useful ally for imperialism and for the local reactionary bloc. It has always been a fierce enemy of the Egyptian democratic movements.

And the multibillionaires currently leading the Brotherhood are not destined to go over to the democratic cause. Political Islam throughout the Muslim world is quite assuredly a strategic ally of the US and its NATO minority partners. Washington armed and financed the Taliban, who they called 'freedom fighters', in their war against the national/popular regime (termed 'communist') in Afghanistan before, during and after the Soviet intervention. When the Taliban shut the girls' schools created by the 'communists' there were 'democrats' and even 'feminists' at hand to claim that it was necessary to 'respect traditions'. In Egypt the Muslim Brotherhood are now supported by the 'traditionalist' Salafist tendency, who also are generously financed by the Gulf states. The Salafists (fanatical Wahhabites, intolerant of any other interpretation of Islam) make no bones about their extremism, and they are behind a systematic murder campaign against Copts. It is scarcely conceivable that such operations could be carried out without the tacit support (and sometimes even greater complicity) of the state apparatus, especially of the courts, which had mainly been turned over to the Muslim Brotherhood. This strange division of labour allows the Muslim Brotherhood to appear moderate, which is what Washington pretends to believe. Nevertheless, violent clashes among the Islamist religious groups in Egypt are to be expected. That is on account of the fact that Egyptian Islam has historically mainly been Sufist, the Sufi brotherhoods even now grouping 15 million Egyptian Muslims. Sufism represents an open, tolerant, Islam – insisting on the importance of individual beliefs rather than on ritual practices (they say 'there are as many paths to God as there are individuals'). The state powers have always been deeply suspicious of Sufism although, using both the carrot and the stick, they have been careful not to declare open war against it. The Wahhabi Islam of the Gulf states is at the opposite pole from Sufism: it is archaic, ritualist, conformist, declared enemy of any interpretation other than repetition of its own chosen texts, enemy of any critical spirit – which is, for it, nothing but the Devil at work. Wahhabite Islam considers itself at war with, and seeks to obliterate, Sufism, counting on support for this from the authorities in power. In response, contemporary Sufis are secularistic, even secular; they call for the separation of religion and politics (the state power and the religious authorities of Al Azhar recognised by it). The Sufis are allies of the democratic movement. The introduction of

Wahhabite Islam into Egypt was begun by Rachid Reda in the 1920s and carried on by the Muslim Brotherhood after 1927. But it only gained real vigour after the Second World War, when the oil rents of the Gulf states, supported by the US as allies in its conflict with the wave of popular national liberation struggles in the 1960s, allowed a multiplication of their financial wherewithal.

## US strategy: the Pakistan model

The three powers that dominated the Middle East stage during the ebb tide (1967–2011) were the US, the boss of the system, Saudi Arabia and Israel: three very close allies, all sharing the same dread that a democratic Egypt would emerge. Such an Egypt could only be anti-imperialist and welfarist. It would depart from globalised liberalism, would render insignificant the Gulf states and the Saudis, would reawaken popular Arab solidarity, and force Israel to recognise a Palestinian state.

Egypt is a cornerstone in the US strategy for worldwide control. The single aim of Washington and its allies Israel and Saudi Arabia is to abort the Egyptian democratic movement, and to that end they want to impose an Islamic regime under the direction of the Muslim Brotherhood – the only way for them to perpetuate the submission of Egypt. The 'democratic speeches' of Obama are there only to deceive a naïve public opinion, primarily that of the US and Europe.

There is much talk of the Turkish example in order to legitimise a government by the Muslim Brotherhood ('converted to democracy'!), but that is just a smoke screen. For the Turkish army is always there behind the scenes, and though scarcely democratic and certainly a faithful ally of NATO it remains the guarantor of secularism in Turkey. Washington's project, openly expressed by Hillary Clinton, Obama and the think tanks at their service, is inspired by the Pakistan model: an 'Islamic' army behind the scenes, a 'civilian' government run by one or more 'elected' Islamic parties. Plainly, under that hypothesis, the 'Islamic' Egyptian government would be recompensed for its submission on the essential points (perpetuation of economic liberalism and of the self-styled peace treaties permitting Israel to get on with its policy of territorial expansion) and enabled, as demagogic compensation, to pursue its projects of Islamisation of the state and of politics and of assassinating Copts. Such a beautiful democracy has Washington designed for Egypt! Obviously, Saudi Arabia supports the accomplishment of that project with all its (financial) resources. Riyadh knows perfectly well that its regional hegemony (in the Arab and Muslim worlds) requires that Egypt be reduced to insignificance. Which is to be done through Islamisation of the state and of politics; in reality, a Wahhabite Islamisation with all its effects, including anti-Copt pogroms and the denial of equal rights to women.

Is such a form of Islamisation possible? Perhaps, but at the price of extreme violence. The battlefield is Article 2 of the overthrown regime's constitution. This article stipulating that '*sharia* [the Islamic canon] is the origin of law' was a novelty in the political history of Egypt. Neither the 1923 constitution nor that of Nasser contained anything of the sort. It was Sadat who put it into his new constitution with the triple support of Washington ('traditions are to be respected'!), of Riyadh ('the Koran is all the constitution needed') and of Tel Aviv ('Israel is a Jewish state').

The project of the Muslim Brotherhood remains the establishment of a theocratic state, as is shown by its attachment to Article 2 of the Sadat/Mubarak constitution. What is more, the organisation's most recent programme further reinforces that medievalistic outlook by proposing to set up a council of *ulemas* empowered to assure that any proposed legislation is in conformity with the requirements of sharia. Such a religious constitutional council would be analogous to the one that, in Iran, is supreme over the 'elected' government. It is the regime of a religious, single super-party, all parties standing for secularism becoming 'illegal'. Their members, like non-Muslims (Copts), would thus be excluded from political life. Despite all that, the authorities in Washington and Europe talk as though the recent opportunist and disingenuous declaration by the Brotherhood that it was giving up its theocratic project (its programme staying unchanged) should be taken seriously. Are the CIA experts, then, unable to read Arabic? The conclusion is inescapable: Washington would see the Brotherhood in power, guaranteeing that Egypt remain in its grip and that of liberal globalisation, rather than that power be held by democrats who would be very likely to challenge the subaltern status of Egypt. The recently created Party of Freedom and Justice, explicitly on the Turkish model, is nothing but an instrument of the Brotherhood. It offers to admit Copts, which signifies that they have to accept the theocratic Muslim state enshrined in the Brotherhood's programme if they want the right to participate in their country's political life. Going on the offensive, the Brotherhood is setting up unions and peasant organisations and a rigmarole of diversely named political parties, whose sole objective is to foment division in the now-forming united fronts of workers, peasants and democrats – to the advantage, of course, of the counter-revolutionary bloc.

Will the Egyptian democratic movement be able to strike Article 2 from the forthcoming new constitution? The question can be answered only by going back to an examination of the political, ideological, and cultural debates that have unfolded during the history of modern Egypt.

In fact, we can see that rising-tide periods were characterised by a diversity of openly expressed opinions, leaving religion (always present in society) in the background. It was that way during the first two-thirds of the 19th century (from Mohamed Ali to Khedive Ismail). Modernisation themes (in the form of enlightened despotism rather than democracy) held the stage. It was the same from 1920 to 1970: open confrontation of views among bourgeois democrats and communists staying in the foreground until the rise of Nasserism. Nasser shut down the debate, replacing it with a populist Pan-Arab, though also modernising, discourse. The contradictions of this system opened the way for a return of political Islam. It is to be recognised, contrariwise, that in the ebb-tide phases such diversity of opinion vanished, leaving the space free for medievalism, presented as Islamic thought, that arrogates to itself a monopoly over government-authorised speech. From 1880 to 1920 the British built that diversion channel in various ways, notably by exiling (mainly to Nubia) all modernist Egyptian thinkers and actors who had been educated since the time of Mohamed Ali. But it is also to be noted that the opposition to British occupation also placed itself within that medievalistic consensus. The Nahda (begun by Afghani and continued by Mohamed Abdou) was part of that deviation, linked to the Ottomanist delusion advocated by the new Nationalist Party of Moustapha Kamil and Mohammad Farid. There should be no surprise that toward the end of that epoch this deviation led to the ultra-reactionary writings of Rachid Reda, which were then taken up by Hassan el Banna, the founder of the Muslim Brotherhood.

It was the same again in the ebb-tide years 1970–2010. The official discourse (of Sadat and Mubarak), perfectly Islamist (as proven by their insertion of sharia into the constitution and their yielding essential powers to the Muslim Brotherhood), was equally that of the false opposition, the only one tolerated, which was sermonising in the mosque. Because of this, Article 2 might seem solidly anchored in general opinion (the 'street' as American pundits like to call it).

The devastating effects of the depolarisation systematically enforced during the ebb-tide periods is not to be underestimated. The slope can never easily be re-ascended. But it is not impossible. The current debates in Egypt are centred, explicitly or implicitly, on the supposed cultural (actually, Islamic) dimensions of this challenge. And there are signposts pointing in a positive direction: the movement making free debate unavoidable – only a few weeks sufficed for the Brotherhood's slogan 'Islam is the solution' to disappear from all the demonstrations, leaving only specific demands about concretely transforming society (freedom to express opinions and to form unions, political parties and other social organisations; improved wages and workplace rights; access to landownership, to schools, to health services; rejection of privatisations and calls for nationalisations, etc). A signal that does not mislead: in the elections to the student organisation, the Brotherhood's share of the vote fell to 20 per cent where five years earlier (when its discourse was the only permitted form of supposed opposition) the Brotherhood's candidates had obtained a crushing 80 per cent majority. Yet the other side likewise sees ways to parry the 'democracy danger'. Insignificant changes to the Mubarak constitution (continuing in force), proposed by a committee made up exclusively of Islamists chosen by the army high command and approved in a hurried April referendum (an official 23 per cent negative vote but a big affirmative vote imposed through electoral fraud and heavy blackmail by the mosques), obviously left Article 2 in place. In the eyes of the corrupt elements still in charge, the legislative and presidential elections under that constitution were clearly meant to perpetuate a grand democratic fraud. The democratic movement, in contrast, seeks a longer 'democratic transition', which would allow its discourse actually to reach those big layers of the Muslim lower classes still at a loss to understand the events. But as soon as the uprising began Obama made his choice: a short, orderly (that is to say without any threat to the governing apparatus) transition, and elections that would result in victory for the Islamists. As is well known, elections in Egypt, as elsewhere in the world, are not the best way to establish democracy but are often the best way to set a limit to democratic progress.

Finally, some words about 'corruption'. Most speeches from the transition regime concentrate on denouncing it and threatening prosecution. Mubarak, his wife and some others have been arrested, but what will actually happen remains to be seen. This discourse on corruption is certainly well received, especially by the major part of naïve public opinion. But the transition regime takes care not to analyse its deeper causes and to teach that corruption (presented in the moralising style of American speech as individual immorality) is an organic and necessary component in the formation of the bourgeoisie – and not merely in the case of Egypt and of the Southern countries in general, where if a comprador bourgeoisie is to be formed the sole way for that to happen is in association with the state apparatus. I maintain that at the stage of generalised monopoly capitalism, corruption has become a basic organic component in the reproduction of its accumulation model: rent-seeking monopolies require the active complicity of the state. Its ideological discourse (the 'liberal virus') proclaims 'state hands off the economy' while its practice is 'state in service to the monopolies'.

## The storm zone

Mao was not wrong when he affirmed that actually existing (which is to say, naturally imperialist) capitalism had nothing to offer to the peoples of the three continents (the periphery made up of Asia, Africa and Latin America – a 'minority' consisting of 85 per cent of the world population) and that the South was a storm zone, a zone of repeated revolts, potentially (but only potentially) pregnant with revolutionary advances toward the socialist transcendence of capitalism.

The Arab spring is enlisted in that reality. The case is one of social revolts potentially pregnant with concrete alternatives that in the long run can register within a socialist perspective. Which is why the capitalist system, monopoly capital dominant at the world level, cannot tolerate the development of these movements. It will mobilise all possible means of destabilisation, from economic and financial pressures up to military threats. It will support, according to circumstances, either fascist and fascistic false alternatives or the imposition of military dictatorships. Not a word from Obama's mouth is to be believed. Obama is Bush with a different style of speech. Duplicity is built into the speech of all the leaders of the imperialist Triad.

I do not intend in this chapter to examine in as much detail each of the on-going movements in the Arab world (Tunisia, Libya, Syria, Yemen and others) The components of the movement differ from one country to the other, just like the forms of their integration into imperialist globalisation and the structures of their established regimes.

The Tunisian revolt sounded the starting gun, and surely it strongly encouraged the Egyptians. Moreover, the Tunisian movement has one definite advantage: the semi-secularism introduced by Bourguiba can certainly not be called into question by Islamists returning from their exile in England. But at the same time the Tunisian movement seems unable to challenge the extraverted development model inherent in liberal capitalist globalisation.

Libya is neither Tunisia nor Egypt, the ruling group (Gaddafi) and the forces fighting it being in no way analogous to their Tunisian and Egyptian counterparts. Gaddafi has never been anything but a buffoon, the emptiness of whose thought was reflected in his notorious Green Book. Operating in a still-archaic society Gaddafi could indulge himself in successive nationalist and socialist speeches with little bearing on reality, and the next day proclaim himself a liberal. He did so to 'please the West!' as though the choice for liberalism would have no social effects. But it did have such effects, and, as is commonplace, it worsened living conditions for the majority of Libyans. Those conditions then gave rise to the well-known explosion, of which the country's regionalists and political Islamists took immediate advantage. For Libya has never truly existed as a nation. It is a geographical region separating the Arab West from the Arab East (the Maghreb from the Mashreq). The boundary between the two goes right through the middle of Libya. Cyrenaica was historically Greek and Hellenistic, then it became Mashreqian. Tripolitania, for its part, was Roman and became

Maghrebian. Because of this, regionalism has always been strong in the country. Nobody knows who the members of the National Transition Council in Benghazi really are. There may be democrats among them, but there are certainly Islamists, some among the worst of the breed, as well as regionalists. The president of the National Council for the transition is Mustafa Muhammad Abdeljelil, the judge who condemned the Bulgarian nurses to death, was rewarded by Gaddafi, and named Minister of Justice from 2007 to February 2011. For that reason the prime minister of Bulgaria, Boikov, refused to recognise the Council, but his argument was not given any follow up by the United States and Europe. From its outset the movement in Libya took the form of an armed revolt fighting the army rather than a wave of civilian demonstrations. And right away that armed revolt called NATO to its aid. Thus a chance for military intervention was offered to the imperialist powers. Their aim was surely neither 'protecting civilians' nor 'democracy' but control over oilfields and acquisition of a major military base in the country. Of course, ever since Gaddafi embraced liberalism the Western oil companies had control over Libyan oil. But with Gaddafi nobody could be sure of anything. Suppose he were to switch sides tomorrow and start to play ball with the Indians and the Chinese? More important than oil are the gigantic underground water resources of Libya. Gaddafi was considering the possibility of using those resources to the benefit of the Sahelian African region. This is now over. Well-known French companies will monopolise the access to those resources and make a more profitable use of them, perhaps for agrofuels. But there is something else more important. In 1969 Gaddafi had demanded that the British and Americans leave the bases they had kept in the country since the Second World War. Currently, the United States needs to find a place in Africa for its Africom (the US military command for Africa, an important part of its alignment for military control over the world but which still has to be based in Stuttgart). With the African Union refusing to accept it, no African country has dared to do so until now. A lackey emplaced in Tripoli (or Benghazi) would surely comply with all the demands of Washington and its NATO lieutenants.

The components of the Syrian revolt have yet to make their programmes known. Undoubtedly, the rightward drift of the Baathist

# An Arab Springtime?

regime, gone over to neoliberalism and singularly passive with regard to the Israeli occupation of the Golan, is behind the popular explosion. But CIA intervention cannot be excluded: there is talk of groups penetrating into Diraa across the neighbouring Jordanian frontier. The mobilisation of the Muslim Brotherhood, which had been behind earlier revolts in Hama and Homs, is perhaps part of Washington's scheme seeking an eventual end to the Syria/Iran alliance that gives essential support to Hezbollah in Lebanon and Hamas in Gaza.

In Yemen the country was unified through the defeat of progressive forces that had governed independent South Yemen. Will the movement mark a return to life of those forces? That uncertainty explains the hesitant stance of Washington and the Gulf states.

In Bahrain the revolt was crushed at birth by massacres and intervention by the Saudi army, without the dominant media (including Al Jazeera) having much to say about it. As always, the double standard.

The Arab revolt, though its most recent expression, is not the only example showing the inherent instability of the 'storm zone'.

A first wave of revolutions, if that is what they are to be called, had swept away some dictatorships in Asia (the Philippines and Indonesia) and Africa (Mali) which had been installed by imperialism and the local reactionary blocs. But there the United States and Europe succeeded in aborting the potential of those popular movements, which had sometimes aroused gigantic mobilisations. The United States and Europe seek in the Arab world a repetition of what happened in Mali, Indonesia and the Philippines: 'to change everything in order that nothing changes.' There, after the popular movements had gotten rid of their dictators, the imperialist powers undertook to preserve their essential interests by setting up governments aligned with their foreign-policy interests and with neoliberalism. It is noteworthy that in the Muslim countries (Mali and Indonesia) they mobilised political Islam to that end.

In contrast, the wave of emancipation movements that swept over South America allowed real advances in three directions: the democratisation of state and society; the adoption of consistent anti-imperialist positions; and entry onto the path of progressive social reform.

The prevailing media discourse compares the 'democratic revolts' of the third world to those that put an end to East European 'socialism' following the fall of the Berlin Wall. This is nothing but a fraud, pure and simple. Whatever the reasons (and they were understandable) for those revolts, they signed on to the perspective of an annexation of the region by the imperialist powers of Western Europe (primarily to the profit of Germany). In fact, reduced thenceforward to the status of one of developed capitalist Europe's peripheries, the countries of Eastern Europe are still on the eve of experiencing their own authentic revolts. There are already signs foretelling this, especially in the former Yugoslavia. Revolts, potentially ripe with revolutionary advances, are foreseeable nearly everywhere on those three continents – Africa, Asia and Latin America – which more than ever remain the storm zone, by that fact refuting all the cloying discourse on 'eternal capitalism' and the stability, the peace, the democratic progress attributed to it. But those revolts, to become revolutionary advances, will have to overcome many obstacles: on the one hand they will have to overcome the weaknesses of the movement, arrive at positive convergence of its components and formulate and implement effective strategies; and on the other they will have to turn back the interventions (including military interventions) of the imperialist Triad. Any military intervention of the United States and NATO in the affairs of the Southern countries must be prohibited no matter its pretext, even seemingly benign 'humanitarian' intervention. Imperialism seeks to permit neither democracy nor social progress to those countries. Once it has won the battle, the lackeys whom it sets up to rule will still be enemies of democracy. One can only regret profoundly that the European left, even when it claims to be radical, has lost all understanding of what imperialism really is.

The discourse currently prevailing calls for the implementation of international law authorising, in principle, intervention whenever the fundamental rights of a people are being trampled. But the necessary conditions allowing for movement in that direction are just not there. The international community does not exist. It amounts to the US embassy, followed automatically by those of Europe. No need to enumerate the long list of such worse-than-unfortunate interventions (Iraq, for example) with criminal outcomes. Nor to cite the double standard common to them all (obviously one thinks of the trampled rights of the Palestinians and the unconditional support of Israel, of the innumerable dictatorships still being supported in Africa).

## Springtime for the people of the South and autumn for capitalism

The springtime of the Arab peoples, like that which the peoples of Latin America have been experiencing for two decades now and which I refer to as the second wave of awakening of the Southern peoples – the first having unfolded in the 20th century until the counteroffensive unleashed by neoliberal capitalism/imperialism – takes on various forms, running from explosions aimed against precisely those autocracies participating in the neoliberal ranks to challenges by 'emerging countries' to the international order. These springtimes thus coincide with the autumn of capitalism, the decline of the capitalism of globalised, financialised, generalised, monopolies. These movements begin, like those of the preceding century, with peoples and states of the system's periphery regaining their independence, retaking the initiative in transforming the world. They are thus, above all, anti-imperialist movements and so are only potentially anti-capitalist. Should these movements succeed in converging with the other necessary reawakening, that of the workers in the imperialist core, a truly socialist perspective could be opened for the whole human race. But that is in no way a predestined 'historical necessity'. The decline of capitalism might open the way for a long transition toward socialism, but it might equally well put humanity on the road to generalised barbarism. The on-going US project of military control over the planet by its armed forces, supported by their NATO lieutenants, the erosion of democracy in the imperialist core countries, and the medievalistic rejection of democracy within Southern countries in revolt (taking the form of 'fundamentalist' semi-religious delusions disseminated by political Islam, political Hinduism and political Buddhism) all work together toward that dreadful outcome. At the current time the struggle for secularist democratisation is crucial for the perspective of popular emancipation, crucial for opposition to the perspective of generalised barbarism.

### Complementary readings

Hassan Riad (1964) *L'Egypte nassérienne*, Paris, Editions de Minuit
Samir Amin (1978) *The Arab Nation*, London, Zed Books
Samir Amin (2006) *A Life Looking Forward, Memoirs of an Independent Marxist*, London, Zed Books

Samir Amin (2008) *L'éveil du Sud*, Paris, Le temps des cerises. The reader will find there my interpretations of the achievements of the viceroy Muhammad Ali (1805–48) and of the Khedives who succeeded him, especially Ismail (1867–79); of the Wafd (1920–52); of the positions taken by Egyptian communists in regard to Nasserism; and of the deviation represented by the Nahda from Afghani to Rachid Reda.

Gilbert Achcar (2010) *The Arabs and the Holocaust: The Arab-Israeli War of Narratives*, New York, Metropolitan Books. The best analysis of the components of political Islam (Rachid Reda, the Muslim Brotherhood, the modern Salafists).

# Concerning the relationship between the North/South conflict and the opposition between the beginning of a socialist transition and the strategic organisation of capitalism, see:

Samir Amin (2011) *Ending the Crisis of Capitalism or Ending Capitalism?*, Oxford, Pambazuka Press

Samir Amin (2011) *The Law of Worldwide Value*, New York, Monthly Review Press

Samir Amin (2008) *The World We Wish to See*, New York, Monthly Review Press

Samir Amin (2011) 'The trajectory of historical capitalism and Marxism's tricontinental vocation', *Monthly Review*, 62(9)

Gilbert Achcar (2011) *Le choc des barbaries*, Brussels, Editions Complexe

# 2

# The Geostrategic Plan of the United States in Trouble

"The revolution has not changed the regime, but it changed the people."

– *written on the walls of Cairo*

Since the first edition of my book *The People's Spring: The Future of the Arab Revolution* (September 2011) much has changed in Cairo, which I have to take into account. As an observer of, and actor on, the Egyptian political scene, I also felt the need to publish in Arabic an update of my first analysis of the ongoing revolution. A book published in Arabic with the title of "The Egyptian Revolution after June 30" (English translation of the title) was released in September 2013 in the aftermath of the Sisi triumph. I also published some fifty articles and interviews, mostly in Arabic, French, and subsequently in English, between summer 2011 and spring 2015.

It is useful to recap for the reader the events that punctuated this story from 25 January 2011, when 15 million protesters demanded the departure of Mubarak, demands that the Muslim Brotherhood condemned:

- *28 January 2011*: mass escape from the Cairo prison of the Muslim Brotherhood and common criminals released by Hamas militia (the Muslim Brotherhood that governs Gaza) who had penetrated Egypt illegally.
- *11 February 2011*: Mubarak's abdication in favor of the Supreme Council of Armed Forces (SCAF) headed by Marshal Tantawi.
- *March 2011*: reform of the constitution drafted by a group of lawyers appointed by SCAF, all close to the Muslim Brotherhood, adopted in haste by referendum.

- *October/November 2011*: parliamentary elections won by the Muslim Brotherhood (50 percent of the votes) and the Salafis (25 percent).
- *April 2012*: invalidation of parliamentary elections by the Constitutional Court on account of massive fraud.
- *June 2012*: presidential elections occur, whose early date was decided by Marshal Tantawi, with the agreement of the Ambassador of the United States (Anne Patterson), and after the release of Khairat el-Shater (the de facto supreme leader of the Muslim Brotherhood). Four to five million votes go to each of the four major candidates: two Muslim Brotherhood people, including Morsi, Hamdeen Sabbahi (Nasserite), and General Shafiq (former Minister of Mubarak). In the second round Morsi overpowered Shafiq. At least, this is what the US Embassy was quick to declare even before the Constitutional Council had given its ruling.
- *December 2012 and following weeks*: repeated coups by Morsi, who makes arbitrary changes to the constitution, establishes a 'Legislative Council' consisting almost exclusively of the Muslim Brotherhood, and appoints the members of a committee (also all Muslim Brothers) to prepare a draft of an 'Islamic constitution.'
- *30 June 2013*: huge demonstration against Morsi and the government of the Muslim Brotherhood (30 million participants).
- *3 July 2013*: Abdel Fattah el Sisi, who succeeded Tantawi (who had been retired by SCAF), dismisses Morsi, dissolves the Legislative Council, and cancels the proposed Islamic constitution.
- *December 2013*: the Muslim Brotherhood are banned and declared to be a terrorist organisation.
- *4 January 2014*: second constitutional referendum occurs; the constitution is approved by 98 percent of voters.
- *May/June 2014:* presidential elections are held: Sisi wins with over 95 percent of the votes cast against his rival, Sabbahi.
- *March 2015*: major international economic conference is held in Sharm el-Sheikh with the goal of obtaining foreign financial contributions for the major Egyptian projects (doubling the Suez Canal, oil and gas exploitation).

Of course I will return repeatedly in this text to these electoral farces, to the unfailing support provided by the United States to their preferential ally (the Muslim Brotherhood), and to the acts of fascist gangsterism practiced by Morsi and his cronies while in government for a year, which was a decisive factor in their fall.

## The single-mindedness of the media on Egypt

Since 2011, international information about Egypt has consistently been mostly misinformation. Some facts are blown up (a few hundred Muslim Brotherhood demonstrators are presented as a huge show of force), others hidden (such as the signature campaign demanding the resignation of President Morsi with twenty-five million signatures collected). But beyond the selection of these so-called facts, there is misinformation about the situation analysis and about the definition of challenges in Egypt. The media clergy, serving the financial aristocracy of NATO and its Gulf allies (especially the media chain Al Jazeera), dominate the scene. The discourse reproduces ad nauseam the same song:

- The concepts and ambitions of nationalism – Nasserite in this case – and of communism all come from a past irrevocably gone, the days of the Cold War.
- Electoral democracy and adjusting to the demands of liberal globalisation are the only realistic ways forward, the only bearers of possible progress.
- People, especially those from Muslim countries, have always given, and give now more than ever, a priority to the expression of their identity through their religious beliefs.
- The only mass movement that exists in Egypt, and in many other countries, is represented by the Islamic current.
- This Islamic current is plural and differentiated and is not inherently incompatible with democracy.
- The Muslim Brotherhood, especially in Egypt, is able to convert to democracy.
- Egypt has been governed since 1952 by military dictatorships.
- The first free election in Egypt was carried out by civilians, and

the Muslim Brotherhood and the Salafists had a strong majority in Parliament and in the presidency.
- President-elect Morsi was overthrown by a military coup on 3 July 2013.
- The only acceptable way out of chaos and to avert the threat of civil war demands the return to power of the elected civilian president.

Each of these statements is contrary to what any serious analysis of the history and current events in Egypt and elsewhere in the world would conclude. There is therefore no objective information nor realistic analysis but simply poisoning propaganda by the current major powers: international financial capital and the policy instruments at its sole devotion.

## Conspiracy or imperialist conquest strategy?

The widespread explosion of popular anger in Tunisia and Egypt in 2010 and 2011 was predictable. There were strong warning signs – the Gafsa miner strikes in Tunisia, the repeated strikes in Egypt, the first daring demonstration in Cairo by Kefaya – announcing that the explosion was imminent. The explosion nevertheless surprised the prevailing consensus, with the exception of a few individuals and perhaps the embryos of potentially radical parties. It certainly also surprised the dominant powers and their sponsors (the CIA, amongst others). These two popular movements expressed themselves through huge peaceful demonstrations that were largely spontaneous and involved a broad range of social forces whose anger and motives were therefore many and varied, even if they could be potentially broadly convergent. The diversity of the anger of the general movement, the fragmentation of the claims (democratic rights, social justice), and the absence, or extreme weakness, of their organisations, are the obvious reasons for the reduction of their claims, at this stage, to one specific aim: to expel Ben Ali and Mubarak, respectively.

Up to the end, the Western powers supported the regimes and subjected them to the dictates of neoliberal globalisation. But, facing a growing movement and the danger of its radicalization, these same powers felt it was useful to drop their support in order to save the system.

And to do that, the United States and its subordinate European allies have chosen to involve the Muslim Brotherhood to disorient and reverse the 'revolution.'

The rainbow of the reactionary political currents of Islam – the Muslim Brotherhood, Salafists, and Jihadists – may seem to constitute only a diverse and varied nebula, and the mainstream media present it that way. I will return later to the question of the dual common denominator that unites these organisations, which are called terrorists by some, 'democratic' Islam by others because of (1) their undemocratic theocratic project and (2) their adherence to ultra reactionary neoliberal capitalist management and to their anti-popular economic and social system, the only real objective of the imperialist triad.

We know – or should know – that the Muslim Brotherhood had initially been against the popular uprisings in Egypt. They joined them later, with the encouragement of the United States and Europe.

The intervention of the imperialist powers is multifaceted. It is manifested by the open and renewed political alliance between Washington (and behind it the European capitals) and reactionary political Islam. I say renewed, since, as I have shown in the first chapter of this book, this alliance has already been operational for a long time (I would go so far as to say since the creation of the Muslim Brotherhood in 1928). But this intervention also puts in place other 'modern' means of intervention: the infiltration of popular movements by the CIA through the plethora of NGOs in its service. Amir Sharif, in his book, *L'histoire secrète des Frères Musulmans* (*The Secret History of the Muslim Brotherhood*, 2014) and Michel Raimbaud (*Tempête sur le Grand Moyen Orient*, or *Storm on the Greater Middle East*, 2014) have provided proof. These manipulations pursue the objective of maintaining and deepening the fragmentation of the movement, thus condemning demonstrators to be unable to formulate and implement a positive strategy of initiating a progressive transformation of society, of sowing ideological confusion by substituting a radical critique of globalised and imperialist liberalism with praise for diversity, and of drifting towards the defense of allegedly paramount 'identities.'

Is this a 'permanent conspiracy'? No, it is a coherent and, unfortunately, effective strategy to date, for there is a lack of an alternative left that is radical and daring, and therefore able to unite – in diversity – the legitimate claims of the victims of the system. However this strategy does not exclude 'conspiracies'; far from it. The diplomacy of Washington and CIA interventions are complementary. The overthrowing of President Allende on 11 September 1973, the murder (now with the use of drones) of a particular opponent, these are processes that should be called by their real names: conspiracy and/or state terrorism.

Having learned from being taken by surprise by the Tunisian and Egyptian explosions, Washington has decided to forestall similar movements, real or otherwise, this time by initiating a 'revolution' and simultaneously, and immediately, taking direct brutal intervention and 'preventive' war in Libya, Syria, and Yemen. And armed reactionary political Islam has been sought for this purpose.

From the beginning of the alleged Libyan 'revolts' that actually were neither popular nor pacifist, but consisted of small armed groups that attacked the security forces (police and military), and in the same vein, on the day of their intervention, they called on NATO forces for their aid. We know what it produced. Beyond the assassination of Gaddafi, the country was broken up by warlords, obviously without the slightest democratic progress. Was this a miscalculation of the NATO powers? No, that strategy had achieved its true purpose.

In Syria, where a breeding ground for the popular explosion had been fermenting since the late Baath regime's 'infitah' (submission to the demands of globalisation), peaceful demonstratios were beginning another Arab Spring. But simultaneously, and from the first day, the Muslim Brotherhood and armed Jihadists attacked the police and demanded in turn intervention by NATO (and by Turkey, which is both Islamist and a NATO member). And that has been granted. Laurent Fabius – an unconditional friend of Israel – has not gone so far as to dare to say that the Jihadists of Nosra have done 'a good job in Syria.' As they cut off the heads of Syrian soldiers, Alawites, and Christians, they were helpful friends whose only act of terrorism was to have cut off the head of a Frenchman. But one should know that Islamist fascists, like all fascists, are unable to prevent derailing abuses, as I mentioned elsewhere (see, 'Fascism returns to contemporary capitalism', *Monthly Review,* 2014). But the Syria of Bashar held, thanks in part to support from Iran and Russia, mainly because his army had not disintegrated as hoped for by Washington and European capitals.

Since 1945, the strategy that the US has developed regarding the 'green belt,' stretching from Morocco to Indonesia, is based on a strategic alliance with Saudi Arabia and reactionary political Islam. The alliance is directed not only against the communist adversaries of yesteryear (the Soviet Union and China) but equally against the Arab anti-imperialist nationalism that forced imperialism into decline at the time of Bandung. Today, despite the collapse of the Soviet Union, the shift of China, and the submission of Arab governments to the dictates of neoliberal globalisation, Washington continues the same strategy, without fail, for fear of an always-possible revival in the Arab world and Russia, capable of imposing a reorganisation of the world system based on the principle of negotiated multipolarity. The 'Islamic' ally (Wahhabi, Salafist, Jihadist) is valuable, because their eventual governing of the region condemns its people to impotence. Certainly this model of despotic government also remains unable to prevent terrorist excesses directed against the West. But in the end these abuses are useful for the further strategy of destroying Arab societies: they provide the arguments that give the appearance of legitimacy to NATO aggression and strengthen the consensus, or 'Western opinion,' which is also manipulated in this manner. With the cynicism with which it is customary, Washington diplomacy then wins both ways.

This strategy is equally that of Zionism. One could even go so far as to say that Zionism inspires the extreme attitudes taken by subalterns of the imperialist alliance, particularly France. The work of Michel Raimbaud gives convincing evidence. Washington, in contrast, reserves the right not to go to the extreme, if it is, deemed tactically necessary.

## The ephemeral triumph of the Muslim Brotherhood

Did the intervention of the Muslim Brotherhood in Egypt and of the Nahda (the Tunisian branch of the Brotherhood), as is too often claimed without much reflection, contribute to the success of the explosion of anger by providing the force demonstrators lacked to gain victory? An analysis of the facts leads to other conclusions: this intervention weakened and divided the movement, thus permitting the United States and their subaltern European allies to intervene and prevent the success of the democratic forces.

Washington and its subaltern allies have fuelled a campaign to clear the name of the Brotherhood and to make them appear as the indispensible partners of the new Arab 'democracy.' Washington thus emphasised the need, for the sake of appearances, to hold elections quickly in both Tunisia and Egypt. And in that it has been successful. But, as we should know, the use of elections is nearly always the means of halting the spread of struggles. We have seen many such examples in history (including, for example, in France in 1968).

The electoral victories of the Brotherhood and the Salafists in Tunis and in Egypt in 2011 and 2012 were not surprising. We can see the obvious explanation in the conjuncture of three dangerous developments in the societies concerned: the social catastrophe produced by economic liberalism, the depoliticisation associated with the exercise of despotism by dictators in the service of this liberalism, and the erosion of the education system, something equally required by liberalism.

The degradation produced by contemporary capitalist globalisation has led to a prodigious swelling of activities referred to as 'informal,' which in Egypt provides a means of survival for more than half of the population (the statistics indicate some 60 percent). The Muslim Brotherhood is well placed to take advantage of this degradation of existence and to perpetuate its reproduction. Their simple ideology legitimises this miserable market/bazaar economy, the antithesis of the requirements of a development worthy of its name. The fabulous financial wealth that is available to the Brotherhood (from the Gulf states) permits them to transform these resources into effective action: providing financial advances to the informal economy and supporting charitable activities (care centers, and so on). It is in this manner that the Brothers have implanted themselves in society and placed it under their control. The Gulf countries have never had the intention of supporting the development of Arab countries through industrial investments, for example. They support a model of lumpen development

– to use the phrase proposed by Andre Gunder Frank – that imprisons the societies concerned in a downward spiral of impoverishment and exclusion, which in turn strengthens the influence of reactionary political Islam in that society.

Moreover, the management of contemporary 'liberal' capitalism by the governments in power is based on systematically organised depoliticisation.

In the capitalist centers, the rallying of the historic left towards social liberalism, the foundation for an appearance of a 'consensus' society, has eliminated the significance of the previous political and social distinctions between left and right.

In the peripheries, the exhaustion and repression of all historical currents of popular nationalism has created a vacuum that religion (Islam, Hinduism, Buddhism) or ethnicity (as in Yugoslavia, Africa, and elsewhere) has filled by moving from the wings to center-stage. Under these conditions, the gibberish of dogmatic liberalism is accepted as hard cash by the dominant opinion. In the case of Egypt, reactionary political Islam has endorsed without hesitation the 'recipes' of liberal economic policies ('long live the market,' it repeats ad nauseam). Reactionary political Islam has thus contributed to shifting the center of the debate from the field of social interests and social struggles (class struggles, taking into account all practical complexities) to the arena of supposedly theological questions.

Nonetheless, democratic opinion that rejects the theocratic response (as shown by the impressive demonstrations of 30 June 2013) is itself contaminated by the 'liberal virus.' It contributes, in turn, to a shifting of the debate from economic and social issues that control reality to that of the abstract choice in favor of electoral democracy and nothing more. The general repoliticisation that has characterised the Egyptian scene since 2011 is real, visible to all. It certainly constitutes a good sign for the future. But it remains hitherto weak, in the sense that its awareness amongst the broad masses of the current real challenges in Egypt (the social devastations produced by economic liberalism) remains very inadequate. The contemporary world pays dearly for this regression of the political culture, in particular the erasure of Marxism. It is a regression characteristic of the hollowing of the historical wave, the pages of the rise and advances of the 20th century being turned, and the rebirth of a socialist movement in the 21st century rendered as a comic sentence.

Finally, it is necessary to mention the disastrous effects of the destruction of the education system. Liberalism requires that education programs meet the needs of the market. And in this spirit, the US bosses have systematically dismantled the education system in Iraq, from primary school to university, retaining ultimately little more than two courses: religion and business. Without even this brutal and cynical response, the education systems in the Arab world, as almost everywhere else on the planet, have succumbed, by privatization amongst other things, to the reforms that have deliberately excluded all 'unnecessary' teachings – philosophy, history, social thought – that are indispensable for building a society worthy of its name, with citizens free and able to express themselves in effective political terms. These reforms have favoured above all the terrorist drift. What the Western media call 'modern Islam' is nothing more than the product of the implantation of 'religion' (understood as ritualistic practice) and 'business.' The 'modern Muslims' in question are individuals incapable of critical thinking, even if they know how to use a computer to perfection.

Nevertheless, the success of the Muslim Brotherhood, even if it had been transitory, would have been difficult if it had not fully responded to the political objectives of the Gulf countries, Washington, and Israel. These three close allies share the same concern: to derail the recovery of Egypt. For the existence of a strong Egypt would be the end of the triple hegemony of the Gulf (a strong Egypt means submission to the discourse of the Islamisation of society), the United States (a compradorised and impoverished Egypt remains in their fold), and Israel (an impotent Egypt leaves them, to do what they will in Palestine).

The rallying of regimes to neoliberalism and to submission to Washington was brutal and total in Egypt under Sadat, slower and more measured in Algeria and Syria. I recalled in the first chapter of this book that the Muslim Brotherhood – a party involved in the system of power – should not be considered simply as an 'Islamist party' but above all as an ultra-reactionary party, albeit Islamist. Reactionary not only in regard to so-called 'social issues' (the veil, Sharia, discrimination against Copts), but also in the fundamental areas of economic and social life: the Brotherhood are opposed to strikes, to claims concerning work, to the power of independent unions, and to the resistance movements against the expropriation of peasants, and so on.

The planned abortion of the 'Egyptian revolution' guarantees thus the continuity of the system put in place since Sadat, which is founded on the alliance between the army and political Islam. Certainly, strengthened by their electoral victory, the Brotherhood was able to demand more power than had hitherto been granted by the military. Nevertheless, a revision of the sharing of the benefits from this alliance to the benefit of the Brothers proved ultimately impossible.

The government of the Brotherhood demonstrated in record time its inability to implant itself in society. Just weeks after their electoral victory, parliament and the president lost their legitimacy in the eyes of the overwhelming majority of citizens, including those who had naively voted for them. The arrogance of the Brotherhood certainly contributed to this reversal of opinions about them. Morsi thought he could set up the theocratic state defined by the program of the Brotherhood as rapidly as Khomeini had done in Iran. He forgot that the Iranian revolution was led by the Islamists, while in Egypt the Islamists had only jumped on the bandwagon once the mass mobilizations had occurred. Thus Morsi systematically removed all responsible officials and replaced them on the spot with members of the Brotherhood, who were generally incompetent and greedy for self-enrichment. He did not hesitate to say that having been elected that he had that right! Can you imagine, furthermore, an elected president revoking all members of the Superior Council of Magistracy, the Media Council, and all national institutions (universities, museums, power, railways, and so on) in defiance of all the regulations of these institutions? Yet the term 'permanent coup d'état' that was on the lips of all Egyptians was not the subject of any commentary from the Western media! Furthermore, the Brotherhood did not understand that they had to deal with SCAF (the Supreme Council of the Armed Forces): they chose to try to eliminate immediately its political presence. This was the Brotherhood's mistake.

## The electoral farce of 2011 and 2012

Egypt's parliamentary elections in October 2011 and the presidential elections in 2012 were anything but fair and transparent.

The first round of presidential elections on 24 May 2012 was organised to achieve the goal that the powers in place and Washington pursued: to reinforce the alliance between the two pillars of the system, the army command and the Muslim Brotherhood, and to resolve their different roles (to determine which of the two would take center-stage). In this spirit, the two 'acceptable' candidates had been the only ones to benefit from enormous campaign finances. Yet Morsi collected only 24 percent of the votes and Shafiq (the army) just 23 percent. The only authentic candidate of the movement, Hamdeen Sabbahi, who had not benefitted from the resources put at the disposal of the other candidates, collected 21 percent of the votes (the figure itself is debatable). After lengthy negotiations, a deal was concluded to declare Morsi the winner of the second round.

The assembly, like the president, was elected through the massive organisation for the distribution of boxes stuffed with meat, oil, and sugar that were distributed to voters who gave their votes to the Islamists. We should also mention the massive fraud (ballot stuffing by militiamen, Brotherhood members seizing polling stations), the prohibition against Coptic villagers from participating in the vote, and so on. Moreover, the foreign observers' failure to notice this has made them the laughingstock of the Egyptian streets.

So when the Constitutional Court invalidated the parliamentary elections in April 2012, it did nothing more than to note the actual massive fraud. We can note, nevertheless, that this dissolution was delayed by the army command who wanted, perhaps, to give the government stemming from this assembly time to discredit itself in the eyes of the public by its stubborn refusal to address social issues (employment, wages, school, health).

In Egypt the drafting of a new constitution has not been the subject of much attention. The Nasser constitution, itself revised by Sadat, has never been questioned. The presidential system that it establishes, as in the United States, France, Latin America, and Africa, is, in my view, a step backwards in comparison to the parliamentary systems invented in Europe in the 19th and 20th centuries. This is because this system contributes significantly to reducing politics to false debates between celebrities who avoid calling into question the policies of the economic liberal consensus. So this is a perfect system for consolidating the real power of the financial oligarchy.

In the Egyptian case, the debate has focused only on the proposed amendments regarding the place of Sharia in the law: should it be an exclusive source, or one source amongst others. The amendment submitted by referendum in May 2011 accentuated the Islamic character of the law. The amendment was opposed by the majority of active players in the movement, but it was nevertheless adopted under the pressure of the Islamists (who did not shrink from fraud, as usual) and the neutrality adopted in its place by the army command.

Moreover, the Egyptian constitution is not just a presidential constitution of the usual format. It prohibits elected civilian authorities any control over the actions of the Supreme Council of the Armed Forces, thus always guaranteeing public order as a final resort.

The constitutional drift came later, under the reign of Morsi. The constitutional project created by the Muslim Brotherhood would have allowed the establishment of a theocratic regime, inspired by the example of Iran. It's important to acknowledge that Khomeini's revolution of 1979 was greeted with enthusiasm by the Brotherhood, despite its Iranian Shiism. The Egyptian project would provide for the substitution of a council of Ulemas (scholars of Muslim religious law) for the Constitutional Court. This council would have benefitted from a right of inspection and of veto, which would in fact have eliminated the division of powers between the judiciary, executive, and the legislature. The council of Ulemas would in fact be entitled to halt any bill passed by the deputies if deemed inconsistent with its own interpretation of Sharia. In the same way, the council was empowered to reverse any decision of the executive and the administrative and any judgment of any court. So when Sisi annulled the project in July 2013, he did nothing more than to support the virtually unanimous opinion that opposed the theocratic drift.

The reason for the subsequent rift between the Muslim Brotherhood and the Iranian regime was not based on a different assessment of a desirable regime (theocracy in both cases) but on other conjunctural political considerations.

In the Gulf, Wahhabism is associated with tribalism. The alliance sealed in the 18th century between the founder of Wahhabism and the Saud clan had defined once and for all the model of the regime: Wahhabi theocracy controls the society while political management of the country is ensured by the absolute monarchy of Saud in alliance with the tribal leaderships. But now, certain currents of Salafism (including with Wahhabi allegiance) that aspire to rid the theocracy of its royal tutelage could challenge this covenant: Bin Laden had initiated this development. The Saudi monarchy therefore requires its allies of political Islam to separate themselves decisively from these 'too fundamentalist' aspirations! Having failed to do so, the Brotherhood were then forced to barter the support of Riyadh for that of Qatar. Furthermore, the confrontation between the Gulf states and Iran for control of maritime traffic in the region took a more acute turn: the United States feared Iran would adopt an independent political stance, even if its adherence to the principles of economic liberalism would not be questioned. Of course, in this conflict, the competitors then mobilised their religious affiliations (Shia and Sunni).

The system in place, 'chaired' by Morsi, was the best guarantee of the pursuit of lumpen development and the destruction of state institutions, which are the objectives pursued by Washington. The movement, which has lost none of its firm commitment to the struggle for democracy, social progress, and national independence, thus continued after the electoral farce that gave power to Morsi and the Brotherhood. The movement eventually managed to create the conditions for the fall of Morsi and his henchmen and to put a stop to the outrageous excesses of the despotic government of the Brotherhood.

However, none of these fundamental questions recalled here appear to have bothered the major political actors, beyond some vigilant intellectuals. Everything happened as if the ultimate goal of the 'revolution' was to have quick elections. As if the sole source of legitimacy of power lay in the ballot box. But there is nevertheless another superior legitimacy – the pursuit of the struggles for social progress and the authentic democratization of societies. These two aspects are called upon in the serious confrontations to come. One can already see them emerging clearly in Egypt.

## Is political Islam compatible with democracy?

We are assaulted by reassuring speeches about the compatibility of political Islam and democracy, some incredibly naive, and some sincere or deceptive. Some say: 'It was inevitable. Our societies are permeated by Islam. We wanted to ignore it, but it imposed itself on us.' As if this success of political Islam was not due to the depoliticisation and social degradation that most people want to disregard. 'This is not so dangerous. Their success is fleeting and the bankruptcy of power exercised by political Islam will result in people disengaging themselves from it.' As if the Brotherhood in question were committed to the principle of respect for democratic principles! Washington pretends to believe the 'opinions' fabricated by the dominant media and the cohort of some Arab 'intellectuals' through their opportunism or lack of lucidity.

We hear that there are Christian democrat parties, so why not Islamist democrats? Yes, in abstract theory, why not? If the equivalent does not hold, however, it is simply because the Brotherhood have created a fascist party. The Brotherhood has been headed since 1928 by a Mourchid, a name inspired by the Brotherhood's admiration of the Duce and the Führer. The Mourchid is chosen by a committee whose members' names are kept secret. The Brotherhood provides in its founding documents the parallel creation of a 'secret organisation,' which gives it the right, for example, to set fire to churches. I ask Europeans: do you know of a Christian democrat party that gives itself the right to burn synagogues?

No. The exercise of power by the reactionary political Islam would be expected to last, say, fifty years? And while it would help push societies into insignificance on the world stage, 'others' would continue their progress. At the end of this sad transition, countries concerned will gather at the bottom of the ladder of world classification.

Depoliticisation has been decisive in the rise of political Islam. This depoliticisation is certainly not unique to Nasserist Egypt and post-Nasserism. It has been the dominant practice in all popular national experiences of the first awakening of the South and even in those historical socialisms after the first phase of revolutionary ferment was outworn. The common denominator is the suppression of democratic practice (which I do not reduce to being merely the holding of multiparty elections), that is to say, the lack of respect for the diversity of opinions and political propositions and for political organisation. Politicisation requires democracy. In every case, the process of depoliticisation is responsible for the subsequent disaster. Such depoliticisation takes the form of returns to former ideologies or beliefs (religious or otherwise), or it takes the form of an adherence to the consumerism and the false individualism proposed by Western media. The latter was the case with the peoples of Eastern Europe and the former Soviet Union. It is also the case not only amongst the middle classes of Egypt (who are attracted to the potential benefits of development) but also amongst the popular classes, who, lacking an alternative, aspire to benefit from consumerism even at a very small scale (which is of course perfectly understandable and legitimate).

In the case of Muslim societies this depoliticisation takes the principal form in an apparent 'return' of Islam. The articulation, combining the power of reactionary political Islam, the compradorian submission, and impoverishment through informalization of the bazaar economy, is not specific to Egypt. It is already a characteristic of most of the Arab and Muslim societies, as far as Pakistan and beyond. This same articulation operates in Iran: the triumph of this bazaar economy has been described from the beginning as the major outcome of the 'Khomeini revolution.' This same articulation of Islamic power and the bazaar market economy has devastated Somalia, now erased from the map of nations (see 'Is there a solution to the problems of Somalia,' pambazuka.org).

The question of democratic politicisation constitutes, in the Arab world, as elsewhere, the central axis of the challenges we face. Our epoch is not that of democratic advances, but of democratic setbacks. The extreme centralization of generalised, monopolised capital requires and demands the unconditional and total surrender of political power to its command. The emphasis on 'presidential' powers and intense individualised appearances, while actually being completely subject to and in the service of the financial plutocracy, is the form of the projection that annihilates the scope of defunct bourgeois democracy (itself enhanced sometimes by workers' conquests) and substitutes it with a democratic farce.

In the peripheries, the embryos of democracy, when they exist, lose their credibility by being associated with social regression that is even more violent than in the centers of the system. The decline of democracy is synonymous with depoliticisation, for it implies the assertion that citizens are incapable of formulating authentic alternative social projects, not just envisaging 'alternating governments without change of policies' through elections that are without effect. The existence of citizens capable of creative imagination is disappearing, and the depoliticised individuals that have succeeded them are passive spectators of the political scene, consumers modelled by the system that make them think of themselves (wrongly) as free individuals.

Advancement on the path of democratisation of societies and the repoliticisation of peoples are inseparable processes. But where to start? The movement can be initiated from one or the other of these two poles. Nothing here can be substituted for the concrete analysis of situations in Algeria, Egypt, Greece, China, Congo, Bolivia, France, or Germany. In the absence of visible progress along these lines, the world will be engaged, as it is already, in the continued chaotic turmoil associated with the collapse of the system. The consequences are worse than terrifying.

## About Salafism

Salafism is a product of the abortion of the Nahda of the 19th century (see chapter 3 of this book) that ended with the obscurantist proposals of Rachid Reda, a convert to Wahhabism (the most archaic form of Islam), which were adopted out of hand by the Muslim Brotherhood from the beginning (1927). Salafists reject the concepts of freedom and democracy, which, according to them, do not take into account the 'nature' that requires man to obey God ('like a slave must obey his master' – the expression is theirs). Of course only the clergymen are allowed to say what God commands. The way is then open to theocracy (*wilayah al faqih*).

Like Edmund Burke and Joseph de Maistre, Salafists are the enemies of modernity, if by that we mean the claim that humans are individually and collectively – in society – responsible for making their own history. The media pretend nevertheless that the Salafists are 'modern' on the pretext that they do not prohibit computers and 'business management' and that they also teach from textbooks that USAID provides.

Obviously, management of the system requires skilled servants, provided they are devoid of critical capacity.

The Brotherhood, the Salafists, and the Jihadists share the goals of 'Islamisation of society and the state.' Salafists and Jihadists openly say what the Brotherhood always thinks but cannot say so openly so as to qualify for the certificate of democracy that Obama awards them.

## Democracy or destruction of states and nations?

For the Greater Middle East, the objective of the United States and their subordinate NATO allies is certainly not democracy, but rather the guarantee for ensuring the submission of the countries concerned to the requirements for the implementation of globalisation so that it functions for the exclusive benefit of the imperialist monopolies. 'All changes so that nothing changes.' Lumpen development based on exclusion and impoverishment of the vast majority of people is the essential product of this strategy.

Achieving this goal requires the destruction of those states and societies that resist. Iraq provides the model. Here the US rulers have substituted the dictatorship of Saddam Hussein with three more criminal dictatorships in the name of 'religion' (Sunni and Shia) and 'Kurdish ethnicity.' They also carried out the systematic murder of tens of thousands of scientists and professionals, administrators, and others, including poets, and prohibited any form of education other than 'religious' and 'useful' (i.e. business management).

The new objective is the destruction of Syria, the ally of Iran, who is the next target. The nuclear issue has been raised to that effect. Two weights, two measures, as always: Israel's nuclear military arsenal attracts no comment!

But beyond this strategy lies concerns about the 'emerging' countries, primarily China and Russia. The United States has formulated for this purpose a two-pronged strategy. First is to 'contain' the efforts of these countries in their pursuit of modifying globalisation and imposing upon it a polycentric order, thus putting an end to the 'hegemony' of Washington. The word used here is 'containment.' But in the longer term, the aim is it to destroy the capacity of these countries for autonomous movement, to 'recolonise' them in some way. The term used by the US is 'rolling back.' This perspective openly entails the abolition of international law and of respect for the sovereignty of states, and it also entails the recourse to war. The 'preventive wars' (more accurately preparatory wars) that the US has been involved with in the Middle East are part of this perspective.

The objective is to ensure the dominance over the world of the North, that is to say, the dominance of the monopolies of the triad – USA, Europe, and Japan – and in particular to ensure their exclusive access to natural resources of the entire planet, to make use of it in a way that we know to be ecologically disastrous. The pseudo-cultural themes invoked for this purpose ('the defence of democracy,' itself subject to continuous erosion in the North, 'the war of civilisations,' the invention of the so-called right to humanitarian intervention or right to protect) are there to hide the real objectives. This strategy implies for the peoples of the South a lumpen development and nothing else. This system is not sustainable, not only for known environmental reasons, but also for the political and social disasters that are exemplified by it. The Arab 'revolutions' (barely begun) are not the only responses to that strategy. There are those that are more sustained, such as in Latin America, and include the rise of struggles across the entire world, Europe included, that testify to the universality of the contestation.

## Outline of a social disaster response

I don't need to restate here the developments (to which I have devoted the first chapter of this book) on the long waves of the tentative emergence of Egypt (1805–1875 and 1920–1970), on the reasons for their failure, and on the two waves of the restructuring of the economy and of society imposed by the dominant imperialism that followed these failures (1875–1920 and 1970–2011). We have now entered what could be considered as the emergence of a third wave of struggles, which is why a balance sheet of recent years, 2011 to 2015, can only be partial and provisional.

Implemented on a global scale, the principles of liberal capitalism do not produce anything in the South other than crony capitalism hinged on a comprador state. It is not development but lumpen development. Egypt provides a good example.

## Crony capitalism, comprador, and lumpen development (1970–2012)

The Nasserist project of building a national developmental state had produced a model of state capitalism that Sadat pledged to dismantle. The assets owned by the state have been sold. To whom? To some businessmen close to power: senior officers, senior functionaries, and wealthy merchants (who, moreover provide political and financial support to the Muslim Brotherhood). But they were sold also to 'Arabs' of the Gulf states as well as to US and European companies. At what price? At ridiculous prices, prices incommensurate with the real value of the assets. Thus was built the new 'owning' Egyptian and foreign class, which fully deserves the descriptor of crony capitalism (the Egyptian term being *rasmalia al mahassib*). The property granted to the army has transformed its character and the responsibilities it had in working as a state institution. Their powers of supervision have become those of owning private property. Moreover, in the race to privatization, the most powerful officers also 'acquired' property from many other state assets: commercial chains, land, and housing developments in particular. Foreign capital inflows, which remained limited, fit into this framework. The whole operation is completed with the establishment of private monopoly groups that dominate the Egyptian economy.

This domination was reinforced by the almost exclusive access that these new billionaires have had to bank credit, at the expense of small and medium producers. These monopolistic positions were also favoured with huge state subsidies for oil consumption, natural gas, and electricity for the factories transferred by the state to private interests (cement, metallurgy of iron and aluminum, textiles, and others). And the 'free market' has allowed these companies to raise their prices to adjust to those of any competing imports. The rationale for public subsidy, which had compensated for the lower prices charged by the state sector, has been broken in favour of super-profits for private monopolies. The salaries of the vast majority of workers have been seriously worsened by the effect of the laws of the free labour market and by the repression of trade unions. Super-profits for private monopolies and impoverishment go hand-in-hand and result in the continued widening of inequality in the distribution of income, and this is reinforced by a tax system that rejects the principle of progressive taxation. This light tax for the rich and corporations, touted by the World Bank for its alleged support for the virtues of investment, has simply resulted in the growth of super-profits.

These policies have also made it impossible to reduce the public deficit and the balance of trade. They have led to the continued deterioration of the value of the Egyptian pound and imposed a growing internal and external debt. This gave the IMF justification to forcefully impose the principles of liberalism.

## An immediate response program

The response program, whose proposals are summarised in the text below, has been the subject of extensive discussions within the parties of the Egyptian left, unions, and many associations for middle professionals. It has also been aired in the press.

1. The procedures for the disposal of public assets should be subject to systematic probing. Since the buyers have paid ridiculous prices, ownership must be transferred, by law, to public companies in which the state will be a shareholder with its stake equivalent to the difference between the actual value and that paid by the buyers.
2. The law should set the minimum wage at an amount roughly equivalent to the purchasing power of 400 Euros (at 2011 value), which is in fact lower than in many countries where GDP per capita is comparable to Egypt. This wage must be linked to a sliding scale and with the participation of trade unions in its implementation. It will apply to all undertakings of the public and private sectors.
3. The rights of workers – employment, safe working conditions, health, unemployment insurance, and retirement insurance – should be clarified on the basis of a tripartite consultation (trade unions, employers, and state). Independent unions established in recent years should be recognised, as should the right to strike (which is still illegal under current legislation). Social security compensation must be established for the unemployed.
4. Subsidies granted from the national budget to private monopolies should be removed.

5. New legislation must be adopted that introduces the progressive taxation of individuals and an increase of tax rates to 25 percent of corporate profits for institutions with more than twenty workers. Taxation of small and medium enterprises, which is often heavier than on the larger corporations, should be revised downwards. The proposed rates for people in higher income brackets (35 percent) also remains light in international comparisons.
6. The measures proposed in points 4 and 5 can not only eliminate the current deficit, but also produce a surplus. This will be used to increase public spending on education, health, and housing. The reconstruction of a public social sector in these areas does not impose discriminatory measures against the private activities of a similar nature.
7. Credit must be placed under the control of the Central Bank. The facilities granted to monopolies must be removed for the benefit of existing and newly created SMEs.
8. Concerning the agrarian question, the goal is to make it difficult for the eviction of farmers who are unable to pay their rents and to make it difficult to expropriate indebted smallholder farmers. We advocate a return to a law fixing the maximum rents for lease (they were removed by successive legislation). Concrete plans exist for ensuring the growth of smallholder farming: improved irrigation methods, the choice of rich and intensive crops (vegetables and fruits), and the provision of freedom upstream by state control of suppliers of inputs and credit and downstream by the creation of marketing cooperatives linked with consumer cooperatives.

This immediate program of action would initiate the recovery of healthy and sustainable economic growth. The argument advanced by liberal critics – that this would ruin any hope for inflows of external origin – does not hold water. The experience of Egypt and other countries, particularly in Africa, who have agreed to submit fully to the requirements of liberalism and gave up developing an independent development project shows that they attract no external capital despite the uncontrolled opening of the their economies – indeed, they don't attract capital precisely because of it. External capital then merely carries out looting operations on the resources of the countries involved, supported by the comprador state. In contrast, emerging countries that are implementing national development projects offer real opportunities for foreign investment that accept to be part of the national projects.

The program of immediate demands, about which I have only outlined the principal elements, only deals with the economic and social aspects of the challenges faced. Of course the movement has also discussed everything in relation to the political aspects: the draft constitution, democratic and social rights, and the necessary affirmation of 'the state of citizens' (*Dawla al muwatana*) contrasting with the proposed state theocracy (*Dawla al-Gama'a al-Islamiyya*) of the Muslim Brotherhood.

The government, composed exclusively of Muslim Brotherhood members chosen by Mohammed Morsi, declared its unconditional support for all the principles of liberalism, took measures to accelerate their implementation, and deployed for this purpose all the means of repression that they inherited from the fallen regime. The same set of 'liberal' policies have been pursued by Prime Minister Beblawi, and were installed by Sisi but then subsequently removed, no doubt because the unpopularity of these policies might spill over and reflect on Sisi himself. His successor has yet to show proof of having a different commitment.

## Out of the confusion

The greatest confusion nevertheless still dominates the scene.

The constitution adopted by the referendum of January 2014 does not break with the concept of a state religion. Sharia remains the source of the law, and the army command remains the power of last resort. The constitution was nevertheless adopted with a certain enthusiasm because it brought an end to the theocratic project of the Muslim Brotherhood, a demand of the overwhelming majority. The presidential elections of June 2014 confirmed the victory of Sisi. Is this regime to continue the same policy of liberalism that was the original cause of the crisis? That much has been signaled: it is envisaged that the council of the Gulf states, the cornerstone for the adherence to neoliberalism and of the submission to the strategic objectives of the United States in the region, will be enlarged to include Egypt, Jordan, and Morocco!

Nevertheless, Hamdeen Sabahi, referred to as the 'unacceptable Nasserite communist' by the US embassy, received as many votes as Morsi in the last presidential elections. This active 'minority' (in electoral terms) is the only one capable of driving the actions of the majority of the movement. The struggle to force an exit from neoliberalism and for the adoption of the above action program thus continues. The pursuit of the ongoing struggles could then compel Sisi to change his tune, just as was the case with Nasser in 1956, shifting from a naïve adhesion to economic liberalism to the project of national and social liberation. Of course the conditions of our epoch, so different from those prevailing during the epoch of Bandung, prevents us from pushing that comparison too far. The future is open, for 'if the revolution did not change the regime, it changed the people'.

## Back to the debate of the 1950s

The return to the debates that were concerned in the past with the relationship between the Nasserite nationalists and the communists allows us to identify the true nature of the challenge that the Egyptian people confronted and continue to confront. We come up against two visions, or strategies, to be implemented. On the one hand, we are dealing with a vision of the 'national bourgeoisie,' that is to say an 'anti-imperialist/anti-feudal' project (in the language of that epoch) in which the national bourgeoisie, supported by a nationalist state, could lead to a desired conclusion. And on the other hand, a 'popular national' vision founded on the idea that the bourgeoisie (in this case the Egyptian bourgeoisie) cannot move the movement to the desired end because it is inconceivable for it to step outside of compromise (or capitulation) with imperialism and 'feudalism,' and that, consequently, only a broad popular movement led by a 'communist' vanguard could achieve it. This second vision was, at times, that of the Egyptian communists. But they remained vacillating and at other times abandoned the vision in favor of rallying to the bourgeois nationalist project (Nasser in this case). In those distant times, when the debate about nationalism versus communism occupied the center stage, 'Islamism' was pushed to the sidelines, and the people's attachment to religion did not influence their political position.

Yet it must be remembered that the Nasserist national project was not a project of the Free Officers who took power, a group of men without a political culture, for most of them were close to the Muslim Brotherhood. From 1952 to 1955, they implemented the program of the Federation of Egyptian Industries, which included appeals to international capital and to the landed aristocracy to 'develop' the country, friendship with the United States, and so on. Nasser only became 'Nasserite' after Bandung, having then realised that he had to part with these reactionary officers and to replace their support with the support of the nation and the people. I refer the reader here to my previous work, *Nassérisme et communisme égyptien*.

The same questions that were asked seventy years ago are emerging once again today. Similar responses to those that had been given in the past reappear like a tideline. For neither Mubarak nor Morsi were ousted by the army. They were defeated by popular anger, by the events that brought together 15 million citizens against Mubarak, and 30 million against Morsi. But this movement remained divided and without a strategy from the start. The movement was unable to link, on the one hand, the need for unity in action for the setting of common strategic objectives and the need to give recognition to the diversity of specific social (class) interests of the different constituents of the movement on the other. This inability benefited the army command that apparently joined the movement, ousted Mubarak and then Morsi, but kept control over the reins of power to themselves.

The army in power revives nostalgia about the Nasserist past, and General Sisi feeds this nostalgia in a systematic way by gestures and allusions, but nothing more. And facing the return (possible or impossible?) to Nasserism, the same posturing, similar to the way it was at the heart of the conflicts of the 1950s, is reappearing. Sisi in control, being ambiguous and intelligent to boot, seems to be the only option. This ambiguity is reflected then amongst the different currents of opinion. There are those who are unconditionally pro-Sisi, a camp that obviously attracts all the beneficiaries of the arrangements that were in place from 1970 to date, but there are also those who are undecided, those frigid with fear of disorder who prefer to leave in place a system that they know rather than risk the unknown. Then there are those who think that 'Sisi is not bad, and he can evolve in the right direction'; that is to say, Sisi can engage slowly but surely toward 'Nasserism,' the affirmation of sovereignty and progressive social reforms. Proponents of this stance might then think, 'Let us give him our confidence. Let us help him, instead of fighting him.' These positions are strangely reminiscent of many of the democrats, progressives, socialists, and communists during the period 1955–1965. And then there are those who are 'anti-Sisi' on principle, who say, 'No. No to any military. No to any alternative but a return to elected civilian government.' In this debate, the center of gravity is shifted. The movement accepts placing itself on the terrain defined by those in power, whose only concern is how to stay in control. The movement refuses to go on the offensive and challenge those in power so that they have to respond to the movement's initiatives.

The future of the 'Egyptian revolution' remains uncertain. Who will win? Will the senior officers and their SCAF who have been systematically corrupted by 'US aid' impose their point of view to continue the policies of Sadat and Mubarak? Or will Sisi, like Nasser did yesteryear, dare to part with them in order to allow the emergence of Egypt? This optimistic but not unrealistic hypothesis implies that the movement becomes more mature in the formulation of its three interlinked objectives (new ways of development for the benefit of the all the people, democratisation, and affirmation of national independence) and that it becomes capable of setting strategic objectives for common progress for various social components of the alternative bloc to the one led by the comprador bourgeoisie.

## The future of the Arab revolutions

It is certainly too early to take stock of the Arab Spring, other than provisionally and step by step, for the simple reason that the ambitions expressed by the peoples concerned are a long way from becoming achieved.

These ambitions are not many, varied, nor conflicting; they constitute, rather, the embryo of a coherent and authentic alternative based on three inseparable transformations of the system itself: undertaking a new path of development in which all people benefit, the democratisation of political and social life, and the assertion of national independence.

It is essential to dispel the illusion that it is possible to reconcile the establishment of democratic forms of political management in these countries with the pursuit of liberal economic policies. The market and democracy are not complementary to one another: they are contradictory. Important sections of the movements have probably not yet taken account of this antinomy. The selection by Western countries of reactionary coalitions involving the parties of the right, heirs of the fallen regimes, and the Islamists is perfectly consistent with the only aim of these powers: to guarantee the interests of monopoly capital. That this option negates the chances of democracy in the countries concerned is not seen as their problem.

The aspirations of the Arab peoples, expressed daily, despite the different conditions of their struggles, are always grounded in three slogans which recur persistently: (1) social justice (*el adala el Ijtimaia*), (2) respect for people (*karama al insan*), and (3) respect for nations (*karama al watan*).

We need to give a more precise meaning for each of these slogans. A new path of development, the only guarantee of social justice claimed by the vast majority of people, is excluded in the current economic model and is synonymous with a rupture with economic liberalism. And because this option comes into open conflict with the logic of the global system dominated by the imperialist powers, the assertion of national independence, in turn, is the condition for progress in this direction. It is therefore necessary to relinquish the exploration of 'friendship' with the United States and Europe, to give up seeking their 'economic aid,' to revive the spirit of Bandung, to open negotiations with China and the BRICS, and to flesh out the prospect of rebuilding a front of the South. Could a project of this kind be implemented from above by national powers? This was the case in the era of Bandung and of national popular but undemocratic projects of that era (1955–1980). But today a replay of those projects seems hard to imagine because the new ruling classes, shaped and enriched by their adherence to the liberal globalisation established over four decades, aspire only to maintain the system from which they benefit. Moreover, sections of the peoples concerned today aspire to something better than enlightened despotism. Democratic demands must be seen in this context. They cannot be reduced to the application of the recipe of 'multiparty elections.' This would instead be the safest way to derail the democratisation process and, ultimately, to annihilate its credibility and legitimacy, by substituting 'the alternative without change' in place of a search for new alternatives. Democratisation is above all the opening, in law and in fact, of the possibility for the popular classes organising to take over for themselves the defense of their rights and interests. In this perspective, democratisation opens the doors to prospects for its permanent enrichment by taking into account all the dimensions of the challenges faced by humanity: the global ecological dimension, the ideological dimension (by substituting the principle of solidarity for that of competition in the process of social reconstruction), and the polycultural dimension (by refusing to consider modernisation and Westernisation as synonyms).

For all these reasons I set the goal of 'exiting from economic liberalism' at the heart of the challenges we face. Without commitment to this goal, the discourse on democracy and on national independence is meaningless. And in the absence of progress in this direction, the cultural drifts (into Islam, Hinduism, Buddhism, and Christianity, known as the fundamentalisms) and the terrorist actions that accompany them are inevitable. I think we need more than ever to insist on this point.

The criminal acts of terrorism suffered by Western citizens (the recent attacks against *Charlie Hebdo* in Paris and the Bardo Museum in Tunis) serve to perfection the justification for the deployment of an aggressive strategy by imperialist powers. These powers helped to frame an ideology of security whose abundant smoke was spread by the media clergy, enabling them to forget that the soil in which the seed of terrorism was itself nurtured was through liberal economic policies that these same powers have not given up imposing on the people of the South. That ideology invites people to consider irrelevant the support that Washington and its subordinate European allies have given to terrorists who were helpful in their strategy of domination in Arab countries. It invites us all to join a 'global front against terrorism,' in which the leaders parade from coast to coast the very powers responsible for stoking the fires of terrorism (why not Netanyahu?) and their victims. The only common front that people need is not this one, but one that would unite – against global liberalism – all victims, the people of the South and those of the North. Moving in this direction is the only way to turn off the terrorist blaze.

Measured in terms of advancing a genuine alternative to liberal and imperialist globalisation, which are both anti-democratic by nature, the conquests that the Arab Spring has made to date are rather meager.

Yet the rulers keep pointing out as examples the advances such as those seen in Tunisia, which, we are told, is well on its way to democracy.

The commitment to democracy of important segments of the Tunisian people who courageously opened the Arab revolts is not in question. Their distinct gain is the fruit of the seeds that Bourguiba had sown in his support of women's rights. Thus the Tunisian revolution was largely supported by the emergence of a female component that was significantly more visible than elsewhere. For my part I just want to say that democratic progress in Tunisia, for a large part, is indebted to the struggles of women. Another advantage that Tunisia had was the existence of a powerful national workers union, UGTT (*Union Générale Tunisienne du Travail*, The Tunisian General Labor Union), which had been at the forefront of the struggle for independence and which understood the need, thereafter, to maintain their real autonomy, albeit relative, in spite of the efforts by Bourguiba, and by Ben Ali in particular, to try to domesticate or eliminate their influence. The UGTT thus has managed to become the major organising center for the popular movement. Its renewed fight for social justice should be at the core of the Tunisian movement.

Yet the fact remains that major sections of the movement subscribed, with much naïveté, to encouragements from Western powers (the United States and France in particular) and, in the process, agreed to holding immediate elections. The success of Nahda as the local branch of the International Muslim Brotherhood, which was no surprise, threatened in turn to sink the country into a theocratic project. The goals of the movement were then displaced – as in Egypt – and priority had to be given to fighting the implementation of this theocratic project instead of continuing the struggles for social justice, democratisation, and national independence. The price paid for the retreat that Nahda represented was heavy: to this end a pseudo-national unity had to be constructed, based on the return to the tracks set by the politicians of the ousted regime. More than that, the process has enabled the integration of Nahda into the government of national unity, thus making the government powerless in the face of the requirements of the open liberal market economy and imperialist globalisation.

There is no reason to welcome this development. The spark for effective responses to real social challenges has not been primed. This is probably why the Western media continue to praise it: 'These developments demonstrate that political Islam can be democratic,' they claim. Nahda leaders have also condemned the terrorist attack on the Bardo museum. But one should be aware that the Muslim Brotherhood boast of practicing *taqia*, the right to lie in order to advance by all means their theocratic project. We should be even more concerned to see Western opinion – represented by 'pro-South' NGOs – subscribe to the same theses, at best naïvely, or perhaps inspired by their rallying to social liberalism.

So the situation in Tunisia remains unstable as elsewhere, in Egypt, for example, and for the same reasons: the reluctance to break with the dogmas of economic liberalism, which is considered as the only alternative. What Westerners greet as the Tunisian gain (national unity) seems to many Tunisians as a real handicap for the continuation of the struggle for a genuine and viable alternative.

The silence of the Algerian people contrasts with the surge of popular movements in Tunisia and Egypt. The Western media attributed this silence to the autocratic character of the Algerian government. This is another lie: the power of the Algerian government is clearly less repressive than it is elsewhere in the Arab world today. This silence must be explained in other ways.

The two experiments – Algeria and Egypt – share many common characteristics, which – in their strength – enable one to understand the importance they have as models for Arab countries and beyond. But the differences between the two, which are not minimal, merit explanation.

The political leadership in both Algeria and Egypt, which was built on the framework of Boumediénism and Nasserism, respectively, were basically similar: these projects need in fact to be assessed in the same way – they were both truly national and popular (not 'populist') projects. It is not important that both described themselves as socialist – socialist they were certainly not, and could not be. Probably more serious is the fact that much of the radical left – of the communist tradition – believed that they were indeed socialist with the encouragement of Soviet diplomacy. In both experiments, their achievements have been significant, to the point that they truly transformed from top to bottom the face of the countries concerned for the better, not for the worse. But also, in both countries, these achievements quickly reached the limits of what they could deliver. Their internal limits – identical in both cases – prevented them from moving ahead in order to pursue their project.

But beyond these similarities, their differences are worth noting. The Algerian model showed clear signs of a much greater consistency, which is why it has been more resilient to its further decline. Thus the Algerian ruling class remains complex and divided, divided between those that still have national aspirations on the one hand, and those rallying toward compradorisation on the other hand. (Sometimes we even find these two conflicting components combined in the same individuals!) In Egypt, in contrast, this ruling class has become fully integrated, with Sadat and Mubarak, a comprador bourgeoisie, not nourishing any kind of national aspiration.

Two major reasons account for these differences.

The liberation war in Algeria had produced organically a social and ideological radicalisation. In Egypt, Nasserism came eventually in the period of the rise of the mass movement, initiated by the 1919 revolution, which radicalised in 1946. The equivocal coup of 1952 thus comes in response to the impasse of the movement.

Furthermore, Algerian society had suffered, with colonisation, major destructive incursions. The new Algerian society emerging after regaining independence had nothing in common with that of the pre-colonial epoch. It became a plebeian society, marked by a strong aspiration for equality. Such aspirations are not found to the same degree anywhere else in the Arab world, nor in the Maghreb (think of the strength of the archaic tradition of respect for the monarchy in Morocco!), nor in the Mashriq. By contrast, modern Egypt was built from the beginning (since Mohamed Ali) by its aristocracy, gradually becoming an 'aristocratic bourgeoisie' (or 'capitalist aristocracy').

From these differences follows another about the future of political Islam (in Algeria this is the FIS, *Front Islamique du Salut*, Islamic Salvation Front), which unveiled its hideous face and was veritably routed. This certainly does not mean that this issue has been finally resolved. But the difference with Egypt is substantial: it is characterised by a strong convergence between the power of the comprador bourgeoisie and that of the political Islam of the Muslim Brotherhood. All these differences between the two countries have consequences for the different possible solutions to their current situations. Algeria seems better placed (or less misplaced) to meet these challenges, at least in the short term. Economic, political, and social reforms coordinated from within seem to have more possibilities in Algeria. In Egypt, the confrontation between the movement and the anti-revolutionary reactionary bloc seems to have become inexorably worse.

The issue of democratic politicisation is, in any case, in Algeria and Egypt, as elsewhere in the world, the core of the challenge.

The imperialist powers have not renounced their desire to destroy the conquests of the Algerian people. They had, for this purpose, supported the FIS, who tried to reemerge on the occasion of the Arab Spring by calling for demonstrations supposedly against high prices, a call that had no resonance. We even saw the intervention by the police to prevent the FIS leader, Belhadj, from being lynched by the crowd. But if the 'Algerian Spring' still seems to be on the agenda of the probable, the fact remains that this non-event was held up by the Western media as a significant event, as stated by Samia Zennadi in her intervention at the Tunis Social Forum on 25 March 2015. The explosion that would erase the gains of the past and restore the imperialist order is still expected, and has been since September 1962.

Algeria and Egypt are two magisterial examples of the impotence of their societies to face the challenge. Algeria and Egypt are the two Arab countries that are potential candidates for being considered as 'emerging.' The major responsibility for failing to become so lies certainly with the ruling classes and their existing power systems. But also the societies, their intellectuals, their activists, and their movements in struggle share the responsibility in this failure to move ahead.

## The geostrategy of the United States in trouble

One will have seen in the preceding pages how the interactions work between the various kinds of movements in which the Arab peoples organise and the interventions of the United States through which it seeks to give expression to the geopolitical strategies it is trying to implement in the region.

The objective of the global and regional geostrategy of the United States is to destroy the states and societies that would threaten – or could threaten – the exclusive domination by Washington (and, behind them, their subaltern allies in Europe and Japan) over the entire planet. The opponents of this goal are potentially all countries of the South and of the former Soviet Union. And in this context, the US does not hesitate to use preventive wars, conspiracies, and the massacre of hundreds of thousands of human beings. This therefore makes the US the number one rogue state in the contemporary world, a state whose leaders are major war criminals and perpetrators of crimes against humanity.

The regions envisaged as being the primary place for the implementation of this geostrategy are Asia/the Pacific and the Greater Middle East regions.

The United States knows that its main adversary is China. China has taken the initiative in implementing its own strategy of emergence in the field of economic development, thereby avoiding the nuclear arms race that the US had imposed on the Soviet Union. I refer the reader here to Barthélémy Courmont's compelling book, *Une guerre pacifique* (ESKA, 2014). And this 'soft' Cold War that China has chosen gives them, hitherto, considerable advantage for becoming the leading world economic power. The United States is thus forced to contain the possible advances of its major opponent by building a wall of states that submit to the deployment of American geostrategy in the Asia/Pacific region. This bloc includes a major subordinate ally, Japan, which has placed itself voluntarily in this position, as has Europe, an important potential ally, India, and the neutralised or destroyed states of Southeast Asia. The strengthening of the US military presence in the Indian Ocean (Diego Garcia), the Western Pacific (Guam), South Korea, and elsewhere through establishing a comprehensive land base completes the tableau.

It is said that because the United States knows that China is its major opponent, the US recently decided to focus less on the Middle East and more on Asia. This is only partially true. Yes, perhaps, the United States, finding it more and more difficult to bear the huge cost of its growing military presence in both regions, is forced to transfer part of its western-intervention budgets eastward. But there is no question of the US withdrawing from the Middle East, especially since the region borders the south of Russia, which is possibly in the throes of reemergence. The Western intervention in Ukraine must therefore be considered as part of the deployment of American geostrategy in the greater Middle East.

The geostrategy of the United States has set as its goal in the greater Middle East the annihilation of any resistance capacity of a number of potentially dangerous states, primarily Egypt, Iraq, Syria, Algeria, and Iran. And so far, Washington has not given up this goal, which implies the permanence of its presence and its activities in the region. Washington has, to this end, four allies: the two staunchest allies (Israel and Turkey, an important NATO member), the constellation of Arab Gulf states led by Saudi Arabia, and finally, even within the societies concerned, reactionary political Islam (the Muslim Brotherhood, Salafists, and Jihadists). The interventions of the four allies allow the implementation of the destruction of a number of states and societies of the region.

Two societies in the region have already been destroyed: those of Somalia and Libya. Both countries, now 'wiped off the map of nations,' are stateless, having been handed over to the warlords, in good part comprising Jihadis and major players in regional terrorism, such as Al Shabaab in Kenya, and Jihadis in Mali and Niger, who find weapons and refuge in Libya. The intervention, conducted deliberately for this purpose, was relatively easy because of the fragility of national construction in the two countries. A similar fate threatens Sudan.

The Iraq of Saddam Hussein had constituted a major objective of the devastatingly criminal deployment of the US plan. And the decision to intervene for this purpose had been decided and planned well before the first intervention during the Kuwait war (1991) and followed by the aggression of 2003 on the grounds of impeding the weapons of mass destruction. The deliberate lies of the secretary of state, Colin

Powell, should have resulted in his appearance before the so-called International Criminal Court (ICC) for his crimes against humanity. But the ICC has only the right to condemn the poor wretches of Serbia and Africa, never the major criminals of the contemporary world. Most African and other states are thus left wanting to quit this farce of justice.

Iraq's infrastructure and industries were deliberately destroyed, its museums ransacked, its elites systematically massacred, all on orders from Washington. Iraq no longer exists: four caricature states were put in place by Paul Bremer (the US gauleiter[1]) with the intention of creating permanent civil war between Shiites and Sunnis, Arabs and Kurds. To this end the US armies have protected those who subsequently had to take the direction of the Daesh[2] (or ISIL), the Caliph himself!

Nevertheless, the success of this geostrategy that sows death produced a situation that allows Iran to penetrate the region, supporting the Shiites in Iraq and elsewhere. Washington should have known. And, if we assume that its leaders are smart enough (the hypothesis is mine) to have known, why then have they ventured there? The reason is that the United States thought that, in the aftermath, they could destroy Iran in its turn, which was what the Gulf states and Israel encouraged them to do. The case of the Iranian nuclear threat was invented for this purpose. But the resistance of Tehran, supported by Russia and China, weakened the impact of sanctions and forced Washington to retreat.

It was then that the US implemented their Plan B: weaken Iran before attacking it head-on and destroying its Syrian ally. The false 'Syrian Spring' was coined for this purpose based on the Libyan model, as I mentioned above. But again Syria, Iran, Russia, and China have managed to thwart this geostrategy. The Syrian army has not fallen apart. To seriously threaten it, it required bringing to the Daesh the support (arms and financing) by some Gulf countries, without which his Caliphate would not have emerged. To advance their plan, the US has relied on the intervention of their Turkish ally, which has become Islamist in turn (under Erdoğan), and the support of the European diplomats at their service (that of France being the in then first line), and that of Israel.

The geostrategy of the United States is clearly in trouble. The US is thus forced to make a tactical retreat on Iran and Syria. The statements of John Kerry, renouncing the designation of Bashar al-Assad as the primary enemy to be defeated (March 2015) testifies to this tactical retreat. Simultaneously in the same month of March, the US agreed to discuss the nuclear issue with Tehran (I refer here to the Lausanne Agreement). With great intelligence, Tehran understood that its eventual access to the production of a few atomic bombs (in contrast to the over two hundred possessed by Israel) – in addition to the impossibility of keeping the secret – would serve as a pretext for open aggression against Iran, meaning Israel would then get the green light to drop a nuclear bomb on Iran. But on its side, Washington has not lost hope of buying the Iranian ruling class, inviting it to operate in the region as a 'normal' actor, that is to say, one ultimately subservient to the US. This class, which, as in Egypt and elsewhere, cannot imagine relinquishing economic liberalism, could find its reward – that is, its own enrichment, not that of its people – in the removal of sanctions, and would be welcomed on world markets. Iran could then withdraw its support for Syria, hopes Washington, and the offensive to destroy this country could be revived. But this is only one possible scenario among others. In contrast, Iran could persevere in its project to become an independent player in the region, approaching the BRICS and forcing Washington to accept it as such. The Lausanne Agreement has nevertheless raised the ire of Israel, the Europeans who unconditionally support the Zionist state, and the Gulf states. Certainly these stooges (Israel, France, the Gulf) know they cannot take bold initiatives without a green light from Washington. But they are nonetheless upset. For the accepted return of Iran as a regional player ruins the hopes of the Gulf of being alone to exercise control over the Strait of Hormuz under the military protection of the United States.

The new Yemeni war and the military intervention of Saudi Arabia from the end of March 2015 was invented to heat up the conflict with Iran, who was accused, without proof, of wanting to install a Shiite power in Yemen (Shiites are the majority in the country). The case is more complex. The man put in place by Washington and Riyadh, Ali Abdullah Saleh, had never been able to convince the heads of tribes and clans, Shiites or Sunnis, nor the militants in the south, of his legitimacy. I refer the reader to chapter 4 of this book regarding the reasons for the suicide of the South in the name of unity of Yemen. Certainly, the permanent chaos in Yemen does not bother the

Western powers, for whom only the military security in Aden matters. But this chaos bothers Saudi Arabia because it permits refuge for the Wahhabi Salafists who dare to want to release Wahhabism of Saudi tutelage, as I have mentioned earlier.

Has Erdoğan's Turkey descended into the neo-Ottoman and Islamist-demented grandiloquence? I refer the reader here to my analysis of the reasons for the failure of the emergence of Turkey, at its heart in the success of Islamists (see *The implosion of contemporary capitalism*, chapter 2). Turkey's active intervention in Syria, in support of Jihadists and Daesh (among others by facilitating the transit of Jihadists from Tunisia and Europe and providing arms, as established by the newspaper *Cumhuriyet* in May 2015), and approved by Washington and Europe, are part of this plan. For here also the semi-theocratic and hardening fascist project is necessary to enable the only card that the imperialist powers can play in this country located on the edge of Europe, Russia, the Arab Mashreq, and Iran. The reason is simply that the growing resistance of the Turkish people to the neo-fascist trends could open the way for what Westerners fear most: the commitment of Turkey to leave the path of lumpen development generated by economic liberalism (the condition among others for entry into the European Union), and to establish a rapprochement with BRICS. In other words, what Westerners fear is the option for a real – and possible – political emergence of the Turkish nation. The ball is now in the court of a radical left, which is still embryonic. For a replay of the days of Atatürk in Turkey is also as difficult to imagine as a replay of Nasserism in Egypt, and for the same reasons. In contrast, a consequential left could give the general democratic movement that is emerging the strategic organisation that it currently lacks. It is necessary here, and elsewhere, that the radical left understands that only audacity pays in a polarizing situation provoked by far-right politics.

Egypt, on which I devoted most of this text, remains the key to the Arab world. The geostrategy of the US has thus made its major objective the annihilation of the real potential for the emergence of Egypt. To this end, Plan A of Washington counted on the Muslim Brotherhood, whose theocratic project would have effectively guaranteed the triumph of US, Gulf, and Israeli objectives. And although the Egyptian people have routed the Muslim Brotherhood, Washington certainly has not given up this plan. But in the absence of anything better, the United States could shelter behind their Plan B, the success of which they hope for, for the short term and visible future at least: the return to the original point of departure, that is to say, the economic and political system of the time of Sadat and Mubarak. Having then renounced the desire to leave the beaten tracks of imperialist globalisation, Egypt would be doomed to insignificance. It would then be kept alive – with its head just above water – by the Gulf's financial pump and the corrupting 'aid' of the US, nothing more.

## Notes

1. A *gauleiter* was the party leader of a regional branch of the Nazi Party, appointed directly by the Führer.
2. Daesh is also an acronym for an Arabic variation of the *al-Dawla al-Islamyia fil Iraq wa'al Sham*. In the English-language media they are referred variously as ISIS or ISIL.

## References

The author published four books (in Arabic) on current developments in Egypt between 2011 and 2014 and tried to put them in the broader context of the systemic crisis of contemporary capitalism. This text summarises the conclusions of these works.

## Bibliography

Amir, Chérif (2014) *Histoire secrète des Frères Musulmans*, Paris, Editions Ellipses.
Raimbaud, Michel (2015) *Tempête sur le Grand Moyen Orient*, Paris, Editions Ellipses.
Courmont, Barthélémy (2014) *Une guerre pacifique*, Paris, ESKA, 2014.
Amin, Samir (2014) *The Implosion of Contemporary Capitalism*, New York, Monthly Review Press.
Amin, Samir (2014) *Egypte : Nassérisme et communisme, diversité des socialisme*, Paris, Les Indes Savantes.

## Articles by and interviews with Samir Amin:

"An Arab springtime?" in *African Awakening: The Emerging Revolutions*, Firoze Manji and Sokari Ekine (eds.), Oxford, Fahamu Books, 2011.
"Les germes d'un cocktail explosive", *Afrique Asie*, March 2011.
"L'Islam politique comme horizon?" *Afrique Asie*, December 2011.
"La désintégration de la Libye est possible", *Afrique Asie*, December 2011.
"An Arab Springtime?" *Monthly Review*, Volume 63, Number 5, October 2011.
"L'Egypte en mouvement", *Pambazuka News*, Issue 177, February 14, 2011.
"Les Frères Musulmans dans la révolution égyptienne", *Pambazuka News*, Number 178, February 21, 2011.
"Egypte : les Etats Unis en quête d'un modèle pakistanais", *Pambazuka News*, Number 178, February 21, 2011.

# The Geostrategic Plan of the United States

"Le printemps arabe?" *Pambazuka News*, Number 191, May 30, 2011.
"Libye: un risque de désintégration sur le modèle somalien", *Pambazuka News*, Number 204, September 12, 2011.
"Au lendemain des élections tunisiennes", *Pambazuka News*, Number 211, October 31, 2011.
"Tunisia: West could scupper genuine democracy with 'Islamic alternative'", *Pambazuka News*, Number 514, January 27, 2011.
"Movements in Egypt: the US realigns", *Pambazuka News*, Number 515, February 02, 2011.
"Is there a solution to the problems of Somalia?" *Pambazuka News*, Number 515, February 17, 2011.
"Egypt: how to overthrow a dictator", *Pambazuka News*, Number 518, February 24, 2011.
"An Arab springtime?" *Monthly Review*, June 6, 2011, www.monthlyreview.org/commentary/2011-an-arab-springtime/.
"The future of Arab revolts", *MRZine*, August 15, 2011, www.mrzine.monthlyreview.org/2011/amin110811.html.
"Libya could break up like Somalia", *Pambazuka News*, Number 546, September 7, 2011.
"After the Tunisian elections, what next?" *Pambazuka News*, Number 556, November 3, 2011.
Préface; in Hocine Belalloufi, *La démocratie en Algérie, réforme ou révolution?* Alger, Ed Apic, 2012.
"Origines et réalités du printemps égyptien", in *La face cachée des révolutions arabes*, Eric Dénécé (ed.), Paris, Editions Ellipse, 2012.
"Le printemps arabe, l'Egypte", *Journal des Anthropologues*, Number 128/129, 2012.
"Le printemps arabe dans la tempête", *Le Patriote*, septembre 2012.
"Egypte, changement, demandez le programme", *Afrique Asie*, Decmber 2012.
"Les révolutions arabes deux ans plus tard," *Recherches Internationales*, Number 94, January-March 2013.
"Ni islamisme, ni néo liberalism", *Afrique Asie*, Septembre 2013.
"Les Etats effaces", *Recherches Internationales*, Number 97, October-December 2013.
"L'Islam politique est-il soluble dans la démocratie?" *Pambazuka News*, Number 270, February 20, 2013.
"Chute de Morsi : une importante victoire du peuple égyptien," *Pambazuka News*, July 10, 2013.
"Le régne des Frères Musulmans n'a duré qu'un an", *Pambazuka News*, Number 288, Septembre 5, 2013.
"Egypt: pour une libération du people," *La Pensée*, Number 379, July-September 2014.
"Fascism returns to contemporary capitalism," *Monthly Review*, Volume 66, Number 3, September 2014.
"La démocratie sans progrès social est impossible", *Afrique Asie*, April 2015.

# 3

# The Middle East as the Hub of the Ancient World System

The oldest civilisations in the eastern hemisphere consolidated in limited regions of the Middle East (Egypt, Syria, Mesopotamia, Western Iran), India and China. At the beginning they were isolated from one another but from 500 to 200 BCE there was enough contact between them to be able to talk of a 'global system'. I have therefore identified three centres of this system that were to last until they were superseded by the new, globalised capitalist system:

A) The Middle East, which, in the narrow sense of the term, consisted of what became the Arab Mashreq (Egypt and the Fertile Crescent), Iran and Turkey. In a broader sense, this region extended into central Asia
B) The Indian sub-continent region
C) The Chinese region.

The other regions of the ancient world (Europe, Korea, Japan, South East Asia, sub-Saharan Africa) remained for a long time peripheral to these systems centred on the three major regions A, B and C.

Geography is important. Apart from the more intensive trade between the three central regions, it was geography that made region A the hub of the global system. This was the only region that was in direct contact with all the other regions, both central and peripheral. Relationships between China and India had to pass through it, as did those between the European and African peripheries. This lasted up until the sea routes enabled the Europeans to be in direct contact with eastern and southern Asia, without passing through the Middle East (until, later on, transit through the Suez canal became possible).

Trade between the three centres, A, B and C, used two routes: the one by land through central Asia, and the maritime one by the Indian Ocean. The former was disputed between the Muslims, who ended by integrating its western part into the Great Middle East, and the Chinese, who still today control the eastern part. It has been among the most stable frontiers in world history.

The latter route was controlled by the Muslims (above all, the Arabs) and the Chinese until it was taken over by the Portuguese, the Dutch and then the English (and, to a lesser extent, the French).

What became the Arab Mashreq was the key to the control of trade between Europe and the important 'rest of the world'. The Arab Maghreb, which remained somewhat isolated from this trade (geography is important!) mainly traded with the European countries of the western Mediterranean, such as Spain and Sicily, as well as with western sub-Saharan Africa.

Region A was not synonymous with the Arab world, which was formed later and gradually. The Arab countries that now constitute the Arab League, that is the countries whose populations are arabophone (at least the great majority of them), are the countries that little by little became 'Arabised' – sometimes slowly and partially, together with their Islamisation, which, too, was a gradual process – as from 700 CE. This presentation of the formation of the Arab world does not conform to the discourses of the Arab nationalists (the *qawmiyin* and the *ourouba* to which I shall return later, in Chapter 4): I contest that they have substituted a veritable mythology for real history.

Region A was never limited just to the Arab Mashreq. It always included Iran (and, beyond it, central Asia) as well as the countries of the Byzantine empire (Anatolia and the Balkans). It therefore always associated the Muslim caliphate (itself more Iranian than Arab, then largely Turkish) with the Byzantine empire. And it was only with the late formation of the Ottoman empire, which coincided with the time that Europe entered into the mercantilist capitalism era and freed itself from having to pass through the Middle Eastern hub, that the two sub-regions of region A were brought together by one political power, which was Muslim, but not Arab.

But region A existed before its Islamisation and partial Arabisation. It dates back to the Hellenisation that followed Alexander's conquests which, without merging them, closely associated the oldest centres of the former civilisation (Egypt, Syria, Mesopotamia, Iran, Greece). And this region already played the role of a hub, which it maintained until the 16th century. One cannot therefore talk about the Arab world/hub when one dissociates this Arab world from its eastern partners, Iranians, Turks and Byzantines.

The following remarks on the region's function as a hub first describe the pattern of trading between the A, B and C regions, among themselves and with the peripheries of the pre-modern (pre-capitalist) global system. They show the decisive weight of China and India in this system, while the comparative advantage of the Middle East region was mainly due to its geographical position as an unavoidable corridor. We then examine the characteristics of the system, which divide the writers on global history. Some consider these characteristics of no importance, but I put forward an analysis of this system which stresses its tributary, even proto-capitalist, nature. This chapter proposes nothing more.

My only observation here is that the decline, which is the subject of the next chapter, began early, even before the Islamisation of the region. It has been continually, apparently 'inexorably', prolonged over the centuries between the formation of the Byzantine empire and the industrial revolution of the 19th century. This poses some questions that I shall raise here.

## Trading between the regions of the ancient world

For 20 centuries China remained not only the most important centre but the one whose development was the most continuous, in spite of the upheavals that occurred during the inter-dynastic periods.

The population of China was 70 million at the beginning of the current era (28 per cent of the world population at the time, which was 250 million). It increased regularly, reaching 200 million in 1700 (still 28 per cent of the world population, estimated at 680 million at that time). Between 1700 and 1800 the demographic increase accelerated and China's population reached 330 million, representing 35 per cent of the world total, estimated at 950 million.

Throughout China's long history, it was the most advanced region in every way. It had the highest per capita agricultural productivity, the largest number of towns with an educated administrative population and skilled artisans and it was considered by all as the model. When the Europeans discovered it in the 18th century, when it was at the height of its glory, they tried to emulate it (see Etiemble, *L'Europe chinoise*). Much earlier the peoples of the Middle East knew of its wealth and power (see the Hadith of the Prophet Mohamed: 'go and seek science in China').

During the whole period China maintained close, continual and intense relationships with the Middle East centre (Hellenistic, then Byzantine and Islamic Arab, Persian and Turk).

India was the second centre of human concentration and civilisation after China. It took off very early on, during the third millennium BCE: in other words, at the same time as Egypt and Mesopotamia, with which the civilisations of the Indus were perhaps in contact. Like China, and in contrast with the Middle East, India had a constant dynamism from its origins up until 1700. At the beginning of the current era it had a population of 45 million, 200 million in 1700 (as many as in China at that time). But from then on it entered into crisis, marking time at around 200 million in 1800 and only catching up later, in the 19th century. The Indian sub-continent remains today the region with the highest population density after China.

But the history of India is more chaotic than that of China. It was frequently invaded (always from the west) and unification was difficult (it was only achieved in the ancient Maurya era, at the dawn of the current era). According to all the historians it was less open to external trade than China. Its main trading partner was the Middle East, either along the land route via Iran–Afghanistan, or by sea. As for trade with South East Asia, this did not become important until India became Hinduised between 600 and 1000 CE, after which Indonesia and Malaysia became Islamised and Chinese penetration intensified.

The Middle East centre had a very different historical evolution from China. In 200 BCE its population was the same as that of China (50 million) and probably its general level of development was at least the same. But by the current era, its population was only 35 million (as against 70 million for China) in the more restricted sense of the region (Greece–Anatolia, Egypt, Syria–Iraq–Iran) and if we add in Italy and the Maghreb, which constituted its prolongation westward through the Roman empire, a population of 50 million. Over the following centuries the population of the Middle East centre (Byzantium plus the caliphate) remained relatively stagnant. The population of the heirs of the Ottoman empire as from 1500, the Persian empire and the emirates and khanates of Turkish central Asia hardly reached 50 million compared with 200 million for China and as many for India in 1700. The relative decline in the position of the Middle East has been virtually continuous since the current era, in spite of brilliant though brief moments and attempts at renewing itself (the Justinian epoch, the first two Abassid centuries).

In contrast, the relative position of the Middle East in the more ancient times was dominant at the world level. For the 2,000 years preceding the current era its population was perhaps 30 per cent of the world population (which grew slowly from 100 to 250 million during this period), as against only 18 per cent at the beginning of the current era and 7 per cent in 1700. The population of ancient Egypt, which had been over 10 million, fell to 2 million in 1800, only returning to its pharaonic levels in the contemporary world, in the 20th century. This is not the place to go into the reasons for this early and inexorable decline, but it is important to mention the tremendous devastation in central Asia, Iran and Iraq, caused by the Turkish–Mongolian invasions which reduced Iran and Mesopotamia, one of the cradles of universal civilisation, to a desert wasteland. Russia and the Islamic east were the main victims of invasions, China having been far more capable of resisting them. The fact remains, however, that as from the current era the dynamism of the Middle East centre was not comparable to that of China.

For this reason, trading between China and the Middle East was relatively more intense in ancient times, subsequently tapering off. Instead, China intensified its trade with Korea and Japan, Vietnam, South East Asia and finally Europe, first by the Mongol route (13th century), then by the sea routes (in modern times).

The relative stagnation of the Middle East meant that the surplus generated in the region, which was comparable to that of China at the beginning of the period under consideration (as from 500 BCE), hardly exceeded one-third of China's surplus by 1300–1500, taking into account the population growth of the populations concerned. The declining position of the Middle East was, however, partially offset by its geographical position, which acting as a hub, was an obligatory intermediary for almost all transcontinental trade in the pre-modern epochs. The economy was commercialised and there was a marked relative increase in the volume of foreign trade on account of the transit commerce.

Although the China–Middle East trade declined in relative terms it was still of major importance in the system of relationships between the regions of the pre-modern world. These transfers of goods, technologies, ideologies and religions through the Middle East enabled the spread – particularly to Europe – of the most advanced Chinese science and techniques. The unchanging silk route left China through the Gansu corridor, passing to the south of the Tian Shan range, skirting the Taklamatan desert, either to the north (Hami–Aksu–Kashgar) or to the south (Kokand–Kashgar), then towards Persia through the south of former Soviet central Asia (Samarkand–Bokhara–Khiva).

The fact that this vital route remained so permanent explains certain phenomena that are otherwise inexplicable, like the early and deep penetration of religions coming from the Middle East: Nestorian Christianity and Manicheism, after Zoroastrism (it is often forgotten that central Asia had been Christian before the Germanic tribes), then Islam (which immediately put down strong roots in this region – in Khorezm) and in India (Buddhism). This process was accompanied by the early settlement of local populations: as from the 9th century, in eastern Turkestan (Uighuristan) the inhabitants were completely sedentarised. From the frontiers of China proper to that of Persia, the route was studded with large commercial towns, centres of intellectual activity and surrounded by intensively irrigated agricultural areas.

It is therefore understandable that the main geostrategic conflict of pre-modern times focused on the control of this route. It is striking, however, that the military frontier between the zone controlled by the Chinese and that of the Middle East (the caliphate and Persia) remained extremely stable, more or less at the present Chinese borders. It is also remarkable that, in spite of its Islamisation, eastern Turkestan has always been under the political and military control of China, while western Turkestan, under that of the Middle East (when it did not actually take over the power there), before being conquered by the Russians.

What has just been said about the Middle East is still more applicable to the central Asian region. As the obligatory passage between the main centres of the pre-modern world, linking in particular China to the Middle East, central Asia has always been sparsely populated, thus probably producing no more than a negligible surplus. It is true, however, that in certain epochs the region of central western Turkestan, around the water routes of Syr and Amu Dar'ya, experienced brilliant development. Trade flows that passed through this region were considerable. More than any other region in the world, central Asia profited from this transit with a proportion of its value, no doubt impossible to estimate exactly but not negligible, being creamed off in the region.

It is therefore important to avoid too many generalisations concerning this region which has never been homogenous or reducible only to nomadism. In fact, central Asia is more or less divided by the Tian Shan range into a southern region – the real silk route – and a northern region, which has always been only marginal in East–West relationships that have been intense since at least the 6th century BCE.

The southern part of the region is itself easily divisible into three distinct sub-regions: eastern Turkestan (the Chinese province of Xinjiang), western Turkestan to the south of contemporary Kazakhstan, and Afghanistan. The trade flows that crossed central Asia, reflecting China–Middle East commerce, have always taken the same route through Xinjiang and the Syr and Amu Dar'ya valleys. Variations in this route, avoiding the desert of Taklamatan either to the north or the south of it, choosing the route of Dzungaria or the passes that lead to Fergana, are all located in the regional cluster under consideration. The eastern part of this southern central Asia (the Xinjiang) is particularly arid, with just a scattering of oases that prevents dense settlement except when oasis towns can be supplied either by small irrigated zones close by, or through long-distance commerce in transit. There has never been any question in this zone of a social formation that was predominantly nomadic. Urban mercantilism dominates the local social formation but it is out of the question that it could exist without the East–West relationship upon which it had been grafted. Whether the local powers had profited at this time from autonomy, or even independence, or that at another period they had been closely controlled by China, does not change the fact that the social formation was only a sub-system of articulation between the tributary formations of China and the Middle East.

This objective dependency in no way limited the importance of the region and the brilliance of its civilisation, characterised by early settlement (that was complete at the latest by the 9th century) and the intellectual life of its open urban centres (which easily adopted advanced, universalist religious forms such as Nestorianism, Manicheism, Buddhism and Islam). To the west of the mountain barrier that separates Xinjiang from western Turkestan, geographical conditions permit a more nomadic population of the steppes, or the irrigated agriculture around the Syr and Amu Dar'ya rivers. The region, a kind of extension of the Iranian plateau and the Afghan landmass, is the meeting place par excellence between the sedentary populations (farmers and urbanites) and the nomads. According to the vagaries of history, the dominance of social formations in the region has been either urban/mercantilist (supported by irrigated agriculture) or nomadic. Obviously East–West commerce was more stimulated in the former case and hindered in the latter. The Turkish–Mongolian invasions, contrary to widespread belief, were a favourable factor in this trade.

Afghanistan had a special place in this regional system. India had always maintained close contacts with the Middle East which, apart from the sea route, took the land route passing north of the Afghan mountain mass, thus joining the China–Middle East route at Amu Dar'ya. Here, through this tripartite contact (Middle East–India–China) civilisations with a particularly interesting synthesis (like the Kushan state) were able to flourish. Trade between India and China also passed by this route, avoiding the impassable barriers of the Himalayas and Tibet, and going round by the west. This was the route taken by Buddhism.

The northern half of internal Asia corresponds roughly to contemporary Mongolia (to the north of Tian Shan) and the steppes of Kazakhstan (to the north of the Aral Sea and the Syr and Amu Dar'ya valleys), which extended without hindrance as far as central Europe, passing to the north of the Caspian Sea and the Black Sea. This region played only a minor role in East–West relationships, at least for two reasons: the lateness in Europe's development until the year 1000 and the domination of the turbulent population of the steppes. This northern route was only taken during the short period between European growth, from the 12th century to the conquest of the seas from the 16th century, which corresponds to the conquest of the whole region by Genghis Khan.

The dominant social formation in the region was different from those that prevailed in its southern half. Here the weak trading relationships of numerically dominant nomadism could not be compared with those along the veritable silk route. Mongolia remained without traces of important towns and even at the time of Genghis Khan, the capital Karakorum was just a small market town of perhaps 5,000 inhabitants. As the main East–West trading route did not pass through it, this region had nothing like the towns of southern central Asia. Furthermore, the trade between China and regions to the north of Tian Shan (Mongolia and Siberia) was extremely limited, virtually confined to the importation of horses and skins by China. In fact the control of this trade by the China of the Qing dynasty, after the collapse of the Mongolian khanate of Genghis, built up a new articulation between nomadism, feudal Buddhism and Chinese mercantilism, which was dominant from the 16th to the 20th century. At the same time Russian expansion brought about a new conflict between the Russians and the Chinese for geopolitical control. Russia, however, was not at this time – and we are already into the modern era – at the heart of capitalist Europe, but a poor semi-peripheral region. Hence its external trade was of secondary importance.

The reference to Buddhism in the Mongolian formation raises a question that merits further study. It is striking to note the failure of Buddhism in the centres of the Asian civilisations: in India, its country of origin, and in China, where Hinduism and Confucianism quickly recovered and dominated, as well as along the silk route where Islam asserted itself. On the other hand, Buddhism established itself definitively in the two marginal regions of the central Asia system, Tibet and Mongolia.

To the west of Mongolia, the region of the northern Asian interior remained, as has been mentioned, without precise borders, including Kazakhstan and southern Russia. It is in this region that almost all the nomadic invaders became Islamised (but late, so this conversion did not have a deep cultural impact) and came into conflict with the no less invasive Russians.

Europe did not participate in the general development of the pre-modern system until very late, after the year 1000. Until then it had remained a backward and barbaric periphery.

At the dawn of the current era, the population of Europe, including Italy, was some 30 million (8 per cent of the world population, less than 30 per cent of that of China and half of that of the Middle East), of which half were in Italy and in land dominated by the Gauls. The take-off of Europe was very slow because, by the year 1000, Europe, including Italy, had barely more than 30 million inhabitants. However, between the year 1000 and 1350, its population rose to 80 million (18 per cent of the world population, estimated at 440 million), although it dropped to 60 million in 1400 (because of the Black Death). It rose again, reaching 120 million in 1700 (18 per cent of the world population of 950 million). The precipitous increase in European demography had begun and it was to explode in the 19th century.

Up to the year 1000 European agricultural productivity was greatly inferior to that of the civilised regions of China, India and the Middle East and there were no towns on the continent. The take-off was, however, rapid as from that time and two centuries later Europe was covered with lively towns and monuments that show the extent of the increase in surplus generated by its agriculture. For the last two to three centuries of the period under consideration, which ended in 1492 with the beginning of world hegemony by modern and capitalist Europe, the continent became a new centre in gestation, with a weight equal to half that of China. It was already double or triple that of the Middle East, if one accepts the hypothesis, which is very likely, of agricultural productivity and the degree of urbanisation as equivalent. This contrasts with the 15 preceding centuries when Europe represented little or almost nothing in the world system as its weak productivity of labour prevented the development of a significant surplus.

Most of this trade came from the Middle East, even if many of the products imported by Europe came from further away – China and India – and only transited through the Middle East. In the 13th century, however, for the first time a direct link was established between Europe and China through Mongol territory, thus cutting out the Middle East.

The conquest of Genghis Khan in fact coincided exactly with the European take-off, which soon caught up with the most advanced regions constituted by the three eastern centres. Europe–China trade was thus intense even if the period in which the Mongolian route was used was brief – less than a century. From 1500 the sea route superseded the ancient land routes. The assessment of Genghis Khan's conquests was distorted by the Europeans who discovered China. So the dominant discourse – Eurocentric as always – attributed a positive role to the Mongol empire in that it established an East–West link that in fact had already existed for ages, even if the Europeans did not know about it. Indeed, the negative effects of the Turkish–Mongolian conquests, which impoverished the main ancient trading partners through the massive destruction wrought in northern China, south-west central Asia, Iran, Iraq and Russia, has always, because of this European perspective, been under-estimated. Overall, the Mongol conquests were more negative than positive as far as East–West trade as a whole was concerned.

Even during the last centuries of our period, Europe, which was peripheral in the ancient system, remained backward. In fact the European balance of trade was always heavily in the red, as the continent did not have many products to trade, while it imported luxury goods and technology from the East and it had to make good the deficit by exporting metals.

## A few first conclusions

The global structure of the world tributary system over the 20 centuries under consideration proved to be remarkably stable. This, given the relative importance of each of the regional blocs – in population and wealth – gradually overturned the relationships between them and created the new structure characteristic of modern capitalism.

The most significant developments in this evolution can be summarised as follows:

1) For the whole period of the 20 centuries China's progress was sustained and continuous. It held a position that was remarkable (but not dominant – see below) as well as stable in the ancient world tributary

system. The same was true, although to a lesser degree, of India, the second sub-continent of the system.

2) In contrast, the stagnation of the Middle East over the whole period was an ominous sign that the region's position in the system had slipped back.

3) The most outstanding evolution was that of Europe. A marginal periphery for 15 centuries, Europe underwent, during the five centuries preceding the capitalist revolution, a gigantic leap forward. This upheaval became even more evident in the two centuries following our period because of the conquest and construction of America by Europe, inaugurating the transformation of a system that up until then had concerned the ancient world, into a total, planetary system.

4) Central Asia had become a key region in the system, the obligatory passageway linking all the most advanced regions of the ancient epochs (China, India and the Middle East, with Europe being a latecomer). Studies of central Asia emphasise the decisive importance of the interactions and commercial, scientific and technological exchanges that passed through this key region. But it was to lose its functions in the world capitalist system and hence become definitively marginalised.

5) The capitalist system that started to develop as from 1500 was qualitatively different from the preceding one. It was not only a question of upsetting the relative positions of the regions concerned to the benefit of Europe. This became the dominant centre at the world level, a centre that was enlarged by the European expansion in North America and the emergence of Japan. The concept of domination that was now characteristic of the new world system had not existed in the previous tributary system. Associated with this transformation I have stressed the importance of another, no less qualitative transformation: the transfer of dominance in the social system from the politico-ideological plane to the economic.

## The earlier Arab-Islamic and Mediterranean systems

Everybody knows that the Arab-Islamic Mediterranean and Middle East region enjoyed a brilliant civilisation even before the Italian cities.

But did the Arab-Islamic world constitute proto-capitalist systems? The proto-capitalist forms are present and, at certain times and places, inspired a glorious civilisation. The views I have put forward on this subject (see my books *The Arab Nation*, 1978 and *Eurocentrism* 2011a) tie in with Fawzy Mansour's book (1990) on the historical roots of the impasse of the Arab world and, in some regards, with the works of the late Ahmad Sadek Saad. Beyond possible divergences – or shades of meaning – we are of the common opinion that the Arab-Islamic political system was not dominated by proto-capitalist (mercantilist) forces but, on the contrary, that the proto-capitalist elements remained subject to the logic of the dominant tributary system power. In fact, I consider the Arab-Islamic world as part of a larger regional system, which I call the Mediterranean system.

I have suggested (in *Eurocentrism*) that we can date the birth of this Mediterranean system from the conquests of Alexander the Great (3rd century BCE) and conceptualise a single long historic period from this date to the Renaissance, encompassing at first the 'ancient Orient' (around the eastern basin of the Mediterranean), then the Mediterranean as a whole and its Arab-Islamic and European extensions.

I have in this regard put forward the thesis that we are dealing with a single tributary system from 300 BCE (unification of the Orient by Alexander the Great) to 1492. I refer to a single cultural area whose unity is manifested in a common metaphysical formulation (the tributary ideology of the region), beyond the successive expressions of this metaphysics (Hellenistic, Eastern Christian, Islamic, Western Christian). In this tributary area I find it useful to distinguish between its central regions (the Mediterranean Orient) and its peripheral regions (the European West). Within this entity exchanges of every kind have (nearly always) been highly intensive and the associated proto-capitalist forms highly advanced, particularly evident in the central regions (in the period of the first flowering of Islam from the 8th to the 12th centuries and in Italy for the succeeding centuries). These exchanges have been the means of a significant redistribution of surplus. However, the eventual centralisation of surplus was essentially tied to the centralisation of political power. From that point of view the cultural area as a whole never constituted a single unified imperial state (except for the two brief periods of the Alexandrine empire and the Roman empire occupying all the central regions of the system). Generally speaking, the peripheral region of the European West remained extremely fragmented under the feudal form (and this is the very expression of its peripheral character). The central region was divided between the Christian Byzantine Orient and the Arab-Islamic empires (the Umayyad, then the Abbasid dynasties). It was first subject to internal centrifugal forces, then belatedly unified in the Ottoman empire, whose establishment coincided with the end of the period and the overall peripheralisation of the eastern region – to the benefit of a shift of the centre towards the previously peripheral region of Europe and the Atlantic.

Could this system be described as proto-capitalist? In support of the thesis is the presence of undeniable proto-capitalist elements (private ownership, commodity enterprise, wage labour) throughout the period, expanding in certain places and times (especially in the Islamic area and in Italy), declining in others (especially in barbarian Europe of the first millennium). But in my view the presence of these elements does not suffice to characterise the system. On the contrary, I would argue that, at the crucial level of ideology, what began in the Hellenistic phase of this period (from 300 BCE to the first centuries CE), and then flourished in the (Eastern then Western) Christian and Islamic forms, is purely and simply the tributary ideology, with its major fundamental characteristic: the predominance of metaphysical concerns (Amin 2011b).

What we are talking about is indeed a system, but not a proto-capitalist system, that is, a stage in the rapid transition form tributary society to capitalist society. On the other hand, we are dealing with a tributary system, not a mere juxtaposition of autonomous tributary societies (in the plural), which just happened to share some common elements, such as religion, for example, or integration – albeit of limited duration – in an imperial state, such as that of Rome, Byzantium, the Umayyad or Abbasid dynasties.

The distinction implies in my view a certain degree of centralisation of surplus, which took the form of tribute and not, as in capitalism, that of profit from capital. The normal method of centralisation of this tributary surplus was political centralisation, operating to the advantage of imperial capitals (Rome, Byzantium, Damascus, Baghdad). Of course this centralisation remained weak, as did the authority of the centres concerned. Byzantium, Damascus and Baghdad could not prevent their staging-posts (Alexandria, Cairo, Fez, Kairouan, Genoa, Venice, Pisa, and so on) from frequently achieving their own autonomy. The entirety of barbican Christendom (the first millennium in the West) escaped such centralisation. In parallel, the logic of the centralisation of authority stimulated proto-capitalist relations to the point that mercantile handling of part of the surplus never disappeared from the region, and took on great significance in some areas and epochs, notably during the glorious centuries of Islam, and the emergence of the Italian cities following the Crusades. On this basis I have described the social formations of the Arab world as tributary-mercantile formations. All this leads me to conclude that capitalism might have been born in the Arab world. This takes me back to other discussions on this issue with which I have been associated. I have argued that once capitalism had appeared in Europe and the Atlantic, the process of evolution towards capitalism was brutally halted in its development elsewhere. The reason why the evolution towards capitalism accelerated in the Atlantic West (shifting the centre of gravity of the system from the banks of the Mediterranean to the shores of the Atlantic Ocean), it seems to me, is mainly due to the colonisation (of America, then of the entire globe) and contingently to the peripheral character of Western feudalism.

## Did a single world tributary system exist?

My methodological hypothesis leads me to regard the other cultural areas as further autonomous tributary systems. In particular, it seems to me that the Confucian-Chinese tributary system constituted a world on its own and of its own. It had its own centre (China), characterised by a strong political centralisation (even if the latter under the pressure of internal centrifugal forces exploded from time to time, it was always reconstituted), and its peripheries (Japan especially) had a relationship with China very similar to that of medieval Europe with the civilised Orient. I leave a dotted line after the question of whether the Hindu cultural area constituted a (single) tributary system.

This having been said, the question is: was the Mediterranean system isolated or in close relation with the other Asiatic and African systems?

# The Middle East as the Hub

Can the existence of a permanent world system, in constant evolution, be argued beyond the Mediterranean area and prior to its constitution? A positive response to this question has been suggested to some (notably Frank) by the intensity of exchange relations between the proto-capitalist Mediterranean, the Chinese and Indian Orient and sub-Saharan Africa, and perhaps even the significance of the exchanges in earlier times between these various regions of the ancient world. For my part, I do not believe that it is possible to answer the questions, given the current state of knowledge. It is, however, useful to raise it in order to provoke a systematic exchange of views on what can be deduced from our knowledge, the hypotheses it may inspire, and the directions of research indicated for verification of these hypotheses.

I do not intend to substitute my own intuitive views for the eventual results of these debates. I advance them here only provisionally, to open the discussion. I should therefore suggest the following (provisional) theses.

First, humankind is one since its origins. The itinerary of the earth's population begins from the nucleus of hominids appearing in East Africa, going down the Nile and populating Africa, crossing the Mediterranean and the isthmus of Suez to conquer Europe and Asia, passing the Bering straits and perhaps crossing the Pacific to install themselves (in the most recent epoch) in the Americas. These successive conquests of the planet's territory are beginning to be dated. The following may be the pertinent question: has the dispersal brought a diversification of the lines of evolution of the various human groups, installed in geographical environments of extreme diversity and hence exposed to challenges of differing kinds? Or does the existence of parallel lines of evolution suggest the conclusion that humankind as a whole has remained governed by laws of evolution of universal application? And as a complement to this question, it might be asked what effect have relations between the scattered human populations had on the fate, intensity and rapidity of the transfer of knowledge, experience and ideas?

Intuitively, it might be imagined that some human groups have found themselves fairly isolated in particularly difficult circumstances and have responded to the challenge by particular adaptation unlikely to evolve of themselves. These groups would then be located in 'impasses', constrained to reproduce their own organisation without the latter showing signs of its own suppression. Perhaps included here would be the (still highly fragmented) societies of hunters/fishers/gatherers of the Arctic, the equatorial forest, small islands and some coasts.

But other groups have found themselves in less arduous circumstances that have enabled them to progress simultaneously in mastery of nature (passage to settled agriculture, invention of more efficient tools and so on) and in tighter social organisation. In regard to the latter the question arises of possible laws of social evolution of universal application and the role of external relations in this evolution.

Second, in regard to societies that have clearly advanced, can one detect similar phasing followed by all, albeit at faster or slower rates? Our entire social science is based on this seemingly necessary hypothesis. For the satisfaction of the spirit? As legitimation of a universalist value system? Various formulations of this necessary evolution succeeded one another up to and during the 19th century. They were based either on the succession of modes of exploitation of the soil and instruments utilised (Old Stone Age, New Stone Age, Iron Age), or on the succession of social forms of organisation (the ages of savagery, barbarism, civilisation). Various evolutions in these particular domains were regrafted onto what we regarded as fundamental general tendencies. For example, the matriarchal–patriarchal succession, the succession of the ages of philosophical thought (primitive, animist, metaphysical, Auguste Comte-style positivist), and so on. I shall not spend time here discussing these theories, which are almost always more or less overridden by subsequent research. I merely point to their existence as evidence of the persistence of the need to generalise, beyond the evident diversity that is the property of the scientific approach.

It seems to me that the most sophisticated formulation of all the theories of general evolution was that proposed by Marxism and based on the synthetic notions of modes of production. The latter comes from a conceptualisation of the basic elements of the construction (forces of production, relations of production, infrastructure and superstructure, etc). They are then enriched by the grafting on of particular theories articulated to those of modes of production (such as theory of the family, of the state, etc). Here again I shall not discuss whether these Marxist constructs are indeed those of Marx himself, or the product of later interpretations that may or may not be consonant with the spirit of the Marxism of Marx. Nor shall I discuss the validity of these theories in the light of our present-day greater knowledge of the societies of the past. Once again I merely point to the formulations as the expression of this same need to understand, which implies the possibility of generalising.

Third, on the basis of the conceptualisation proposed, it is not difficult to identify several tributary societies at more or less the same level of maturity of general development: production techniques, instruments, range of goods, forms of organisation of power, systems of knowledge and ideas, and so on. Noteworthy too is a fairly dense web of exchanges of all kinds between these societies: exchange of goods, knowledge, techniques and ideas. Does this density of exchange justify speaking of a single world system (albeit described as tributary) in the singular? Frank provides an explicit criterion: an integrated system arises when reciprocal influences are decisive (A would not be what it is without the relation it has with B). So be it. But the overall question remains: were these relations decisive or not?

However, the universality of the laws of social evolution in no way implies the concept of a single system. Two distinct concepts are involved. The first refers to the fact that distinct societies – separated in geographical distance or time – have been able to evolve in a parallel manner for the same underlying reasons. The second implies that these societies are not distinct from one another but ingredients of the same world society. In the evolution of the latter – necessarily global – the laws in question are inseparable from the effects of the interaction between the various components of the world society.

I would in this context make two prefatory comments. First, economic exchanges are not necessarily a decorative element, making no lasting impression on the mode of production and hence on the level of development. Exchanges may be a significant means of distribution of surplus, decisive for some segments of the inter-related societies. The question is not one of principle but of fact. Were they? Where and when? I discount any hasty generalisation that they were always (or generally) so or that they were never (or with rare exceptions) so. In the case of the Arab-Islamic region, for example, I have said that the exchanges were significant. They were enough to mark the formation of a tributary–mercantile character essential to an understanding of its involuted history of succession from a 'glorious' phase to one of 'degeneration', and of shifts of the centres of gravity of wealth and power in the region. I have also said that the proto-capitalist formation of mercantilist Europe (17th–18th centuries) rapidly climbed the step towards capitalism thanks to these exchanges it dominated. But whether the exchanges had a matching role in China, India, the Roman empire, etc, I personally am in no position to say. Second, the exchanges in question must not be limited only to the economic field; far from it. The writing of the history of the precapitalist epochs puts greater emphasis on cultural exchanges (especially the spread of religions) and military and political exchanges (rise and fall of empires, 'barbarian' invasions, etc), whereas the accent is on the economic aspect of relations within the modern world system. Was this distinction wrong?

I do not think so. I believe, on the contrary, that the historians – albeit intuitively – have grasped the reversal of dominance, from the political and ideological to the economic, which is the central core of my own thesis. At this level is it possible to speak of a single tributary political and ideological world system? I do not believe so. I have therefore preferred to speak of distinct tributary 'cultural areas' founded precisely on broad systems of particular reference – most often the religious: Confucianism, Hinduism, Islam, Christianity. Of course there is a certain relationship between these various metaphysics since they express the fundamental requirement of the same type of (tributary) society. The relationship in turn facilitates mutual borrowings. To approach an answer to the question (of one or more systems), it is necessary to combine three elements: the density of economic exchanges and transfers of surplus distributed through this channel; the degree of centralisation of political power; and the relative diversity/specificity and hence autonomy of the ideological systems. Autonomy of the various tributary systems does not preclude economic relations and other exchanges among them, nor even that such exchanges could be significant. It would be impossible to understand many historical facts and evolutions without reference to these exchanges: the transfer of technology of all kinds (the compass, gunpowder, paper, silk that gave its name to the roads in question, printing, Chinese noodles becoming Italian pasta, etc); the spread of religious beliefs (Buddhism crossing from India to China and Japan, Islam travelling as far as Indonesia and China, Christianity as far as Ethiopia, south India, and central Asia), etc.

There is certainly no centralisation of surplus at the level of a world system comparable to that characterising the modern world in the exchanges that led here and there to lively proto-capitalist links (from China and India to the Islamic world, the African Sahel and medieval Europe) and transfers of surplus – perhaps even decisive at key points of the network of exchanges. The explanation is that centralisation of surplus at the time operated mainly in association with the centralisation of power, and there was no kind of world empire or even a world power comparable to what British hegemony would constitute in the 19th century or United States hegemony in the 20th. The ancient (tributary) epochs had nothing comparable to the polarisation on a global scale of the modern capitalist world. The earlier systems, despite significant levels of exchange, were not polarising on a world scale, even if they were on a regional scale to the benefit of the centres of the regional systems (for example, Rome, Constantinople, Baghdad, the Italian cities, China, India). By contrast, the capitalist system is truly polarising on a global scale and is therefore the only one deservedly described as a world system. This methodology for the analysis of the interactions between the tributary systems may call for a reassessment of the traditional findings in the history of the notorious 'barbarians' who occupied the interstices of the great tributary cultural areas. Was the role of these barbarians really as it has been made out, a purely negative and destructive role? Or did their active role in inter-tributary exchanges give them a certain vocation to take decisive initiatives? The latter would explain their success (not only military) in unifying immense territories (Genghis Khan's empire), their capacity to situate themselves at the heart of ideological initiatives (Islam born in Arabia, the barbarian crossroads of Mediterranean–Indian–African exchanges), their capacity to hoist themselves rapidly to central positions in a tributary system (the glorious example of the Khwarism area in the first centuries of Islam), etc.

A final reservation concerning the systematisation of the hypothesis of the existence of a single world system throughout history: is it possible to speak of tributary systems and significant exchange networks among them before the 5th to 3rd centuries BCE? I do not think so for the following three reasons at least: (1) because the social systems of the greater part of humankind were still backward at the stage I have described as communal; (2) because the islets of civilisation at the stage where the state was the recognised form of the expression of power had not yet found complete tributary ideological expression (see the argument on the ideology of the ancient world in *Eurocentrism*); (3) because the density of the exchange relations between these islets remained weak (this did not preclude some exchange relations, for example, technological borrowings that were able to travel unexpected distances).

## The diversity of tributary formations

Marx made his abstract model of capitalist production before considering the emergence of its concrete historical forms. Likewise, and for the same reasons, I shall first make an abstract presentation of the tributary mode before examining its concrete and diverse historical forms. Such an examination is no less important as there is great diversity in response to the challenges.

The tributary form of China, in the long run the main protagonist in universal history, has been the object of analysis – particularly by Pomeranz (2000) and Giovanni Arrighi (1994) – that I find very convincing (as opposed to the simplified interpretation of Frank 1998), which I have taken up and developed elsewhere (Amin 2011b). These theses make it possible to understand how China was able to invent modernity even before Europe. I find it quite justified to refer to the proto-capitalist tributary formation of China as from the 13th century.

I have studied the successive forms of tributary 'Arab' (and Middle East) formation. Discussion on these issues has been animated but it has not spread much beyond Arab circles of reflection in which I have participated with, among others, Sadek Saad, Fawzy Mansour, Fayçal Darraj ('non orthodox' Marxists). Our criticisms were especially addressed to the political popularisers (*qawmiyin*), whose writings outrageously simplified those of leading thinkers on the nationalist question (like Constantin Zirrik, Yassine el Hafez, Elias Morcos). I have emphasised the importance of commerce, together with its function as a hub of the region, therefore I describe it as a tributary/proto-capitalist form. The question of the 'Arab nation' is to be considered in this context (see my book *The Arab Nation*, 1978). In this sense, an Arab proto-nation has certainly existed (like the Chinese proto-nation), built by the 'warrior merchants' who, in turn, characterised Mameluk power. The 'mercantile' interpretations of Islam also make sense in this context. The bibliographies of my participation in these debates can be found in my book *Global History: A View from the South* (2011b).

## The mercantalist transition in Europe 1500–1800

The world system is not reducible to the relatively recent form of capitalism dating back only to the final third of the 19th century, with the onset of imperialism (in the sense that Lenin attached to this term) and the accompanying colonial division of the world. On the contrary, we say that this world dimension of capitalism found expression right from the outset and remained a constant of the system through the successive phases of its development. The recognition that the essential elements of capitalism crystallised in Europe during the Renaissance suggests 1492 – the beginning of the conquest of America – as the date of the simultaneous birth of both capitalism and the world capitalist system, the two phenomena being inseparable.

How should we qualify the nature of the transition from 1500 to 1800? Various qualifications have been suggested, based on the political norms prevailing at the time (the *ancien régime* or the age of absolute monarchy) or character of its economy (mercantilism). Indeed, the old mercantilist societies of Europe and the Atlantic and their extension towards central and eastern Europe are problematic. Let us simply note that these societies witnessed the conjunction of certain key preliminary elements of the crystallisation of the capitalist mode of production. These key elements are a marked extension of the field of commodity exchanges affecting a high proportion of agricultural production; an affirmation of modern forms of private ownership and the protection of these forms by the law; and a marked extension of free wage labour (in agriculture and craftsmanship). However, the economy of these societies was more mercantile (dominated by trade and exchange) than capitalist by virtue of the fact that the development of the forces of production had not yet imposed the factory as the principal form of production.

As this is a fairly obvious case of a transitional form, I shall make two further comments on this conclusion. First, the elements in question – that some have called proto-capitalist (and why not?) – did not miraculously emerge in 1492. They can be found long before in the region, in the Mediterranean precinct particularly, in the Italian cities and across the sea in the Arab-Islamic world. They had also existed for a very long time in other regions: in India, China, etc. Why then begin the transition to capitalism in 1492 and not in 1350, or in 900, or even earlier? Why speak of transition to capitalism only for Europe and not also describe as societies in transition toward capitalism the Arab-Islamic or Chinese societies in which these elements of proto-capitalism can be found? Indeed, why not abandon the notion of transition altogether, in favour of a constant evolution of a system in existence for a long while, in which the elements of proto-capitalism have been present since very ancient times? My second comment explains in part my hesitation in following the suggestions made above. The colonisation of America accelerated to an exceptional extent the expansion of the proto-capitalist elements indicated above. For three centuries the social systems that participated in the colonisation were dominated by such elements. This had not been the case elsewhere or before. On the contrary, the proto-capitalist segments of society had remained cloistered in a world dominated by tributary social relations (feudal in medieval Europe). So let us now clarify what we mean here by the domination of tributary relations.

One question we might ask is whether the dense network of Italian cities did or did not constitute a proto-capitalist system. Undoubtedly proto-capitalist forms were present at the level of the social and political organisation of these dominant cities. But can the Italian cities (and even others, in south Germany, the Hanseatic cities, etc) really be separated from the wider body of medieval Christendom? That wider body remained dominated by feudal rural life, with its ramifications at the political and ideological level: customary law, the fragmentation of powers, cultural monopoly of the church, and so on. In this spirit it seems to me essential to give due weight to the evolution of the political system of proto-capitalist Europe from the 16th to the 18th century. The evolution that led from the feudal fragmentation of medieval power to the centralisation of the absolute monarchy kept pace precisely with the acceleration of proto-capitalist developments. This European specificity is remarkable, since elsewhere – in China or in the Arab-Islamic world for example – there is no known equivalent of feudal fragmentation: the (centralised) state precedes peripheral character of the feudal society – the product of a grafting of the Mediterranean tributary formation onto a body still largely at the backward communal stage (the Europe of the barbarians).

The (belated) crystallisation of the state, in the form of absolute monarchy, implied, at the outset, relations between the state and the various components of the society that differed abstractly from those that were the case for the central tributary state. The central tributary state merged with the tributary dominant class, which had no existence outside it. The state of the European absolute monarchies was, on the contrary, built on the ruins of the power of the tributary class of the peripheral modality and relied strongly in its state-building on the proto-capitalist urban elements (the nascent bourgeoisie) and rural elements (peasantry evolving towards the market). Absolutism resulted form this balance between the new and rising proto-capitalist forces and the vestiges of feudal exploitation.

An echo of this specificity can be found in the ideology accompanying the formation of the state of the *ancien régime*, from the Renaissance to the Enlightenment of the 18th century. I stress the specificity – and in my opinion advanced character – of this ideology, which broke with the tributary ideology. In the latter scheme, the predominance of the metaphysical view of the world is based on the dominance of the political instance over the economic base. To avoid any misunderstanding, I stress that metaphysics is not synonymous with irrationality (as the radical currents of the Enlightenment have painted it), but seeks to reconcile reason and faith (see my discussion of this theme in *Eurocentrism*). The ideological revolution from the Renaissance to the Enlightenment did not suppress metaphysics (metaphysical needs), but freed the sciences from their subjection to it and thereby paved the way to the constitution of a new scientific field, that of the social sciences. At the same time, of course, (far from accidental) concomitance between the practices of the new state (of the *ancien régime*) and developments in the field of ideology began to move rapidly towards the bourgeois revolution (1688 in England, 1776 in New England, 1789 in France). They challenged the absolutist system that had provided a platform for proto-capitalist advances. New concepts of power legitimised by democracy (however qualified) were introduced. It is also from there on that the Europeans developed a new awareness of their specificity. Before the Renaissance the Europeans (of medieval Christendom) knew they were not superior (in power potential) to the advanced societies of the Orient, even if they regarded their religion as superior, just as the others did. From the Renaissance on, they knew they had acquired at least potential superiority over all the other societies and could henceforth conquer the entire globe, which they proceeded to do.

## A critique of evolutionism

The theory according to which all human societies have been forever integrated in a single world system, in continuous evolution (capitalism not representing, therefore, any kind of qualitative break in this respect), arises from a philosophy of history which is in the end based on the notion of competition. Certainly it is based on a realistic observation of facts, namely, that all societies on earth, in all eras, are to some extent in competition with one another – it would not matter whether the relations they did or did not entertain showed their awareness of it. We know that the strongest must carry the day. At this level of abstraction there is indeed a single world, because there is a single humankind. It might perhaps be added that most 'open' societies with intensive relations with the others have a greater chance of measuring up to this competition and facing up to it more effectively. It is otherwise for those who shy away from competition and seek to perpetuate their way of life; they risk being overtaken by the progress made elsewhere and later being marginalised.

This discourse is not wrong, but merely at such a high level of abstraction that it begs the real issue, namely, how this competition is manifested. Two bourgeois historians – themselves philosophers of history – deliberately placed themselves at this most general level of abstraction (in order to refute Marx). Arnold Toynbee in this regard suggests an operative model reduced to two terms: the challenge and the response to the challenge. I suggest that as a model valid for all times and all places, it teaches us nothing that is not already obvious. Toynbee (1947) suggests no law to explain why the challenge is taken up or not. He is satisfied with a case-by-case treatment. There is an almost natural parallel with the contradiction between the axioms of neoclassical bourgeois economics defined in terms claiming to be valid for all times (scarcity, utility, etc) and the historical concept of qualitatively differing successive modes of production, determining specific institutional frameworks in which the 'eternal rationality of human beings' is expressed. Jacques Pirenne (1947), far superior to Toynbee in my opinion, suggests a refinement of constant contradiction between (seagoing) open societies and (land-based) closed societies and does not hesitate to describe the former as capitalist (Sumer, Phoenicia, Greece, Islam in the first centuries, the Italian cities, the modern West) and the latter as feudal (from ancient Persia to the Europe of the Middle Ages). He never hesitated to attribute to what I call proto-capitalist elements the decisive place in the progress of the open societies making the driving force of development of the forces of production. He likewise never concealed that his thesis intended to discount the closed experiences of the Soviet Union and salute the dynamism of the Atlantic world. Hence, Pirenne managed – certainly with skill – to replace class struggle with a constant struggle between the capitalist tendency and the feudal tendency within human societies.

I still believe that Marx's method is superior, precisely because it situates the abstraction at the appropriate level. The concept of modes of production gives back to history its explicit real dimension. At that level the significance and character of the capitalist break can be detected. The break is such that I do not think that competition between societies of earlier times and within the modern world system can be treated in the same way. This is because the competition of earlier times rarely crossed the threshold of consciousness and each society saw, or believed, itself 'superior' in its own way, protected by its deities, even when a looming danger imposed a greater consciousness (as between Muslims and Crusaders). Moreover, the discrepancy between the great tributary pre-capitalist societies is not such that the superiority of one over another is obvious; it is always conjunctural and relative. There is nothing comparable to the subsequent overwhelming superiority of capitalist societies over the rest. That is why I see the seizing of consciousness of this superiority as crucially important and therefore date the beginnings of capitalism to 1492. From then on the Europeans knew that they could conquer the world and went on to do so (see my arguments on this point in *Eurocentrism*). We know, *a posteriori* (but the actors of the time were unaware), that the 'strongest' is the one who has advanced to a qualitatively superior mode of production – capitalism. I would add that in the competition of earlier times geographical distance had a blunting effect. However intensive the exchanges between Rome and China, I find it difficult to believe that the external factor could have a similar impact to that of the discrepancies in productivity of our own times. I believe that this distancing gave strictly internal factors a considerably more decisive relative weight. It also explains why those concerned had difficulty in assessing the real balance of forces. Quite different, it seems to me, is competition within the modern world system, where consciousness is so acute that it is a plaintive chorus in the daily discourse of the authorities.

## An illustration of the tributary regional and world systems

I illustrate my concept of the ancient world system (reduced to societies of the so-called eastern hemisphere: Eurasia–Africa) for the periods covering the 18 centuries between the establishment of the Hellenistic system in the Middle East (300 BCE), the establishment of the Han state in China (200 BCE), the Kushāna and Maurya states in central Asia and India (200 BCE), and the European Renaissance, that is, from 300 BCE to 1500 CE as follows.

As I have already said, all societies of the system in question are, from one end of the period to the other, of a tributary nature. Nevertheless, it is possible to distinguish among all these societies those which I would call central tributaries from those which are peripheral tributaries. The former are characterised by a surplus centralisation at the relatively high state level, with redistribution placed under its control; while in peripheral formations, the embryonic character of the state (and even its virtual non-existence) leads to a complete disintegration of surplus distribution monopolised by local feudal systems. The centres–peripheries antithesis is not, in this case, analogous to

## The Middle East as the Hub

that which characterises the (modern) capitalist world. In the latter, the relationship in question is an economic domination relationship in which the centres override the peripheries (and this is associated with economic dominance). This is not so in the ancient relationship. Dominated by the ideological authority, the tributary structures are either central or peripheral depending on the degree of the completion of the power centralisation process and its expression through a state religion. In the central formations, the latter takes the form of a state religion or a religious-oriented state philosophy with a universal vocation which breaks with the specific local religions of the former periods which I called 'communal formations' (see my book *Class and Nation* (1980)). There is a striking relationship between the establishment of big tributary societies in their completed form and the emergence of great religious and philosophical trends which were to dominate civilisations over the ensuing 2,000 years: Hellenism (300 BCE), Oriental Christianity, Islam (600 CE), Zoroaster, Buddha, and Confucius (all three 500 BCE). This relationship – which in no way excluded the reciprocal concessions provided by the relations that all tributary civilisations maintained among themselves – is not, in my view, an accident, but rather one of the consistent bases of my thesis on the dominant tributary mode.

The establishment of great philosophical and religious movements associated with the formation of tributary systems represents the first wave of revolutions related to universal history, which is expressed by a universalist-oriented vocation transcending the horizons of the local – almost parochial – line of thinking in the ancient periods. This revolution sets up the tributary system as a general system at the entire level of mankind – or almost does so – for 2,000 to 2,500 years. The second wave of universal-oriented revolutions, which opens up capitalist modernity and its possible socialist overtaking, is marked by the Renaissance (and the revolution in Christianity with which it is associated) and, subsequently, by the three great modern revolutions: the French, Russian and Chinese revolutions (see *Eurocentrism*).

The model par excellence of this tributary mode is, in my view, provided by China which, without it seems a long incubation period (there is only one millennium between the Shang and the Zhu and the establishment of the Han dynasty), crystallises in a form which undergoes no fundamental change, either with regard to the organisation of productive forces and production relationships or ideology (the Confucianism–Taoism tandem replaced for only a brief moment by Buddhism), or with regard to power concepts during the 2,000 years between the Han dynasty and the 1911 revolution. Here, surplus centralisation is at its height, at the level of an enormous society, not only during the brilliant periods where political unity was entirely or almost entirely achieved in this continent-country by great successive dynasties (Han, Tāng, Sōng, Yuān, Ming and Qing), but even during the periods of interdynastic disturbances when the country was divided into several kingdoms whose size was nonetheless considerable for the period. At the borders of China, Korea and Vietnam also turned, during the course of the first millennium of our era, into similar tributary systems which, in spite of their political independence with regard to China, borrowed its model of organisation and Confucian ideology.

In the Middle East, the tributary system derived its completed form from the conquest of Alexander the Great. I have recommended in this connection (see *Eurocentrism*) this reading of the successive philosophical and religious orientations of Hellenism, Oriental Christianity and Islam. However, in this region, the incubation period lasted for as long as 30 centuries for Egypt and Mesopotamia, ten centuries for Persia, Phoenicia, etc, and five centuries for Greece. Hellenism, Christianity and Islam were, moreover, to produce a synopsis which borrowed some elements crucial to each of these ancient components and even from Persia and India as well. Here, too, surplus centralisation for the ensuing 2,000 years is remarkable. It is true the region was split after the precarious political unification in the Alexander era; but it was split into large kingdoms for the period. Hence, divided between even bigger empires – those of Byzantium (300 to 1400 CE) and the Sassanids (200 to 600 CE) – and subsequently reunified gradually through the expansion of the Muslim caliphate (formed in the 7th century CE) which conquered Constantinople at the end of our period (in 1453), the spaces of surplus centralisation were still either vast (during the first three centuries of the caliphate), or at the very least, considerable, after the break-up of the caliphate from the year 1000 to the advantage of Arabo-Berber dynasties in North Africa and Turco-Persians in the Mashreq and western part of central Asia. The western Roman empire finds its place in this reading of history as an expression of an expansion of the tributary model to the banks of the western Mediterranean. Of secondary importance in universal history, the Roman empire owes its place to the fact that it has transmitted tributary ideology – in the form of western Christianity – to the European periphery.

A Eurocentric reading of history (see my critical appraisal in *Eurocentrism*) has, in this regard, distorted the achievements which, beyond the Italian peninsula failed to resist barbaric feudalisation (that is, the disintegration of the tributary system).

A third completed tributary centre was established on the Indian continent in 200 BCE from the Maurya period, followed by the Kushāna state (which overlaps the western part of central Asia) and Gupta after the long incubation period which began with the Indus civilisations (Mohenjodaro and Harappa – 2500 BCE). The Muslim conquest from the 11th century on, which followed after a 'pulverisation' period (of the 7th and 9th centuries), re-established, together with the Ghazhavids, the sultanates of Delhi (1200–1500 CE), and subsequently the Mughal empire (1500–1800 CE), a tributary centralisation on a large scale, while the Hinduist states of Dekkan, also tributaries, equally represented considerable kingdoms for the period.

Europe (beyond the Byzantine region and Italian, that is, 'barbaric' Europe), was the product of a tributary graft (transmitted by the ideal of the Roman empire and Christian universalism) on a social body still organised, to a large extent, on deteriorated community bases. Here, I wish to refer to the analysis I made (see *Class and Nation*) which simultaneously gives an account of the disintegration in the control of surpluses, and which defines feudalism as an uncompleted peripheral form of the tributary system, although the collapse of the state system was partially offset by the church. Europe was slowly moving toward the tributary form, as testified by the establishment of absolute monarchies (in Spain and Portugal after the Reconquista, and in England and France after the Hundred Years War). This belatedness constitutes, in my view, the crucial advantage which facilitated the early qualitative strides made by the Renaissance and capitalism (see *Class and Nation*).

Japan constituted, at the other end of the Euro-Asian continent, a peripheral tributary mode whose resemblance to Europe had struck me even before Michio Morishima (1987) came to confirm my thesis. The degraded form of Japanese Confucianism and the feudal disintegration which preceded the belated formation of a monarchical centralisation from the Tokugawa state (1600 CE) bear testimony to this peripheral character (see *Eurocentrism*), which, here, too, explains the remarkable ease with which Japan switched over to capitalism in the 19th century. Sub-Saharan Africa constituted the third periphery. It was still lingering at the communal stage developing towards tributary forms. At this stage the tributary surplus centralisations still operated only on societies with limited size. Disintegration therefore remained the rule.

The status of South East Asia was ambiguous. It seems to me that here it is possible to recognise some central type of tributary formations – even if they only cover smaller spaces than those of other great Asian systems – and peripheral zones (defined by surplus disintegration). To the first type belongs the Khmer empire, followed by its Thai, Burmese and Cambodian successors from the 5th century and, perhaps, in Indonesia, the Majapahit kingdom from the 13th century. On the other hand, the organised societies of Malaysia and Indonesia which crystallised into states under the influence of Hinduism (from the 5th century) and subsequently Islam, seem, in my view, to belong to the peripheral family, crumbled by the scattering of the surplus, collected in very small and relatively numerous and fragile states. The status of the central Asian region was special. The region itself is less defined in its borders than the others. Some large states were established in this region at an early period – such as the Kushāna empire – which directly linked up the Hellenistic Middle East and the Sassanids and then the Islamic Middle East to India and China. The region itself became the centre of gravity of an immense empire at the time of Genghis Khan (1300 CE). Before and after this final crystallisation, it had entered the Islamic orbit. Its modes of organisation were tributary-oriented, at one time advanced (where the expression of centralised power on a large scale makes it possible), at another time relapsing into feudal disintegration. But the major feature of the region was that, by virtue of its geographical position, it was the indispensable transit zone for East–West trade (China, India, the Middle East and beyond to as far as the peripheries of the system). Having been in competition with the sea route

# The Middle East as the Hub

from time immemorial, the continental route lost its importance only belatedly in the 16th century.

As for the second characteristic of the ancient world system: during the entire 18 centuries under consideration, all the societies not only existed together, but still maintained trade links of all types (trade and war, technological and cultural transfers), which were much more intense than was generally thought. In this very general sense, one can talk of the general system without, of course, mistaking its nature for that of the modern (capitalist) world system. To clarify things, I want to distinguish four sets of links:

1) The links mutually maintained between the three major centres (A – Rome and Byzantium, the Sassanid empire, the caliphate; B – India; C – China) were undoubtedly the most intense of all, merely in view of the wealth and relative power of the centres in question, at least in the glorious years of their history.

2) The links maintained by the Arabo-Persian Islamic centre with the three peripheries (Europe, Africa, South East Asia): the trade in question was less intense than that of the previous group (due to the relative poverty of the peripheries), and especially important is the fact that it was asymmetrical (a concept that I clearly distinguish from the specific inequality of the centres–peripheries relationships of the modern world) in the sense that they were perhaps neutral in their effects on the centre, but crucial for the development of the peripheries. These relationships considerably accelerated the establishment of states in the African Sahel and East Africa (see *Class and Nation*) as well as in Malaysia and Indonesia and thus opened the way for the Islamisation of these regions (Islam then replacing the ancient local religions in line with the needs of the tributary world). They also contributed immensely to the emergence of Italian trading cities and, through these cities, of infiltration throughout the whole of feudal Europe.

3) The links maintained by the Chinese centre with the Japanese periphery and the South East Asian periphery are of the same nature as those in the second group. A direct communication between China and Europe was established, using of course the routes of central Asia but without passing through the canal in the heart of the Islamic

caliphate. This direct relation existed only for a relatively short period, within the framework of the Mongol Pax (the Genghis Khan empire in the 13th century). But it was crucial for subsequent events of history because it made it possible for Europe to resort to China's vast technological accomplishments (gunpowder, printing, the compass, etc); Europe was mature enough to do this and take the qualitative leap from a peripheral tributary (feudal) system to capitalism. Furthermore, shortly thereafter, Europe substituted the sea route it dominated for all ancient forms of long-haul transport, thus establishing direct links between itself and each of the other regions of the world (Africa, India, South East Asia), 'discovering' and then 'conquering' America at the same time.

4) The links maintained by the Indian centre (Buddhist and Hindu) with its South East Asian peripheries are similar to the China–Japan links.

It obviously appears that the relative intensity of external flows, as compared with the different masses constituted by the regional formations under consideration, varies considerably from one region to another. The three key central regions, A, B and C (Middle East, India, China), represented, in terms of economic weight, a multiple of what constituted each of the other regions.

Geography has assigned to key central region A an exceptional role without any possible competitor until modern times, when Europe, through its control over the seas, overcame the constraints. Indeed, this region is directly linked to all the others (China, India, Europe, Africa) and is the only one that is. For two millennia, it was an indispensable transit route to Europe, China, India or Africa. Besides, the region does not reflect a relative homogeneity similar to that of China or India, neither at the geographical level (stretching from the Moroccan shores of the Atlantic to the Aral Sea, Pamirs and to the Oman Sea, it does not have the features of a continental block as in the case of China and India), nor at the level of its peoples, who themselves are products of the early proliferation of the most ancient civilisations (Egypt, Sumer, Assyria, Mesopotamia, Iran, Hittites, Phoenicians and Greeks) and speak languages from various families (Semitic, Hamitic,

Indo-European). The conquest of Alexander the Great and the triumph of the Hellenistic synthesis triggered a collective awareness which was subsequently strengthened by Oriental Christianity (limited by the Sassanid border) and subsequently and, above all, by Islam.

One of the keys to the success of Islam relates, in my view, to this reality. The region was finally firmly established within the short period covering the first three centuries of the Hegira. It was thus composed of the three superimposed strata of Islamised peoples, namely, the Arabs from the Atlantic to the Gulf, the Persians beyond Zagros to Pakistan, and the Turks in Anatolia and in the entire Turkestan from the Caspian Sea to China proper. Thus, Islam did not only unify the peoples of the so-called classical 'East' but annexed, at the same time, central Asia, the indispensable transit route to China and northern India. I think that this success should be attributed to the fact that in spite of all the conflicts witnessed by history internal to this region, it created a certain solidarity and strengthened the sense of a particular identity with regard to the 'others'; that is, specifically, the Chinese, Indians, Europeans and Africans that the Muslim *umma* (nation) borders on along each of its frontiers. In central Asia the success of Islam created regional unity, which, until then, was absent. For the civilisation in this region, in which trade flows represent larger volumes than the surplus produced locally, depended on the capacity to capture, in passing, a part of these transit flows.

The magnitude of the links with the others for the entire key central region A and its central Asia annex bestows on its social system a special character which I venture, for this reason, to call 'mercantile-tributary', thus indicating even the magnitude of proto-capitalist forms (commercial links, wage labour, private property or estate) in the tributary societies of Islam. Moreover, beyond the original boundaries of Islam, the gradual conquest of African and South East Asian peripheries is also worth putting into close relationship with its mercantile dynamism of region A (see *The Arab Nation, Class and Nation*).

Third, the world system described above for the period of 18 centuries preceding the Renaissance is not analogous to the modern system that follows it (in time). To talk about the ancient system in its spatial and time universality, or even in its Arab-Islamic component, as the ancestor of the modern system would be misleading. For this is only a platitude – succession in time and nothing more; or it implies that there was no qualitative break but only quantitative development and a shift of the system's centre of gravity from the southern shore of the Mediterranean to its northern shore (Italian cities) and then to the Atlantic shores, and this boils down to eliminating the essential, that is, the qualitative change in the nature of the system: the law of value which governs the dynamics of the modern system but not those of the tributary system. This universalisation of the law of value is exclusively responsible for the establishment of one single antinomy which operates worldwide (a centre composed of historically established national centres as such and peripheries all economically dependent on this centre), thus creating an ever-increasing differentiation from one period to another between the centre and the peripheries, over the entire five-century history of capitalism and for the entirely visible or imaginable horizon within the framework of its immanent laws. In this connection, there is nothing comparable to the lasting relative balance (for 2,000 years) between the key central regions of the tributary period. This qualitative difference forbids talking about interdependence – unequal, as it were – of the different components of the ancient system in terms similar to those that govern the modern world. Key regions A, B and C are certainly in relation with one another (and with the other regions). It remains to be demonstrated that this interdependence would have been essential. The parallelism in their trend is no evidence of the crucial nature of their relations; it only reflects the general character of the laws governing the social development of all mankind (thus defining the status of the specificities). The possible concomitance of the rise and the specificities of states of the past is far from obvious.

Pirenne (1947) had already observed – a view taken up again by A.G. Frank – the concomitance between the fall of the Roman empire and that of the Han dynasty. But the Roman fall was followed by the rise of Byzantium, the Sassanid and the Kushāna state, while the decline of the Hans was followed, right from the year 600 (the height of barbarianism in the West) by the rise of the Tāng and, three centuries earlier, by that of the Guptas, whose fall coincided (also by chance) with the rise of Islam. There are no clues to the identification of the general cycles of the rise and fall. The very term 'fall' is, even in this context, misleading; it is the fall of a form of state organisation in a given region, but, in most cases, as regards the development of productive forces, there is no parallel fall. I am struck rather by the opposite phenomenon, that is, the continuity of these long parallel historical events: from Rome–Byzantium–Sassanids–Islam to the Ottomans and the Safavids, from the Maurya dynasty to that Mughal state, from the Han dynasty to those of Ming and Qing, there were only a few qualitative changes but great quantitative progress on the same organisation (tributary) bases. This does not exclude the fact that, in examining local developments, it is possible to explain any particular political rise (or fall) which may still be relative by a special link in which external relations have occasionally played a role. Once again, there is nothing similar to the cycles of the capitalist economy, whose scope is really global as a result of the universalisation of the law of value, the basis of the modern capitalist economy. The crystallisation of new modernity in Europe which was achieved within a short time (from the rise of Italian cities to the Renaissance: three to four centuries) is not the repetition of a general phenomenon under which would be subsumed all together the birth of civilisations (Egypt, Sumer, Harappa, Shang) and the establishment of empires (Achemenid, Alexander, Rome, Byzantium, Sassanid, Umayyad, Abbasid, Ottoman, Safavid, Maurya, Gupta, the Mughal state, Han, Tāng, Sōng, Ming, Qing and the Genghis Khan empire).

I proposed an explanation of this fact (see *Class and Nation*) that the qualitative break is first made within a tributary periphery (Europe) and not in one of its centres (A, B or C) and is then repeated in another periphery (Japan). I based my explanation on the contrast between the flexibility of the peripheries and the rigidity of the centres, that is, while keeping to the logical context of the general nature of the laws of the evolution of societies (the 'uneven development' which is the general form of an identical overall evolution). I consider this explanation more satisfactory than those proposed by the different characteristically Eurocentric conceptions (see *Eurocentrism*). I also think it is more satisfactory than Pirenne's theory, which I have referred to as being based on the permanent contrast between capitalism (the synonym of openness, especially in maritime terms) and feudalism (the synonym of closure, especially in landlocked terms). Like A.G. Frank's (who is close to the extreme), Pirenne's theory is a transformation of the Eurocentric deformation: it attributes the European miracle to the maritime openness of the region, since each of the theories is based on the negation of the specific nature of the capitalist modernity.

Of course the crystallisation of capitalism in Europe has a history (it is not done by magic, in 1493 for instance) and entails specific consequences for the subsequent evolution of the other regions. The rapid development of Italian cities, which of course accounted for such crystallisation, is in turn a result of the tributary mercantile expansion of the Arab-Islamic region. However, it is because it operated within an outlying zone (feudal Europe) that this Italian expansion set fire to the grassland and accelerated the rate of evolution to the extent of creating in Europe a system that was qualitatively superior to that of the formerly more advanced societies. I have given (in *Class and Nation*) a detailed explanation of this conjuncture, which establishes a link between the state's weakness and the establishment of an area of autonomy for a veritable new class – the middle class – to appear, then the state's alliance with the latter in order to go beyond the breaking up of the feudal system by creating a new absolutist and mercantilist state. The general consequence of the new crystallisation of Europe (capitalist and no longer feudal) is obvious: it blocked the evolution of the other societies of the world, which were gradually marginalised in the new global system. Moreover, the capitalist crystallisation of Europe brought about a specific hostility towards the Arab-Islamic region. We recall at this juncture the observation I made earlier about the specific position of the Islamic world in the old system. In order to establish direct links with the rest of the world to its advantage, Europe had to break the indispensable monopolistic and intermediary position enjoyed by the Islamic world. Ever since the early attempt of the Crusades, which was followed immediately by the establishment of the link between Europe and China that was opened by the Mongolian peace during the era of Genghis Khan, this hostility has been pursued and has found expression in a particularly neurotic attitude towards Muslims which generated in turn a similar response in the opposite direction. It is finally to break up this inevitable intermediate zone that Europeans set off on the seas. Contrary to Pirenne's thesis, such a choice was not the result of some geographical determinism.

Fourth, the remarks made concerning these 2,000 years are not valid for the previous periods: on the one hand, the civilised societies known during previous periods – *a fortiori* the barbarians – were sometimes organised in a manner that was different from those of the subsequent tributary period; on the other hand, the network of relations that they engaged in among themselves was also different. Certainly our scientific knowledge of the past becomes even less as we recede further in time. Nevertheless, it seems to me that two lines of thought relating to the 'pre-tributary' eras can be distinguished (two philosophies of history). Pirenne's theory – which on this basic point is similar to the points of view defended by A.G. Frank – does not recognise any qualitative break around 300 BCE, neither around the current era nor from the end of the Roman empire (the end of antiquity, according to contemporary textbooks), just as it does not recognise any qualitative break separating modern times from ancient times. Indeed, as I already mentioned, according to Pirenne, all periods of human history are marked by the same contrast between open, maritime and capitalistic societies and closed, landlocked and feudal societies. Moreover, like Frank, Pirenne emphasises the exchange relations that existed among the societies at all times, irrespective of the distance separating them (for example, on the exchanges between Sumer, the Indus civilisation, Egypt, Crete, Phoenicia and Greece). Like Frank, Pirenne's theory is based on a philosophy of linear history: the progress is quantitative and continuous, without any qualitative change; in the words of Frank, it is the 'culmination of accumulation'. On the other hand, the commonly accepted theory of Marxism distinguishes three stages of civilisation that are different in terms of quality: slavery, feudalism and capitalism. I do not enter into this field of Marxology, to resolve the question of knowing whether this theory is really that of Marx (and of Engels) – and to what extent – or whether it is only that of the subsequent Marxian common understanding. In any case, this theory states that all the societies are feudal societies: for Europe, from the end of the Roman empire; for the Byzantine and Islamic Middle East, right from their constitutions; for India, since the installation of the Maurya dynasty; and for China, since the Han era. Previously, on the other hand, according to this theory, they must have passed through a phase of slavery whose obvious and indisputable existence would be exemplified by Greece and Rome. In my opinion, people put forward by analogy a stage of slavery in China (from the Shang to the Han), in India (the Indus and Aryan civilisations), in the Middle East (in Mesopotamia). The existence of slavery located elsewhere and later on in certain regions of Africa, produced by the disintegration of earlier communal configurations, proves – according to this theory – that the passage through slavery constitutes a general requirement.

I do not share this point of view (see *Class and Nation*) and have offered instead a theory according to which: (1) the general form of class society that succeeded the previous communal formations is that of the tributary society; (2) the feudal form is not the general rule but only the peripheral form of the tributary type; (3) various conditions determine the specific form of each tributary society (castes, estates of the feudal era in the European sense – Stände; peasant communities subjected to a state bureaucracy, etc); (4) slavery is not a general requirement – it is absent from most of the landmarks of history (Egypt, India, China); it hardly undergoes any important development unless it is linked to a commercial economy and is therefore found within ages that are very different from the point of view of the development of productive forces (Graeco-Roman slavery and slavery in America up to the 19th century). Are the periods before the break of tributary societies not then to be distinguished from the rest of the precapitalist history? For instance, Egypt in particular offers the example of a tributary society having practically nothing to do with slavery whose history begins 3,000 years before the crystallisation of the Hellenistic era. Assyria, Babylon, Iran of the Achemenids and probably pre-Mauryan India and pre-Han China sometimes practised slavery but this practice did not constitute the main form of exploitation of productive labour. Finally, according to my theory, a tributary society is not crystallised into its complete form until it produces a universal ideology – a religion based on universal values that go beyond the ideologies of kinship and country religions peculiar to the previous community stage. In this perspective, Zoroaster, Buddha and Confucius announce the crystallisation of the tributary society. Until then, I prefer to talk about 'incubation' or even the 'long transition from communal forms to the tributary form'. This transition, which is perhaps relatively simple and rapid in China, is made more complicated in India as a result of the Aryan invasion that destroyed the Indus civilisation. In the Middle East the diversity of the peoples and trajectories, as well as the mutual influence of one people by the other, compels us to consider the region as a system. I place within this context the early maturing of Egypt into a tributary society, the distinctive mercantile nature of slavery in Greece, and therefore I give particular importance to the Hellenistic synthesis, the prelude to the Christian and Islamic revolutions which were to take over the unification of the region.

Does the intensity of the exchange relations among the societies of these distant eras make it possible to talk about a 'system'? I doubt it, considering that the civilised societies, that is, those advanced in the transition to the tributary form, still remain islets in the ocean of worlds of communities. Even when they are parallel, the trajectories do not prove that the societies in question do constitute a system but establish only the validity of the general laws of evolution.

## Bibliography

Amin, Samir (1978) *The Arab Nation*, London, Zed Books
Amin, Samir (1980) *Class and Nation*, New York, Monthly Review Press
Amin Samir (2011a) *Eurocentrism*, Oxford, Pambazuka Press
Amin Samir (2011b) *Global History: A View from the South*, Oxford, Pambazuka Press
Arrighi, Giovanni (1994) *The Long Twentieth Century*, London, Verso
Etiemble, René (1988) *L'Europe Chinoise*, Paris, Gallimard
Frank, A.G. (1998) *ReOrient: Global Economy in the Asian Age*, Berkeley and Los Angeles, CA, University of California Press
Mansour, Fawzy (1990) *L'impasse du monde arabe*, Paris, L'Harmattan
Morishima, Michio (1987) *Capitalisme et Confucianisme*, Paris, Flammarion
Pirenne, Jacques (1947) *Les grands courants de l'histoire universelle*, Paris, Albin Michel
Pomeranz, Kenneth (2000) *The Great Divergence: China, Europe, and the Making of the Modern World Economy*, Princeton, NJ, Princeton University Press
Toynbee, Arnold (1947) *A Study of History*, Oxford, Oxford University Press

# 4

# The Decline: The Mameluke State, the Miscarriage of the Nahda, and Political Islam

The decline of region A set in during the first century of the Christian calendar – hence a long time before its conquest by the Arabs. With this decline as the background, how should we view the extraordinary 'renewal' of Islam in its first grandeur: the first three centuries of the Hegira?

Personally, I see this renewal as the last 'firework display' (or swan-song) of Hellenism. After all, this renewal cannot be dissociated from the function of the region as a hub, which was still important in the epoch and facilitated by the caliphate's unification. But it should be stressed that the region at that time was not homogenised, because of the diversity of languages and the continuing presence of Christians, who were still numerous. This is overlooked by contemporary ideologues of Arabness (*ourouba*).

The Arab conquest itself was ambiguous. The Iranians thus distinguish the Islamic *fath* (opening) from the Arabic *ghazw* (conquest). They praise the former and pride themselves for having overcome the latter. In Egypt the Coptic wars that most Arab historians prefer to ignore set in motion the collapse of irrigated agriculture. And historians who are neither Arabophobe or Islamophobe have shown that the stages of desertification both in Syria and North Africa were associated with the invasions of the nomads coming from Arabia.

All that did not prevent the brilliant renewal of the caliphate, which extended into the Maghreb and as far as Andalusia. Apart from simply passing Hellenistic heritage to the Arabs who were forming in the Mashreq, Damascus enabled the enrichment of the caliphate by outstanding scientific and philosophical advances that I analysed in my book *Eurocentrism* (2011). Baghdad made possible the grafting of knowledge from Iran and, beyond it, India, onto a Hellenistic Islamic base. But the firework display gradually petered out as the region lost the origins of its cultural diversity.

The Crusades, known by the Arab writers of that time as the Frankish wars, accelerated this decline and when Saladin reconquered Jerusalem, it turned out to be a Pyrrhic victory. It caused the region to fall back on itself and saw the first success of the Europeans (between 1250 and 1500) in discovering new routes towards China (the Russian route to the north, and later the ocean routes). The region maintained its role as a hub, although it was no longer the obligatory passage. And the Ottoman conquest, which unified almost all the Arabs, but under Turkish yoke, came too late to enable a second renewal. It coincided with the beginning of Atlantic mercantilism and the centre of gravity of the newly born capitalist system shifted to the two shores of the Atlantic.

The decline, even if, *a posteriori*, it seemed inexorable, was not continuous. Egypt of the Mamelukes, before and after the Ottoman conquest, managed to re-establish a flourishing trade with India and China to its own advantage. But the general decline continued over and above the ups and downs of the period. That it became very serious was proved by Napoleon Bonaparte's easy victory over Egypt at the end of the 18th century. Nevertheless, this inspired a brilliant new surge, led by Mohamed Ali and his successors until Khedive Ismail. Egypt at that time was what we would today call an 'emerging' country. The violent reaction of the Ottoman state, supported by Great Britain (as the rope supports the person to be hanged), put a brutal end to this surge and prepared the way for the British invasion.

It was this decline, together with the growth of European capitalism, accelerated by the industrial revolution, that would facilitate the colonisation of the Arab world: the early colonising of Algeria by the French, the semi-colonisation of the Ottoman empire, then at the end of the 19th century, the British colonising of Egypt and Sudan, the French of Morocco and Tunisia and later, in 1920, the colonisation of Greater Syria and Iraq.

This chapter does not deal with these issues so it will not recount their history. These reflections are exclusively about the reactions of the Arab world to its own decline. First, I tackle the invention of the Mameluke state, which lasted during the Ottoman regime and extended into our world of today as the 'autocratic state' in its contemporary deviation. Then I look at the Arabo-Islamic Nahda of the 19th century, which, as I see it, was no more than a miscarriage (a failure insofar as it did not succeed in creating awareness of the reality of the challenge of capitalist modernity). And finally, as a consequence of this miscarriage, there is the crystallisation of triumphant political Islam, with its political deviation.

## The Mameluke state

The Mameluke state, which was invented by Salah El Dine (Saladin) after his victory over the Crusades, survived until the Ottoman conquest, dominating the land from Algeria to Iraq, hence a major portion of the Arab world.

What is it about? It is about a complex system that associated the personalised power of warlords (relatively structured and centralised, or otherwise scattered), businessmen and men of religion. I emphasise men, since women were obviously not allowed to assume any responsibilities. The three dimensions of this organisation were not merely juxtaposed; they were actually merged into a single reality of power.

The Mamelukes were men of war who owed their legitimacy to a certain concept of Islam that placed emphasis on the distinction between Dar El Islam (the Muslim world – a community governed by the rules of peaceful management) and Dar El Harb (an extra-Muslim world, the place for the pursuit of jihad, 'holy war'). It is not by chance that this military concept of political management was fabricated by the conquering Seldjoukide Turks and the Ottomans, who called themselves *ghazi* – conquerors and colonisers of Byzantine Anatolia. It is not by chance that the Mamelukes' system was built from the era of Salah El Dine, liberator of the lands occupied until then by the Crusaders. Populist powers and contemporary nationalists always mention the name of Salah El Dine with respectful admiration without ever considering or making any allusion to the ravages of the system originated by Salah El Dine. At the end of the Crusades, the Arab world (which became Turkish-Arab) entered into a military feudalisation and isolation process reflecting a decline that put an end to the brilliant civilisation of the early centuries of the caliphate, while Europe was beginning to discard feudalism and preparing to embark on the invention of modernity and move on to conquer the world.

In compensation for this service as protectors of Islam, the Mamelukes gave the men of religion monopoly in the interpretation of dogmas, of justice rendered in the name of Islam and in the moral civilisation of the society. Relegated to its purely traditional social dimension – respect for rites being the sole important consideration – religion was absolutely subjugated by the autocratic power of men of war.

Economic life was then subject to the mood of the military–political authority. Whenever possible, the peasantry was directly subjected to the whims of this ruling class and private property was jeopardised (the related principle being indisputably sacralised by the fundamental texts of Islam). The proceeds of trade were no less tapped.

The Mameluke ruling class naturally aspired to the dispersion of its autocratic power. Formally responsible to the sultan-caliph, the Mamelukes took advantage of the long distance then separating them from the capital (Istanbul) to personally exercise full powers within the radius of the land under their control. In areas with an age-old tradition of state centralisation, such as Egypt, there have been successive attempts to discipline the whole military corps. It is not by chance that Mohamed Ali established his centralised authority by massacring the Mamelukes, but only to re-establish a military–real estate aristocracy under his personal authority from that time onwards. The Beys of Tunis tried to do likewise on a more modest scale. The Deys of Algiers never succeeded in doing so. The Ottoman sultanate did so in turn, thereby integrating its Turkish, Kurdish and Armenian provinces of Anatolia and its Arab provinces of historic Syria and Iraq under an authority 'modernised' that way.

Just modernisation? Or just a modernised autocracy? Enlightened despotism? Or just despotism? The fluctuations and variants are situated in this range, which does not usher in anything, making it possible to go beyond.

Certainly, the typical autocratic model of Mameluke had to reckon with the numerous and diverse realities that always defined the real limits. Peasant communities that took refuge in their fortified mountains (Kabylians, Maronites, Druzeans, Alaouites, etc), Sufi brotherhoods almost everywhere and tribes obliged the dominant authorities to reach a compromise with and tolerate the rebellious groups. The contrast in Morocco between Maghzen and Bled Siba is of a similar nature.

## The miscarriage of the Nahda

Modernity is founded on the principle that human beings, individually and collectively, make their own history and that to do so they have the right to innovate and do not have to respect tradition. Declaring such a principle meant making a rupture with the fundamental principle that governed all pre-modern societies including, of course, feudal and Christian Europe. The principle required the renunciation of the dominant forms of the legitimisation of power – in the families, in the communities that organised their way of living and mode of production, and in the state, based up until then on metaphysics, usually expressed in religious terms. It implied the separation between the state and religion and a radical secularisation, a condition for the deployment of modern forms of politics.

This declaration gave birth to modernity. It was not a re-birth, just a birth. The term 'Renaissance' that the Europeans themselves gave to this moment in history is thus misleading. It results from an ideological construction according to which Greek and Roman antiquity had known the principle of modernity, which was buried during the Middle Ages (between old modernity and the new modernity) by religious obscurantism. This was a mythical perception of antiquity which, in turn, founded Eurocentrism, by which Europe claimed to inherit its past as a 'return to its sources' (hence the Re-naissance), when in fact, it had made a rupture with its own history.

The birth of modernity at the same time as capitalism is no chance affair. The social relations characteristic of capitalism's new system of production involve the freedom of enterprise, access to markets and the declaration of the inalienable right to private property (which is 'sacred'). Economic life, which had been emancipated from the tutelage of the political powers that characterised the regimes prior to modernity, developed as an autonomous domain of social life, governed by its own laws. Capitalism replaced the traditional determinism of wealth by a process of inversion that makes wealth the source of power.

## The Arabo-Islamic Nahda

The European Renaissance was the product of an internal social process, the solution found to contradictions peculiar to the then Europe through the invention of capitalism. On the other hand, what the Arabs by imitation referred to as their Renaissance – the Nahda of the 19th century – was not so. It was the reaction to an external shock. The Europe that modernity had rendered powerful and triumphant had an ambiguous effect on the Arab world through attraction (admiration) and repulsion (through the arrogance of its conquest). The Arab Renaissance takes its qualifying term literally. It is assumed that, if the Arabs 'returned' to their sources, like the Europeans (that is what they themselves say), they would regain their greatness, even if debased for some time. The Nahda does not know the nature of the modernity that enhances Europe's power.

This is not the place to refer to different aspects and moments marking the Nahda's deployment. I will just state briefly that the Nahda does not forge the necessary break with tradition that defines modernity. The Nahda does not recognise the meaning of secularism, in other words, separation between religion and politics, the condition to ensure that politics serves as the field for free innovation, and for that matter, for democracy in the modern sense. The Nahda thinks it can substitute for secularism an interpretation of religion purged of its obscurantist drifts. At any rate, to date, Arab societies are not adequately equipped to understand that secularism is not a specific characteristic of the Western world but rather a requirement for modernity. The Nahda does not realise the meaning of democracy, which should be understood as the right to break with tradition. It therefore remains prisoner of the concepts of autocratic state; it hopes and prays for a 'just' despot (*al moustabid al adel*) – even if not 'enlightened' and the nuance is significant. The Nahda does not understand that modernity also promotes women's aspiration to their freedom, thereby exercising their right to innovate and break with tradition. Eventually, the Nahda reduces modernity to the immediate aspect of what it produces: technical progress. This voluntarily over-simplified presentation does not mean that its author is not aware of the contradictions expressed in the Nahda, nor that certain avant-garde thinkers were aware of the real challenges posed by modernity, like Kassem Amin and the importance of women's emancipation, Ali Abdel Razek and secularism, and Kawakibi and the challenge posed by democracy. However, none of these breakthroughs had any effects; on the contrary, the Arab society reacted by refusing to follow the paths indicated. The Nahda is therefore not the time marking the birth of modernity in the Arab world but rather the period of its abortion.

In his splendid book *The Arabs and the Holocaust*, Gilbert Achcar (2010) analysed the writings of Rachid Reda, the last link in the Nahda chain. Reda wrote in the 1920s, inspiring the Muslim Brothers right from the beginning. The Islam that he puts forward, defined as a 'return to sources', is rigorously devoid of any serious thought. It is a conveniently conservative Islam, affirming communitarianism and rituals. The support of Reda and the Muslim Brothers for Wahhabism, which also expressed hatred of the slightest sign of critical thought and that only meets the needs of an archaic society of nomads, heralds the advent of political Islam.

## The limits and contradictions of modernity

Modernity that operates under the constraints of capitalism is thus contradictory, promising much more than it can deliver and thus generating unsatisfied expectations. This rupture, which got under way in Europe during the 16th, 17th and 18th centuries, is far from being completed, either in the regions of its birth, or elsewhere.

Contemporary humanity is therefore faced with the contradictions of this modernity – the only one we have so far known – which is only modernity in the capitalist stage of history. Capitalism and its modernity destroy the human being, who is reduced to the status of goods that provide labour. In addition, polarisation brought about at the global level by the accumulation of capital wipes out the possibility for most of the human race – those in the peripheries of the system – to satisfy their needs as promised by modernity. For the great majority, this modernity is quite simply odious and so it is violently rejected. But rejection is a negative act. The inadequacies of alternative projects obliterate the effectiveness of revolt and finally bring about submission to the demands of capitalism and modernity that people claim to reject.

The main illusion feeds on nostalgia for the pre-modern past and this nostalgia finds its partisans both in the centres and in the peripheries of the system. In the former it takes the form of dreams of no great significance, an expression of conservatism and a way of lessening the dangers of emancipatory demands by the victims of the system, thus reducing modernity to an inconsistent patchwork, confusing manipulated vestiges of the past with requirements of the present. But in the peripheries, nostalgia for the past is the result of a violent and justifiable revolt that becomes neurotic and powerless because it is, quite simply, based on ignorance of the nature of modernity's challenge.

This nostalgia is expressed in different ways, usually in a fundamentalist religious key, which does in fact mask a conventional conservative option, or in an ethnic key, decked out in specific virtues that transcend other forms of social reality, for example, class. The common denominator of all these forms is their attachment to a culturalist thesis in virtue of which religion and ethnicism are characterised by transhistoric specificities that define intangible identities. With no scientific basis, these positions are none the less mobilising for the masses, who are marginalised and confused by the destructions of capitalist modernity. But, by the same token, they are efficient means of the manipulation that supports the strategy of imposing de facto submission to the dictatorship of the combined dominant forces in global capitalism and its local and subordinate conveyor belts. Political Islam is a good example of this way of managing peripheral capitalism. And in Latin America and Africa, there is a proliferation of obscurantist sects of Protestant institutions to stem liberation theology and to manipulate the confusion of the excluded and their revolt against the conservative official church.

The Muslim peoples and Islam have a history, as do those in other parts of the world, which contains different interpretations of the relationships between reason and faith and that of the mutual transformations and adaptations of society and its religion. But the reality of this history is denied, not only by Eurocentric discourses but also by the contemporary movements that claim to be Islamic. In fact, both share the same culturalist bias according to which the 'specificities' peculiar to the different trajectories of peoples and their religions are inalienable, immeasurable and transhistoric. Contemporary political Islam opposes the Eurocentrism of the West by an inverted Eurocentrism.

## The permanence of the autocratic state

Have the forms in which power is exercised in the Arab world been innovated to the point that those described here can be said to belong to bygone times? The autocratic state and the forms of political management associated with it are certainly still in place. But they are in profound crisis which has already greatly eroded their legitimacy, being less and less capable of dealing with the challenges of modernity. This is testified by the emergence of political Islam, the confusion in political conflicts, but also the renewal of social struggles.

There is no democratic state in the Arab world. There are only autocratic states. This is certainly a harsh judgement, but it is essentially correct, even if we later on try to identify the flaws whereby the political and social struggles can initiate the transformation of this reality.

This general autocracy certainly assumes diverse forms. It would not be difficult to cite well-known names corresponding to the identification of each of the common forms of autocracy. The plight of Arab peoples has variously depended on the mood of a general who proved to be an assassin by nature, a junior police officer specialised in torture, a king who built perpetually dark dungeons, a chief of a tribal pyramid, or a religious extremist. In a less negative case, the Arab state has sometimes been ruled by an enlightened despot, in the true sense of the term, or by an easy-going heir, and therefore relatively tolerant. Lebanon partly shares the common feature of the Arab states even if it appears as an exception, as elections are held there regularly and the presidents are actually changed every four years. For one thing, if it is true that the elections are not devoid of a certain interest, it is only because the political authorities that follow one another are so much alike that their difference is negligible.

Although autocratic, the Arab political regimes have not always been denied legitimacy by their own societies. According to Hashem Sharaby (1991), state power has always been synonymous with personal power as opposed to the power of the law defining the modern state. This Weber-like descriptive analysis is worth qualifying since the personal (or personalised) powers in question are legitimate only insofar as they are proclaimed as being respectful of the tradition (and especially of the religious sharia) and are perceived as such. From a more in-depth perspective, it is the relationship Sharaby establishes between autocracy and the 'patriarchal' nature of the system of social values. The term 'patriarchy' is understood here to be more than what is ascribed to the popularised commonplace term of 'male chauvinism' (asserting and practising the marginalisation of women in society). The patriarchy in question is a system that upholds the duty of obedience at all levels: while school and home education put down the slightest critical attempt and sacralisation of hierarchies in the family system (subordinating women and children of course), in the business sector (subordinating the employee to the employer), in public service (absolute submission to the senior in rank), absolute prohibition of religious interpretation, etc.

This observation – which appears indisputable to me – links up with the conclusions that I have drawn from the definition of modernity which I proposed and from the challenge it constitutes.

Autocratic power derives its legitimacy from tradition, beyond the principles of non-modernity. In some cases it can be a traditional national and religious monarchy as in Morocco (and it is in this sense that no Moroccan political party questions the slogan of this monarchy – God, the Nation, the King) or an archaic tribal monarchy, as in the Arabian peninsular, or the enduring Mameluke state.

The dominant fashionable discourse tries to replace analysis of political conflict and social struggle by a language that claims to be rational and hence consensual as regards social management. Thus post-modernism, instead of using the clear language of social *struggle*, has a discourse about social *movements*. This substitution of terms is by no means neutral because it assumes that members of society are already reconciled among themselves and that the movements in question impart an inexorable movement to society – implicitly, towards the best of all worlds. The explosion of what are called the decentralised initiatives of the associations – the women's movements, the ecologist movements, the so-called non-governmental organisations of all kinds – express this qualitative change in 'post-modern' political life.

This discourse, which accompanies the massive return of the brutal dictatorship of capital vis-à-vis its adversaries, who have temporarily been weakened, is daily losing some of the credibility from which it was able to profit for a while. This imbalance that favours capital, far from constructing a peaceful consensus, calls for a return to social struggle, which is a condition for any change in power relationships capable of guiding the movements towards more justice and democracy, and greater effectiveness. These struggles are not occurring in a political and economic vacuum. They are developing, partially at least, against the double power of the contemporary state and dominant capital. In other words, they are developing against the practices of the managerial state and against the globalised economic liberation that constitute the options of dominant capital and the state at its service.

## The deviation of political Islam

The miscarriage of the Nahda led fatally to what became political Islam.

The fatal error lies in thinking that the emergence of mass political movements identified with Islam is the inevitable outcome of the rise of culturally and politically backward people who cannot understand any language other than that of their quasi-atavistic obscurantism. Unfortunately, such an error is not only widely circulated by the dominant simplifying media; it is also echoed in the pseudo-scientific discourses on Eurocentrism and awkward Orientalism. Such views are based on the biased assumption that only the West can invent modernity, thereby confining Muslims in an immutable tradition that makes them incapable of apprehending the significance of the necessary change.

Muslims and Islam have a history, just like those of the other regions of the world. It is a history fraught with diverse interpretations concerning linkages between reason and faith, a history of mutual transformation and adaptation of both society and its religion. However, the reality of this history is denied not only by Eurocentric discourses but also by the contemporary movements associated with Islam. In fact, the two entities have the same cultural bias whereby the specific features ascribed to the different careers of their own peoples and religions are allegedly intangible, infinite and transhistorical. To the Western world's Eurocentrism, contemporary political Islam solely opposes an inverted Eurocentrism.

The emergence of movements claiming to be Islamic is actually expressive of a violent revolt against the destructive effects of actually existing capitalism and against its attendant unaccomplished, truncated and deceptive modernity. It is an expression of an absolutely legitimate revolt against a system that has nothing to offer to the peoples concerned.

The discourse of the Islam proposed as an alternative to capitalist modernity (to which the modern experiences of the historical socialisms are clearly assimilated), is political by nature, and by no means theological. The 'fundamentalist' attributes often ascribed to Islam by no means correspond to this discourse, which, moreover, does not even allude to Islam, except in the case of certain contemporary Muslim intellectuals who are referred to in such terms in Western opinion more than in theirs.

The proposed Islam is in this case the adversary of every liberation theology. Political Islam advocates submission and not emancipation. It was only Mahmoud Taha of Sudan who attempted to emphasise the element of emancipation in his interpretation of Islam. Sentenced to death and executed by the authorities of Khartoum, Taha was not acknowledged by any radical or moderate Islamic group, and neither was he defended by any of the intellectuals identifying themselves with Islamic Renaissance or even by those who are merely willing to dialogue with such movements.

Mahmoud Taha distinguished, in the revelation of the Koran, between the suras of Mecca and those of Medina. The former testify to the emancipatory desire in the message, the aspiration to liberty and equality among all human beings, created in the image of God and who should in all circumstances struggle to move further towards this ideal. The latter, on the other hand, respond to the needs of the moment, to the organising of society in the historical conditions of Arabia at that time.

This interpretation allows Muslim society to conceive an evolution of the sharia in response to the challenge of the times. The liberation theology (*fiqh* in Arabic) of Taha is in opposition to the dominant interpretation of Islam which gives a definitive, transhistoric character to the sharia, as implemented in Medina (see Amin 2005).

The heralds of the so-called Islamic Renaissance are not interested in theology and they never make any reference to the classical texts concerning theology. Hence, what they understand by Islam appears to be solely a conventional and social version of religion limited to the formal and integral respect for ritual practice. The Islam in question would define a community to which one belongs by inheritance, like ethnicity instead of a strong and intimate personal conviction. It is solely a question of asserting a collective identity and nothing more. That is the reason why the term 'political Islam' is certainly more appropriate to qualify all these movements in the Arab countries.

Modern political Islam had been invented by the orientalists in the service of the British authority in India before being adopted intact by Abul Ala Al Mawdudi of Pakistan. It consisted in 'proving' that Muslim believers are not allowed to live in a state that is itself not Islamic – anticipating the partition of India – because Islam would ignore the possibility of separation between state and religion. The orientalists in question failed to observe that the English of the 13th century would not have conceived of their survival without Christianity either!

Mawdudi therefore took up the theme, stipulating that power comes from God alone (*wilaya al faqih*), thus repudiating the concept of citizens having the right to make laws, the state being solely entrusted with enforcement of the law defined once and for all (the sharia). Joseph de Maistre had already written similar things accusing the revolution of inventing modern democracy and individual emancipation.

Refuting the concept of emancipatory modernity, political Islam disapproves of the very principle of democracy – the right of society to build its own future through its freedom to legislate. The shura principle is not the Islamic form of democracy, as claimed by political Islam, for it is hampered by the ban on innovation (*ibda*), and accepts, if need be, only that of interpretation of the tradition (*ijtihad*). The shura is only one of the multiple forms of the consultation found in all pre-modern and pre-democratic societies. Of course, interpretation has sometimes been the vehicle for real changes imposed by new demands. However, the fact remains that by virtue of its own principle – denial of the right to break with the past – interpretation leads into deadlock the modern fight for social change and democracy. The parallel claimed between the Islamic parties – radical or moderate, since all of them adhere to the same anti-modernist principles in the name of the so-called specificity of Islam – and Christian-Democrat parties of modern

Europe is therefore not valid, strictly speaking, even though American media and diplomatic circles continue to make allusion to the said parallel so as to legitimise their support of possibly Islamist regimes. Christian-Democracy is an element of modernity of which it upholds the fundamental concept of creative democracy as the essential aspect of the concept of secularism. Political Islam refuses modernity and proclaims this fact without being able to understand its significance.

Hence, the proposed Islam does not deserve at all to be qualified as 'modern' and the supporting arguments advanced in this regard by friends of dialogue are extremely platitudinous: they range from the use of cassettes by its propagandists to the observation that these agents are recruited from among the 'educated' classes – engineers for instance. Moreover, these movements' discourse solely reflects Wahhabite Islam, which rejects all that the interaction between historical Islam and Greek philosophy had produced in its epoch, as it merely went over the unimaginative writings of Ibn Taymiya, the most reactionary of the theologians of the Middle Ages. Although some of his heralds qualify this interpretation as 'a return to the sources', it is actually a mere reference to the notions that prevailed 200 years ago, notions of a society whose development has been stalled for several centuries.

Contemporary political Islam is not the outcome of a reaction to the so-called abuses of secularism, as often purported, unfortunately. It is because no Muslim society of modern times – except in the former Soviet Union – has ever been truly secular, let alone appalled at the daring innovations of any atheistic and aggressive power. The semi-modern state of Kemal's Turkey, Nasser's Egypt, Baathist Syria and Iraq merely subjugated the men of religion (as often happened in former times) to impose on them concepts solely aimed at legitimising its political options. The beginnings of a secular idea existed only in certain critical intellectual circles. The secular idea did not have much impact on the state, which sometimes retreated in this respect when obsessed with its nationalist project, thereby causing a break with the policy adopted by the Wafd since 1919, as testified by the disturbing evolution inaugurated even at the time of Nasser. The reason for this drift is perhaps quite obvious: whereas the democracy of the said regimes was rejected, a substitute was found in the so-called homogeneous community, with its danger obviously extending to the declining democracy of the contemporary Western world itself.

Political Islam intends to perfect an evolution already well established in the countries concerned and aims at restoring a plainly conservative theocratic order associated with political power of the Mameluke type. The reference to this military caste that ruled up to two centuries ago, placed itself above all laws (by pretending to know no law other than the sharia), monopolised profits from the national economy and agreed to play a subsidiary role in the capitalist globalisation of that era – for the sake of 'realism' – instantly crosses the mind of anyone who observes the declined post-nationalist regimes of the region as well as the new so-called Islamic regimes, their twin brothers.

From this fundamental point of view, there is no difference between the so-called radical movements of political Islam and those that wanted to appear moderate, because the aims of both entities are identical.

The case of Iran itself is not an exception to the general rule, despite the confusions that contributed to its success: the concomitance between the rapid development of the Islamist movement and the struggle waged against the shah, who was socially reactionary and politically pro-American. Initially, the extremely eccentric behaviour of the theocratic ruling power was compensated for by its anti-imperialist positions, from which it derived a legitimacy that echoed its powerful popularity beyond the borders of Iran. Gradually, however, the regime showed that it was incapable of meeting the challenge posed by an innovative socio-economic development. The dictatorship of turbaned men of religion, who took over from that of the 'Caps' (military and technocrats), as they are referred to in Iran, resulted in a major degradation of the country's economic machinery. Iran, which boasted about 'doing the same as Korea', now ranks among the group of 'fourth world' countries. The indifference of the ruling power's hard wing to social problems facing the country's working classes was the basic cause of its take-over by those who described themselves as reformers with a project that could certainly attenuate the rigours of the theocratic dictator, but without renouncing, for all that, its principle enshrined in the constitution (*wilaya al faqih*), which constituted the basis of the monopoly of a power that was therefore gradually

# The Decline

induced to give up its anti-imperialist postures and integrate itself into the commonplace comprador world of capitalism of the peripheries. The system of political Islam in Iran has reached deadlock. The political and social struggles in which the Iranian people have now been plunged might one day lead to the rejection of the very principle of *wilaya al faqih*, which places the college of the men of religion above all institutions of political and civil society. That is the condition for their success.

Political Islam is in fact nothing other than an adaptation to the subordinate status of comprador capitalism. Its so-called moderate form therefore probably constitutes the principal danger threatening the peoples concerned since the violence of the 'radicals' only serves to destabilise the state to allow for the installation of a new comprador power. The constant support offered by the pro-American diplomacies of the Triad countries towards finding this 'solution' to the problem is absolutely consistent with their desire to impose a globalised liberal order in the service of dominant capital.

The two discourses of globalised liberal capitalism and political Islam do not conflict; they are, rather, complementary. The ideology of American 'communitarianisms' being popularised by current fashion overshadows the conscience and social struggles and substitutes for them so-called collective identities that ignore them. This ideology is therefore perfectly manipulated in the strategy of capital domination because it transfers the struggle from the arena of real social contradictions to the imaginary world that is said to be cultural, transhistorical and absolute, whereas political Islam is precisely a communitarianism.

The G7 powers, and particularly the United States, know what they do in choosing to support political Islam. They have done so in Afghanistan by describing its Islamists as 'freedom fighters' (!) against the horrible dictatorship of communism, which was in fact an enlightened, modernist, national and populist despotism that had the audacity to open schools for girls. They continue to do so from Egypt to Algeria. They know that the power of political Islam has the virtue – to them – of making the peoples concerned helpless, consequently ensuring their compradorisation without difficulty.

Given its inherent cynicism, the American establishment knows how to take a second advantage of political Islam. The 'deviants' of the regimes that it inspires – the Taliban, for instance – who are actually not deviants but actually come within the logic of their programmes, can be exploited whenever imperialism finds it expedient to intervene brutally. The 'savagery' attributed to the peoples who are the first victims of political Islam is likely to encourage 'Islamophobia' and that facilitates the acceptance of the perspective of a 'global apartheid' – the logical and necessary outcome of an ever-polarising capitalist expansion.

The sole political movements using the label of Islam that are categorically condemned by the G7 powers are those involved in anti-imperialist struggles – under the objective circumstances at the local level: Hezbollah in Lebanon and Hamas in Palestine. It is not a matter of chance.

## Bibliography

Achcar, Gilbert (2010) *The Arabs and the Holocaust: The Arab-Israeli War of Narratives*, London, Saki Books

Amin, Samir (2005) 'Vers une théologie islamique de la liberation', *La Pensée*, no. 342

Amin, Samir (2011) *Eurocentrism* (2nd edn), Oxford, Pambazuka Press

Sharaby, Hashem (1991) *Al Naqd al Hadari*, Beirut, Markaz Dirasat al Wihda al Arabiya,

# 5

# The Leap Forward: The Bandung Era and Arab Popular Nationalisms

The Arab world moved from the top to the bottom in the world system when modern globalised capitalism reached maturity in the 19th century. The Arab world then became peripheral in the sense I give to the term: it was fully integrated into the world system but submitted and adjusted itself to the requirements of the reproduction of the system in its dominant centres.

The only serious effort to integrate into this modernity and to rise to the rank of an active participant, respected and equal, was made by Egypt during the first two-thirds of the 19th century (from Mohamed Ali to Khedive Ismail). The main reason for this failure, apart from the aggressive hostility of Great Britain, was certainly the absence of a 'bourgeois' social class capable of directing the movement. Its substitute, the enlightened despotism of the leader, did not succeed in transcending the history of the Mameluke state. The beneficiaries of this model of capitalist development ended by passively accepting a subordinate role in the new capitalist globalisation. Egypt, which became a cotton farm for Lancashire, thus prepared itself for subsequent colonisation. The 'nationalist' opposition did not succeed in freeing itself from its nostalgia for the past (as expressed by the Nahda) and the illusion of Ottomanism as protector. Political life was shared between this weak political class (the Nationalist Party – El Hizb El Watany) and the one that agreed to be subordinated (the Umma Party of Saad Zaghoul, forerunner of the Wafd right-wing and the monarchist parties of the interwar years).

The economic histories of colonisation stress the conventional criteria of the 'growth' of GNP, of exports and of the creation of infrastructure. The devastating effects of peripheralisation – the large-scale dispossession of the peasants, the super-exploitation of labour, the pillage of natural resources – are systematically expunged from the record. The praise for cotton-farm Egypt and for Algeria transformed into a vineyard are examples of this blind view of reality.

It is not surprising, therefore, that the people concerned finally rose up. And it is this revolt – the surge after the Second World War, the Bandung era – that will be the subject of this chapter.

The first moment of the awakening of the Arab nations (as we can now describe it) formed part of the awakening of all the peoples of Asia and Africa, who took the offensive in shaping the modern world in the favourable circumstances created by the new balance of power after the Second World War. The Arab world had a remarkable position in the Bandung era, which led to hopes for much more than could be fulfilled.

I think it is necessary here to describe exactly what the Bandung project was. It was ambiguous as it never reached the necessary level which would have resulted in an awareness for the need of a rupture with the fundamental principles of capitalism, which went beyond mere anti-imperialism. I will also show the limited potential of the achievements of Nasserism. In other writings, about the more radical experiences in Algeria under Boumediene, in Morocco, in the Tunisia of the 'moderate' Bourguibists, or in Baathist Syria and Iraq, I have reached similar conclusions, emphasising the negative weight of social and ideological heritages that were not counteracted. In this chapter I shall show how the movement led to remarkable advances, as well as to the crushing defeats of three countries that had been beacons of light for the radical Arab world (Yemen, Iraq and Sudan) and also of the non-Arab country that belongs to the greater Middle East: Afghanistan. The advances and retreats of Kemalist Turkey and Iran, about which I have written elsewhere, show similar contradictions. It is all these 'failures' that prepared the way for further deviations and the growth of the political Islam illusion.

Thus this chapter closes on what I think should be placed at the centre of the analysis: the question of democracy. But it is important here not to fall into the trap of the illusion of democracy as it is formulated by the contemporary dominant ideology, promoted by the imperialist offensive. Rather, I insist on the need for the participation of the Arab peoples in inventing the socialist democracy of tomorrow, the only response to the challenge. We shall see in the following chapter if this objective need has a real chance of imposing itself, in the Arab world as elsewhere.

## Bandung and the first globalisation of struggles (1955–80)

The ruling class of the dominant imperialism – the United States – openly declared its hegemonic ambitions at the end of the Second World War at Potsdam, a few days before the nuclear bombing of Japan. This project was based, from the beginning, on a military advantage at that time, the monopoly of nuclear power. It was not difficult for the US to get vassalised Europe and occupied Japan to rally to its cause. Thus, despite its decisive role in crushing the Nazi monster, the USSR found itself isolated. But the key obstacle to the US implementing its strategy was in fact the victorious struggles of the peoples of Africa and Asia, who were engaged in the final stages of their national liberation. Bandung was therefore a milestone in this process. The Soviet Union and China were thus able, through their support for these struggles, to emerge from their isolation and open the way to the building up of a multipolar system (rather than the bipolar system that the dominant discourse on the cold war would have people believe), giving to the peoples of the South their place.

At Bandung, in 1955, the governments and peoples of Asia and Africa proclaimed their desire to rebuild the world system based on recognition of the rights of nations that had hitherto been dominated. This right to development was at the basis of globalisation at that time, implemented in a negotiated multipolar framework imposed on imperialism, which was forced to adapt to this new requirement. The success of Bandung – and not its failure, as is increasingly said without due thought – was, at the beginning, a gigantic leap forward of the peoples of the South in the fields of education and health, as well as in the construction of a modern state, often reducing social inequalities and finally marking entry into the industrial age. However, there is no doubt that the limits of these achievements, particularly the democratic deficit, by the national populist regimes who 'gave to the people' but never allowed them to organise themselves, must be seriously taken into consideration in drawing up a balance sheet of that epoch.

The Bandung system was articulated to two other systems typical of the post-war situation, that of Sovietism (and Maoism) and that of the welfare state of Western social democracy. There were, of course, systems in competition, even in conflict (although they were easily contained within manageable limits, restricted to localised armed conflict), but also in a way, complementary to each other (the development of each of them supported that of the others). Thus it makes sense to talk about the globalisation of struggles in these conditions and, as it was the first time in the history of capitalism that struggles were occurring in all the regions of the planet and within the nations that constitute it, it inaugurated a first step towards this evolution.

The interdependence of the struggles and the historical compromises ensuring the stabilisation of the management of the societies concerned was conversely proven by what happened after the parallel erosion of the development potential of the three systems. The collapse of Sovietism brought with it the collapse of social democracy, the social advances of which – completely genuine – had been imposed because this was the only way to ward off the communist challenge. In this context we should also remember the echo of the Chinese cultural revolution in the Europe of 1968.

The industrialisation advances that started in the Bandung era did not follow imperialist logic but were achieved through the victories of the peoples of the South. It is true that these advances nourished the illusion that the South was 'catching up', while in fact imperialism, having been forced to adjust to the requirements of the development of the peripheries, recomposed itself into new forms of domination. The old contrast of imperialist countries/dominated countries, which was synonymous with the contrast between industrialised countries/non-industrialised countries, gradually gave way to a new contrast based on the centralisation of the advantages of the 'five new monopolies of the imperialist centres' (the control of new technologies, natural resources, financial flows, communications and weapons of mass destruction).

The achievements of this period, like their limitations, raise the central question of the future of the bourgeoisie and of capitalism in the peripheries of the system. This is a permanent issue because the globalised spread of capitalism, through its polarising effects produced by its imperialist nature, is marked by the fundamental inequality in the potential of bourgeois, capitalist development at the centre and in the periphery of the system. In other words, are the bourgeoisie of the peripheries necessarily forced to submit to the requirements of this unequal development? Is it thus necessarily a comprador bourgeoisie? Is the capitalist path, in these conditions, necessarily at an impasse? Or does the margin of manoeuvre from which the bourgeoisie could benefit in certain circumstances (that have to be specified) permit a national, autonomous capitalist development, capable of progressing toward catching up? To what extent do these limits make the capitalist option an illusion?

## And today?

The Bandung page was finally turned in 1981 at Cancún, when President Reagan began his offensive to re-establish the leadership of the US and the world domination of what I have called the collective imperialism of the Triad. The turnaround of the post-Maoist China of the 1980s and the collapse of the USSR in 1990 were certainly new milestones indicating the end of one epoch and the beginning of a transition towards another, the contours of which remain unclear.

In the immediate post-war period, the Soviet Union had responded to the isolation imposed on it by enacting the Zhdanov Doctrine which, in its way, adopted a similar position to that of the US, dividing the world into two camps, those of the socialist states and those of the imperialist countries. The mounting upsurge of the peoples of the South was not taken into account. At the same time the viewpoint of the Comintern was forcefully laid down by Stalin himself: everywhere, in third world countries, as in vassalised Europe, the bourgeoisie had abandoned the national flag. That meant the national liberation had to be directed by the 'proletariat', in fact, the communist party, as had been proclaimed by the 'New Democracy' of Mao, published in 1952, and which had been confirmed by the Vietnam war and the guerrillas of South East Asia.

Then things stabilised and evolved in a different way. There were signs indicating that the Zhdanov Doctrine was being superseded. The Bandung era thus implemented national popular projects, not exclusively bourgeois, but not escaping from the logic of capitalist accumulation.

Now this page has been turned, but the 're-compradorisation' of the governing classes of the South is more fragile than it could have seemed 20 years ago. And the same question is posed: how to extricate the peoples and nations of the South from the impasse? The governing classes of the emerging countries openly foster renewal projects based on the logic of capitalist accumulation – even if they are 'anti-hegemonic', as the Chinese say, to avoid the expression of 'anti-imperialist'. The question posed yesterday has to be asked again: will the capitalist path allow catching up by those who know how to deal with it as active partners, and who refuse unilateral adjustment to the requirements of imperialism? Any analysis of the opportunities and contradictions of these projects would show that such hopes are based on many illusions.

## The Arab world of radical nationalism

Over the second half of the last century, the Arab world underwent three, distinct stages.

From 1955 to 1975, Nasser's Egypt, Baathist Syria and Iraq, and Boumediene's Algeria were major actors at the front of the Non-Aligned Movement and its spread in Africa. The first conference of the African liberation movements took place in Cairo in 1957, as a result of which the Organisation for Solidarity with the Peoples of Asia and Africa was formed. The new international economic order – the swan-song of the Non-Aligned Movement – was drawn up in Algiers in 1974. These were no mere coincidences.

But whereas the positive social effects of the 'Arab revolutions' (which I have described as national populism) wore out in a brief period, one to two decades on from 1973, the rents from oil took over and gave the illusion of an easy modernisation. The play on words known to all Arabs, *al fawra mahal al thawra* (the gush – understood as oil – instead of revolution), sums up this transfer of aspirations. At the same time, the centre of gravity for strategic decision-making passed from Cairo to Riyadh. And this happened when it began to be apparent that the oil resource was not renewable. It was in this context that the US started to implement what was to become the project for the military control of the planet by which it could ensure exclusive access to this irreplaceable energy resource for its own benefit. As from 1990

US armed intervention became a reality, totally changing the nature of the challenges then confronting Arab societies and others in the region. Mired down in the *infitah* (the 'opening' associated with the oil illusion), the Arab regimes lost the legitimacy that they had hitherto enjoyed. And, in the political vacuum, political Islam stepped into the breach, occupying the stage ever since. 'The old is dying and the new cannot be born; in this interregnum there arises a great diversity of morbid symptoms' (Gramsci).

This involution requires serious study of the reasons for such a dramatic failure. I believe it is due to two main factors. There were those relating to the limits and contradictions of the Nahda (the 'Renaissance' that started in the 19th century), which are at the origin of the continuation of the political model of the Mameluke regime. And then there were those that stem from the global geopolitics of the new collective imperialism of the Triad and the leadership of the US.

## An example: the limits of Nasserism

The year 1957 was that of the great upheaval in Egypt, following the failure of the tripartite aggression of 1956. British, French and Belgian capital, which dominated the industrial and modern sectors of the economy, was impounded. What was to be done? The leading group of Free Officers was split. There were those who wanted to Egyptianise it, i.e. to transfer the property, with or without real payment, to private Egyptian capital which, in fact, had been more associated than competitive with foreign capital (particularly the MISR group). And there were those who wanted to nationalise it to create a public sector that, because of its size, could start planning an accelerated development. Nasser tended to the second alternative which was decided upon with some formal concessions to the first alternative by associating Egyptian private capital, here and there and marginally, with the new state sector.

But how were these national enterprises to be managed and their development planned? The danger was that the responsibility would be given to political clients – officers for the main part – who were virtually unaccountable and formally dependent on different ministries. Not only was the management incompetent but control was also dispersed. Finally, in 1957 a state holding was created, called Mouassassa Iqtisadia, which would choose the administrators.

Because of my functions in this institution I closely followed the way in which the new public sector was to be managed and the discussions and decisions of the board of governors. I thus had first-hand experience of how the 'new class' was constituted, how the private interests of many of these gentlemen (there were very few women among them) affected too many decisions, how the representatives of the workers (an innovation of Nasserism, excellent in principle) were marginalised, taken for a ride – or bought off.

Furthermore, the bureaucracy of the Egyptian state, which was always pharaonic, was beset by all kinds of contradictions and conflicts. The more noble held different political views while among the others, who were more crass, there were conflicts of interest among individuals and clans. In the main, there were four decision-making centres where the disputes were greater than the views on how to direct the development of the country: the Mouassassa, the planning ministry, the finance ministry, on which depended the central bank, and the industrial bank. It was not possible for the Mouassassa to manage the public sector on a daily basis and it was therefore necessary to plan its development. Was that not a task that the new planning ministry should take on? But it did not do so. Its technicians had been trained on the growth model. I am not, on principle, against the use of models, of course. They are necessary to test the coherence of sectoral and partial policies. But the model must come afterwards, not before, the social and political content of objectives has been decided. Technocrats often believe they can escape political responsibility by the illusion that models make it possible to make choices, the rationality of which can be supra-political, supra-social. It was also a fact that the development of the public sector controlled by Mouassassa needed finance. Here we came up against the obstacle of the different vision of finance and the industrial bank.

The finance ministry, an institution as ancient as Egypt itself, had habits that were almost impossible to change. The treasury had always financed irrigation and, since the 19th century, the railways. Following the crisis of the 1930s, which had threatened too many large landowners with failure, the treasury took over land tenure credit from the banks to which these owners were indebted. Finally, since the Second World War, agricultural credit (which advanced loans to smallholders) and a certain number of funding offices, scattered here and there, managed compensation funds created on an ad hoc basis to limit the damage caused by inflation. In all these fields it was impossible to wean the treasury off its old habits, as they were managed by separate services which did not communicate between themselves, which created a lot of waste and many absurdities. Moreover, the treasury had never thought of financing industry which, incidentally, it had never been asked to do. It was satisfied with ensuring its profitability through protective customs tariffs and the granting of public tenders, reinforcing the monopoly of enterprises.

The central bank, whose functions were then taken over by the national bank that had just been nationalised, was ultra conservative, as was its nature. Its responsibility was to ensure monetary stability – which it already did well – but nothing more. There remained only the industrial bank, created by the regime and controlled in principle by the new ministry of industry (independent of the finance ministry). At the ministry of industry, which was the decision-maker of last resort, the 'clans' (*shilal*, in Egyptian, a term familiar to those who know the time-honoured ways in which the country was managed) of officers and others, both more and less corrupt, not very competent and stubborn for any old reason, ruled the roost. It was they who 'planned' the reality, in fact in a total disorder which goes against the very concept of planning.

I am recounting some of the details of this history because I have noticed that the books dealing with this period do not mention them. Instead, they give an abstract and general discourse on planning in the Nasser epoch, as though it had been a rational implementation of the public declarations and texts on the subject. As if its 'failure' was due to its theoretical principle! My book *L'Egypte nassérienne*, published a little later (in 1963) under the pseudonym of Hassan Riad, owes much of its content to the material I put together at that time.

## Revolutionary advances followed by tragic setbacks

This section looks at the conjunction of the external aggression of imperialism and local reactionary forces; the theoretical errors and the practical deficiencies of the revolutionary forces; and the democracy issue: what democracy can 'serve the people'?

The examples of advances followed by dramatic setbacks are numerous. The history of the 19th and 20th centuries is full of them. They constitute the history of the three great revolutions of the modern world (the French, the Russian, the Chinese) and a few others (those of Haiti and Mexico). There is a possibility of similar setbacks elsewhere (Cuba, Vietnam). Less spectacular, but real, advances marked the history of the Asian and African peoples during the Bandung epoch. Everywhere they have been followed by setbacks to the point of re-establishing the power of the compradors at the service of imperialist dictatorship.

## Afghanistan, Iraq, Yemen and Sudan

The second half of the 20th century saw unprecedented transformations in all the societies of the world. But it was in Asia and Africa, as they came out of the colonial night, that these transformations were the deepest, forced as they were to question the different degrees of capitalist logic. The page of 1492 was turned over and the globalisation of the future was not the one that was inaugurated 500 years previously, which had been dominated by Western imperialism.

Nevertheless, after the flood tide of the Bandung era came the ebb flow. I have put forward some analyses of the progress accomplished and the reasons for later retreat, particularly the most radical experiences in the two continents, in my recent book *L'Eveil du Sud*.

I would suggest four recent cases for debate: Afghanistan, Iraq, Sudan and South Yemen. These are little and badly understood by those who are not readers of Arabic and Farsi. Readers could complement the outlines given here with some supplementary writings about Afghanistan and Iraq. These four societies are comparatively less homogenous than others from a religious or ethnic viewpoint. But that happens frequently in history, homogenisation often being a result of modernisation. This does not signify – far from it – that there is a natural animosity between the different elements of a country, whether it is a question of Shiites or Sunnis, Arabs or Kurds (in Iraq), of people speaking Farsi or Turkish (in Afghanistan), of Muslims or non-Muslims (in Sudan) or of subjects of a 'feudal' fragmentation (in South Yemen).

Nevertheless, this heterogeneity has, it seems, benefited the revolutionary response, because it accounts for the relative weakness of local powers, both the old 'independent' powers and those subordinated, through modernisation, to the protection of the imperial powers. The weakness of this power turns – in moments of crisis – into a break-up according to the lines that define this heterogeneity, while the revolutionary forces are able to take advantage of the general aspiration for unity of the people fighting against the existing powers.

These four countries are important from the viewpoint of the global interests of imperialism, which has difficulty in renouncing control over them: Afghanistan, once the frontier state with the Soviet Union and now with the central Asia that the imperialists are trying to build up against Russia; Iraq, whose sub-soil hoards some of the best oil reserves in the world; South Yemen, which commands the entrance to the Red Sea (the oil route); and Sudan, whose control involves the control of Egypt (for the British of yesterday), rich in oil and uranium (today).

In the four countries, the minority 'modern' society, confronted by an apparently traditional mass, has thus been particularly attracted by radical solutions, through a project of 'modernisation from above', supported from below, that had a socialist perspective.

## The remarkable success of the communist parties

In Afghanistan, a monarchy which could be called feudal governed (hardly) a collection of regions with vague borders, which were ruled over by their local masters. The country's long attempt to resist the aggression of Great Britain, concerned to cut off the route of the Russians to the Indian Ocean and then of the Soviets in Turkestan, did not allow it to acquire the homogeneity and strength to meet the challenge of social transformation. It is hardly surprising that the social and intellectual elites, who understood this failure, were naturally convinced, almost unanimously, that the (Soviet) socialist model was able to respond to this challenge.

In Iraq, the 'Sunni' monarchy imported by the British could not maintain itself except by renouncing its real independence. The Iraqi communist party was therefore able to win the hearts of the masses among the Kurds and the Shiite Arabs, winning minds among all the educated class, particularly among the students, of course, but also among large sectors of the new urban middle classes (professionals, army officers, etc).

In South Yemen, the British had reinforced – by creating everything necessary for it – a subordinated pseudo-feudal fragmentation. It divided the apparent local powers into a multitude of *mashiakhas* (the domains of the sheikhs or those that claimed to be such), of sultanates and emirates (reduced to a small town and three villages), reserving the port of Aden to direct colonial administration. The communist movement (unified under the name of the socialist party) had no difficulty in rallying all sectors of modern society (dockers, students, urban middle classes) under the banner of 'abolishing the structures created by the British: unity, liberation, socialism'.

In Sudan, the communist party succeeded in winning over all of the country's modern society: the workers' unions (starting with the railway workers) which, although clearly a minority in the society, nevertheless represented an important force, not so much for itself but for the role it played for the people as a whole by its defence of the social rights of workers and the democratic rights of the popular classes in their own organisations; the peasants in the regions modernised by irrigation, which had been incorporated into capitalism in a more direct way; the women's organisations struggling against patriarchal oppression; the educated youths and students; the professions organised in unions by the party; and even a good number of officers in the army.

The communist parties of these four countries succeeded in making remarkable revolutionary advances: in Afghanistan and Yemen they conquered state power; in Iraq and Sudan they were not far from doing so.

The communist party of Afghanistan (in fact two parties in one: Parcham – the Flag, and Khalq – the People) did not come to power by a military coup d'état fabricated by Moscow (on the model of the CIA coups d'état), as unfortunately is widely believed in Western opinion. It took over the declining power of the monarchy, and the few communist officers that 'invaded' the palace did not set up a dictatorship, but opened the way for power to be exercised by the party. Moscow did not have much to do with it at the beginning; it had been quite happy with the monarchy's neutralist position in international politics. But one part of the communist party, confronted by the (military) aggression of the US, which it had rightly foreseen as being inevitable, felt that Soviet support was necessary. The other part felt that this support would not strengthen the capacity of the country to successfully resist imperialism, but, on the contrary, risked complicating the task.

Afghanistan experienced the best moment of its contemporary history during the epoch of the so-called communist republic. It was a regime of a modernising enlightened despotism, opening up education to both boys and girls and hostile to obscurantism for which it had decisive support within society. The agrarian reform that it undertook was mainly a collection of measures aimed at reducing the tyrannical powers of the tribal chiefs. The support – at least tacit – of the peasant majorities guaranteed the probable success of this evolution that started well. The propaganda transmitted both by the Western media and political Islam presented this experience as one of 'communist and atheist totalitarianism', which was rejected by the Afghan people. In reality the regime, like that of Ataturk in his time, was far from being unpopular.

The fact that its promoters described themselves as communists in their two major sections (Khalq and Parcham) was not at all surprising. The model of the progress accomplished by the neighbouring peoples of Soviet central Asia (in spite of all that could be said on this subject and in spite of the autocratic practices of the system), compared with the permanent social disasters of the British imperial management of neighbouring countries like India and Pakistan, had the effect, as in many other countries of the region, of encouraging patriots to understand the obstacle that imperialism constituted for all efforts at modernisation. The invitation that certain factions of the party addressed to the Soviets to help them get rid of the others certainly weighed negatively in that it impeded the national–popular–modernist project.

In South Yemen, the party (officially socialist) was constituted on the basis of five communist groups of different origins, who realised that they had to merge (while keeping their own identities). The British had decided to hand over a false independence to some of their colonies (Aden, the Emirates and the Trucial Coast) so had developed a plan guaranteeing the 'pacific' transfer of power to feudal bodies (emirates and others) whose powers had been reinforced during the colonial period.

London's plan functioned without a hitch for the Gulf coast, producing the United Arab Emirates. The Socialist Party of South Yemen refused to play the game and succeeded in mobilising all the most active elements of society around its watchwords: real independence, abolition of the systems of political oppression claiming to be traditional and social justice. Its radicalism paid off: the forces that it mobilised entered Aden, and then all the towns that functioned as the administrative centres of the country. They even short-circuited a rival current supported by Nasser and the regime of North Yemen. The advances that followed are equally incontestable, in particular the liberation of women and the rolling back of obscurantism, opening up the way to a modern and democratic interpretation of religion and a secular state. Its popularity was no less undisputed.

In Iraq, too, the fall of the monarchy in 1958 was not the result of a 'military coup d'état'. The intervention of a group of officers (including communists but also progressive nationalists) only crowned the struggles of imposing masses of people, in which the communist party played a decisive role (in cooperation with other Arab and Kurd organisations, which were progressive in different degrees). The Baath party and the Muslim Brothers were remarkably absent in these struggles. Abdel Karim Kassem, who presided over the regime, was therefore supported by a political alliance that brought together the communist party, the progressive Kurds and the nationalists (independent of the Baath party). The rivalry between the latter and the communist party was constant and lively. So much so that at a certain moment, supported by a faction of officers who were communists or sympathisers, the communist party thought it was able to tilt the balance in its favour. Their failure to do so was due to a combination of interventions from the local reactionary forces (supported from outside), Nasserites and allied Baathists.

In Sudan, the strength of the communist party in 'modern' civil society (workers, peasants from the Gezira, students, women, professionals and the army) was why the dictatorship of General Aboud (supported by the British) was overturned, not by a military counter-coup but by an enormous mass movement (the officers, in their turn, having refused to repress them). A long struggle followed, in which the traditional obscurantist parties (Ansar and Ashiqqa), devoted to the colonial power, were mobilised, supported almost unconditionally by the Muslim Brothers and the diplomats of Nasser's Egypt and Libya's Gaddafi. This reactionary, obscurantist and nationalist bloc (considered uncritically as anti-imperialist) was supported by Western opinion against the most democratic forces of the country.

The 'victories' of this reactionary bloc were always limited and fragile and the communist party each time succeeded in getting back on its feet and making its opponents withdraw. The communist party did not try to make a military coup (which would have been fatal for it), as has been said. General Nimeiry was put in power by a military coup supported by the reactionary alliance, the Egyptian and Libyan diplomats, the Muslim Brothers, the US and Great Britain. But not all the army officers were partisans of the coup. It was they (communist officers and sympathisers, progressive nationalists) who, without difficulty, isolated (and arrested) Nimeiry. After this success there was a possibility of a return to democratic civilian power, the place of the communist party having been reinforced. But a third reactionary military counter-coup (with, this time, the direct intervention of foreign powers, as well as Gaddafi) destroyed this democratic perspective. And ever since…

There were various causes of this failure of the four revolutionary advances. Some, of course, were specific to each case, but others were more or less common to all.

The first cause was the deliberate intention of the US, Great Britain and their subaltern European allies to destroy these advances by the most extreme violence, including military intervention, either implemented (as in Afghanistan and later in Iraq) or seriously threatened.

As part of their strategy, the imperialists mobilised all possible and imaginable obscurantist forces, financing and giving them military equipment. In this they were helped by the Muslim Brothers. It has to be said that they also benefited from the benevolent neutrality (and sometimes the complicity) of the nationalist populist regimes of Egypt and Libya.

The second cause stemmed from the very real difficulties in integrating certain parts of the 'middle classes' into the democratic bloc that supported the revolutionary advances. All efforts were made, very systematically, by – among others – the Muslim Brothers, supported by brutal actions of the power in place (prohibiting organisations, mass arrests and torture), to block the access of the communist party to the popular masses.

As for the third cause, it was a result of the 'theoretical' weaknesses of the various parties and of their analysis of a 'summary' Marxism.

The Russian revolution had a strong echo in the East and the communist parties ranged themselves with no hesitation in the 'Marxism–Leninism' camp, to which they remained verbally faithful until the collapse of 1990. This took them by surprise, as they had never really posed questions about the nature of the system and its problems. Perestroika appeared to them as a welcome new stage of development in triumphant socialism. They were ignorant of the profound crisis of Soviet society which was at the origin of the problem. Then they considered the unfortunate choices of Gorbachev as simple mistakes, if not betrayal.

Convinced of the Marxist–Leninist nature of the Soviet communist party, these communist parties always rallied verbally to the positions defended by Soviet diplomacy, which was itself very attentive to the developments in the strategic countries. I say 'verbally' because, in fact, these parties – many of their cadres and leaders – actually maintained, in spite of everything, their own judgement and sidestepped the insistent interventions of Moscow. This was the case, for example, when Moscow insisted that the parties should dissolve and join with the nationalist parties in power (Nasserites and Baathists), described as being engaged in the 'non-capitalist way'.

The combination of all these elements, as well as others, explains the setbacks.

In Afghanistan, the Soviet intervention – 'useless' is the kindest way of describing it – was capitalised on by the imperial powers, thus rallying the moderate nationalists of the Middle East. Without this intervention, it is possible that the progressive Afghan forces might have been able to hold in check the forces of Pakistan, the Taliban and all the obscurantists described in the Western media as 'freedom fighters'!

In South Yemen, the communist power really committed suicide in 1991, by accepting unity with North Yemen. How to explain this incredible decision? Of course Yemen constitutes one nation and there was a real desire among its people to get rid of the separation created by the British colonisation of its southern coast. But the relationship between North and South Yemen was not similar to that of West and East Germany. Here, it was exactly the reverse. The ('backward') society and the political power of the North, even after the 'revolution' had chased away the imam to replace him with a populism inspired by the confused discourse of Gaddafi (whose power, in fact, did not have much to its credit in terms of progressive achievements), had no attraction for the South. This is proved by the fact that, just after 'unity' had been proclaimed, the people of the South revolted against it, considering themselves betrayed by the leaders of their party. Savage military repression was necessary to impose unity. This is only a partial explanation: some of the party leaders (but not all), desperate after the collapse of the Soviet Union, wanted to rally to the camp of those they thought must be victorious in the end. Some of them were afraid (and they were not wrong) of a ferocious economic blockade by the West, perhaps a military intervention on some pretext or other.

In Iraq, the power relations could not be reversed except by the bloody dictatorships of Abdelsalem Aref, and then of the Baath, with the unconditional support of the Muslim Brothers, the autocratic, pro-imperialist regimes of the Gulf and even of Nasserite Egypt. Was not Nasser the 'father' of Kuwait's independence, fabricated by the British in 1961 and then supported by Egypt? The way was then open for the regime of Saddam Hussein.

In Sudan, the defeat of the attempts to stop the counter-revolution of Nimeiry opened the way to a regime that combined the dictatorship of the military with that of the 'Islamists'. But in spite of the brutality of this type of power, the 'modern' sectors of the society constituted a resistance front (but henceforth more passive than active) which was ignored by the Western 'friends of democracy'. The interminable war in the South, the breaking up of the country (provinces of the East, Darfur in the West) are the price that the Sudanese people pay for this undoing of its revolutionary advances. The intervention, for 'humanitarian' reasons among others, of the Western powers does not redeem them from their close association with the assassination of Sudanese democracy – not to speak of the direct economic interests that motivate these interventions (particularly for oil and uranium).

## The aggression against Lebanon

Israel's aggression against the Lebanese people, which erupted on 11 July 2006, was an integral part of Washington's plan for the region. The implementation of the project has gone ahead: Palestine and the Syrian Golan, Iraq and Afghanistan have been occupied and destroyed, and, following on Lebanon, Syria and Iran have been openly threatened. But the failure of the project is also evident: the Lebanese people gave a lesson in unity by defending their fighters, thus belying the attempts of Tel Aviv, Washington and the Europeans. The armed popular resistance of South Lebanon having proved its effectiveness, all the efforts of the US and Europe are now aiming at imposing its disarmament to enable a new aggression by Israel to obtain an easy victory.

## Iran threatened

Both those in the political Islam camp and 'foreign observers' refer to the 'Islamic revolution'. But does it usher in a development that should spread over the whole region, if not over all the Muslim world, which has been rebaptised for the occasion as the *umma* (which means 'nation', which it has never been)? Or is it an exceptional event, particularly confined to the combination of interpretations of Shiite Islam and the expression of Iranian nationalism?

I shall make just two remarks here about what interests us in this context. The first is that the regime of political Islam in Iran is not incompatible with the integration of the country into the globalised capitalist system, such as it is (the principles underlying the regime are commensurate with a liberal approach to the economy). The second is that the Iranian nation as such is a 'strong nation', that is, its main components, the popular classes and the governing classes (even if not all of them) do not accept the integration of their country into a dominated position in the globalised system. It is true that there is a contradiction in these two dimensions of the Iranian reality but the second one takes into account the orientations of Teheran's foreign policy, which testify to the will to resist foreign diktats.

It is indeed true that it is Iranian nationalism – which is powerful and, in my opinion, absolutely positive – that explains the success of the modernisation of its scientific, industrial, technological and military capacities, which have been undertaken by the successive regimes of the shah and Khomeini. Iran is one of the rare countries in the South that could have a national bourgeois project. Whether the achievement of this project will, in the long run, be possible (and that is my view) is not the subject of our discussion here.

It is precisely because Iran constitutes a critical mass and is capable of attempting to impose itself as a respected partner that the US has decided to destroy the country by a new 'preventative war'. The conflict is, as we know, about the nuclear capacities that Iran is developing. Why should this country not have the right to become a nuclear military power, as others have? What right have the imperialist powers and their Israeli toy to boast that they have claim to the monopoly over the weapons of mass destruction? Can one believe a discourse according to which the 'democratic' countries would never use nuclear power as the 'rogue states' could do? As we know, the 'democratic' countries in question are responsible for the greatest genocides of modern times, including that of the Jews, while the US has already used the atomic bomb and today refuses the absolute and general prohibition of its use. Unfortunately, the European countries are now aligned with Washington in its project of aggression against Iran.

Let me voice some useful thoughts for the actors in the new advances (notably in Latin America).

I believe that, although representative democracy enabled, in favourable circumstances, incontestable victories and the formation of governments committed to progressive social transformation, history shows that the process will quickly end in an impasse.

It is necessary to move beyond the formulas of the Bandung epoch. At that time the regimes had emerged from the national liberation struggles of Asia and Africa and were legitimate and popular for this reason. In general, they were 'populist' as could be seen in the practices of the state (often confused with its charismatic hero) and of the party (fabricated at the top in certain cases and never very democratic in its actions even when they were the outcome of popular mobilisations associated with the liberation struggle) in their relations with the 'people' (a vague substitute for the alliance of the identified popular classes). The ideology underlying the legitimacy of power made no reference to Marxism. It was made up of bits and pieces, associating a past that had been largely reinvented and presented as basically 'progressive' (by the forms that claimed to be democratic in their exercise of power in the ancient communities and by religious interpretations of the same order) and founding nationalist myths, as well as an uncritical pragmatism as concerns the requirements of technological and administrative modernisation. The 'socialism' that the Bandung regimes claimed remained vague in the extreme, difficult to distinguish from the populist, redistributing state and guarantor of social justice. Should one point out the existence of many of these same characteristics in the recent advances in Latin America, where people did not have the opportunity of knowing about the experience of Bandung, and thus risked reproducing its limits?

I have developed a completely different vision of the question of socialism. I am careful not to reduce the 'construction of socialism' to the achievement even of a programme that is as maximal as possible. I describe such a programme as national, popular and democratic, opening the way (but no more than that) to a long, secular transition to socialism. I avoid the simple phrase 'socialism of the 21st century', preferring 'advance on the long route of the transition to socialism',

Reflections on 'democracy' should focus on conclusions drawn from these tragic histories.

Democratisation is a process that cannot be reduced to a static and definitive formula like the contemporary 'representative democracy' which is generally proposed (multiparty, elections, human rights). It is about all aspects of social life and not exclusively the management of the political life of a country. It concerns all the relationships between individuals, within the family, in the work place, as well as the relationships between these and the economic, administrative and political decision makers. These relationships are at the same time individual and collective (the class relations are mainly the result of the unequal power relations in contemporary societies). Democracy means associating and not dissociating political democracy and social progress. It also involves the recognition and the definition of the rights of the individual, formulated in terms of legal rights, the institutional guarantee of their being genuinely respected. Individual freedom and the liberation of human beings from all forms of oppression are inseparable from the exercise of power by the people. A society is not advanced if it does not integrate the rights of the individual with those of the workers' and peoples' collective organisations.

The dominant ideology associates 'democracy' with 'freedom of the markets' (that is, capitalism) and claims that they are inseparable: there is no democracy without markets, therefore democratic socialism is inconceivable. It is only an ideological formulation – in the vulgar and negative sense of the term – which is tautological, inferring that the concept of democracy is reduced to that of the truncated US model.

History does not bear out this viewpoint. The advances in democracy did come as a result of popular struggles and have always been in conflict, in different degrees, with the fundamental logic of capitalism. In fact, the history of actually existing capitalism as a world system shows that even that truncated democracy has been the exception rather than the rule. In the very centres of capitalism, the progress of representative democracy has always been the result of popular struggles, resisted as long as possible by the holders of power (the owners). At the world level of the capitalist system – the real unit of operations for capitalism – the association of (truncated) democracy with capitalism still more visibly has no real grounds. In the peripheries integrated into real world capitalism, democracy has never – or hardly ever – been on the agenda of the possible, or even desirable for the functioning of capitalist accumulation.

In these conditions, I would go as far as saying that the democratic advances in the centres, while they have indeed been the result of the struggles by the popular classes, have at least been greatly facilitated by the advantages of their societies in the world system. Marx expected positive effects from universal suffrage: the possibility of a peaceful transition to socialism. History has not confirmed his hopes, as universal suffrage functioning in societies that had become gangrenous through nationalist/imperialist ideology and the real advantages associated with it (see Canfora 2006).

The popular movements and the peoples struggling for socialism and liberation from the imperialist yoke were at the origin of genuinely democratic breakthroughs, initiating a theory and a practice that associated democracy with social progress. This evolution – beyond capitalism, its ideology and its limited practice of representative and procedural democracy – began very early, as from the French Revolution. It was expressed in a more mature and radical way in the later revolutions, in the Paris Commune, the Russian Revolution, the Chinese revolution and a few others (those of Mexico, Cuba and Vietnam).

The Russian Revolution proceeded to make the great reforms that conditioned a possible socialist and democratic evolution: agrarian reform and the expropriation of the capitalists. The state deviations came later. But it was without doubt the Chinese revolution that had posed the principles of a 'popular democracy' (which has nothing to do with the 'popular democracies' of Eastern Europe), conveying real social and democratic advances that define a stage in the long transition to democratic socialism.

The abolition of the private property of land and the guarantee of equal access to it for everyone constitute a major advance. The implementation of communes, of the collective management of agricultural production, of small, associated industries and of public services (schools, clinics, etc) could serve as an effective institutional framework for a gradual democratisation of the management of all these aspects of social life.

The limits, inconsistencies and retreats from popular democracy in China have many causes, which have been well analysed by Lin Chun (2006): they include the objective contradictions that oppose the three necessary thrusts towards a transition project over a long period (national independence, the development of the productive forces, progress towards the values of equality and socialism), but also – and no less important – the absence of formal legal guarantees for the individual and the imprecise institutionalisation of powers. The 'mass line' that invited the popular classes to make their claims, gave them the means of doing it, and did not raise the party as a self-proclaimed avant-garde, which 'taught' the people the truth, of which it had the monopoly, without having to 'learn' from the people: all this stems from the fundamental logic of a democratic project. This principle is at the very opposite to the thesis that theory comes from outside the movement. The mass line is not, however, a substitute for the institutionalisation of rights and of organisations.

The capitalism of the oligopolies is the enemy of democracy. 'The market decides everything, the parliament (where it exists), nothing.' People thus risk being attracted to the illusion of identity (para-ethnic and/or para-religious), which are in their very essence antidemocratic and so they are imprisoned in an impasse.

In the countries that I have mentioned here, the communist parties, far from having been antidemocratic by nature ('totalitarian' as Western propaganda always repeats) have, on the contrary, constituted the most democratic forces in their societies, despite the limitations of their practices (so-called democratic centralism, etc).

Sudan is a tragic example of the contradiction between the practice of representative, multiparty, electoral democracy on the one hand and, on the other, the urgent need for an authentic democracy that serves social progress. Several times in the contemporary history of Sudan (before the setting up of the military/Islamic dictatorship) – in a country that was attached to free elections – the revolution in progress (supported by the people) was challenged by a (correctly) elected parliament, dominated by the traditional parties, who were enemies of both democracy (when necessary) and of social progress (always).

So what is the alternative? The 'enlightened despotism' of the party as in Afghanistan? Some will say that it is an oxymoron: despotism is always antidemocratic, the Enlightenment was always democratic. This is a dogmatic simplification which does not stand the test of the long time of the apprenticeship and deepening of democracy, of the necessary, continuing invention of new forms (including institutional ones) that go well beyond the Western formula of representative, electoral democracy.

So what is the alternative? A single party? Or a front of different forces that are genuinely autonomous (not 'conveyor belts') but concerned to participate in a real convergence in the strategy for a long transition? The parties of the four countries considered here never settled this question, either in the bureaucratic sense that is commonplace elsewhere (which is to their credit) or in the sense of a consistent formulation of the alternative. This weakness stems from their summary interpretation of Marxism.

## 'Democracy' – what democracy?

The stroke of genius of the Atlantic Alliance was to choose the field of 'democracy' for their offensive, which aimed from the start at dismantling the Soviet Union and reconquering the countries of Eastern Europe. This was decided back in the 1970s and gradually took form in the setting up of the Conference on Security and Cooperation in Europe (CSCE), and then the signing of the final act in Helsinki in 1975. In his book with the suggestive title, *Le Piège: Helsinki et la chute du communisme*, Jacques Andréani (2005) shows how the Soviets, who had expected an agreement on the disarmament of NATO and a genuine détente, were simply taken for a ride by their Western counterparts. It was a stroke of genius because the question of democracy was a genuine issue and the least that could be said was that the Soviet regimes were certainly not democratic, whatever the definition used for the concept and its practice. In contrast, the countries of the Atlantic Alliance could claim to be democratic, however limited and contradictory their political practice, linked as they were to submission to the requirements of capitalist reproduction. Comparison between the systems was visibly in their favour.

This democratic discourse gradually substituted the one that was held by the Soviets and their allies, which was for 'peaceful co-existence', associated with 'respect' for the political practices of both and the principle of 'non-interference' in internal affairs.

The discourse of co-existence had some strong moments. In fact, the selection of this strategy was convenient – or could be convenient, depending on the occasion – to the dominant powers of both West and East. For it accepted as a matter of course the reality of the respective qualifications of 'capitalist' and 'socialist' claimed by the countries of the West and the East. It voided all serious discussion concerning the precise nature of each of the two systems, that is, from examining both the actually existing capitalism of our epoch (capitalism of the oligopolies) and the actually existing socialism. In their place the United Nations (with the tacit agreement of the powers of the two worlds in question) substituted the terms 'capitalist' and 'socialist' with 'market economies' and 'centrally planned economies' (or, to be naughty, 'administered economies'). These two descriptions made it possible, depending on the moment, to stress the 'convergence of the systems' – a convergence that was itself imposed by modern technology (a thesis – also false – based on a technical, monistic concept of history) and to give co-existence its place in facilitating this 'natural' convergence. However, on the contrary, at moments during the cold war it put the emphasis on the irreducible opposition between the 'democratic' model (associated with the market economy) on the one hand, and on the other, 'totalitarianism' (produced by the administered economy).

Deciding to concentrate the battle around 'democracy' made it possible to talk of the 'irreducibility' of the systems and offer the countries of the East and the South only one prospect, that of capitulation, through a return to capitalism (the 'market'), which would then – naturally – produce the conditions for democratisation. That this was not the case (for post-Soviet Russia) or only in extremely grotesque forms (for ethnocracies here and there in Eastern Europe), is another matter.

The 'democratic' discourse of the countries of the Atlantic Alliance is, in fact, recent. NATO adapted perfectly well to Salazar, the Turkish generals and the Greek colonels. At the same time the diplomats of the Triad supported (and often put into power) the worst dictators that Latin America, Africa and Asia had ever known.

At the beginning, the new democratic discourse was only adopted with much reticence. Many of the most important political leaders in the Atlantic Alliance considered it inconvenient, upsetting for their favourite realpolitik. There needed to be Carter in the presidency of the US (rather like Obama today) for it to be understood that the moral sermon of the democracy theme was useful. There needed to be Mitterand in France, to break with the Gaullist tradition of refusing the 'severance' of Europe, imposed by the cold war, preached by the US. There needed to be Gorbachev in the USSR not to understand that rallying to this discourse would bring nothing but guaranteed catastrophe.

The new 'democratic' discourse thus bore its fruit. It seemed sufficiently convincing for the opinions of the 'left' in Europe to rally to it. Not only the electoral left (the Socialist Party) but also those of a more radical origin, of which the communist parties were the heirs. With the advent of 'euro-communism', the move towards a consensus was initiated, and developed later.

The dominant classes of the imperialist Triad learnt their lesson from this victory. They therefore decided to pursue this strategy of concentrating the debate on the 'democracy question'. China is not reproached for opening up to the outside, but for its political management being monopolised by the communist party. No notice is taken of Cuba's social achievements, unique in the whole of Latin America, but there is no end to castigation of its single party. Concerning Putin's Russia, there is the same discourse.

Is the aim of this strategy really to see the triumph of democracy? One needs to be really naïve to think so. In fact the only aim is to impose on refractory countries the market economy, open and integrated into the so-called liberal world system which is, in reality, imperialistic, subordinating the countries concerned to the status of dominated peripheries. This is an objective that, once achieved, will become an obstacle to the progress of democracy in the victim countries and in no way is it an advance in response to the 'democracy question'.

The possibilities of democratic advances in the countries practising, at least at the beginning, actually existing socialism would have been much greater in the medium term if not immediately, if they had allowed the dialectic of social forces to develop by itself, thus opening up the prospect of overcoming the limitations of actually existing socialism (deformed, furthermore, by rallying, at least partially, to the opening up to the liberal economy) in order to reach the 'end of the tunnel'.

Moreover, the democracy theme is only invoked against countries that are recalcitrant about globalised liberal opening up. For the others, there is less concern for the extremely autocratic way that they manage their affairs. Saudi Arabia and Pakistan are two good examples, but also (pro-Atlantist) Georgia and many others. At best, the proposed democratic formula hardly goes beyond the multiparty election charade, completely dissociated from the requirements of social progress, but also still – almost always – associated with the social regression that the domination of actually existing capitalism (that of the oligopolies) requires and produces. The formula has greatly discredited democracy, and confused people have replaced it by sticking to backward-looking religious and ethnicist illusions. It is therefore more than ever necessary to reinforce criticism of the *radical* left (I stress radical to distinguish it from confused, vague left-wing criticism), a criticism that associates and does not dissociate the democratisation of society (and not only in its practice of political management) from social progress (in a socialist perspective). In this criticism the struggle for democratisation and the struggle for socialism cannot be separated. There is no socialism without democracy, but also no democratic progress without a socialist perspective.

## Bibliography

Amin, Samir (writing as Hassan Riad) (1963) *L'Egypte nassérienne*, Paris, Editions de Minuit
Amin, Samir (2008) *L'Eveil du Sud*, Paris, Le Temps des Cerises
Andréani, Jacques (2005) *Le Piège: Helsinki et la chute du communisme*), Paris, Odèle Jacob
Canfora, Luciano (2006) *La Démocratie: histoire d'une idéologie*, Paris, Seuil
Lin Chun (2006) *The Transformation of Chinese Socialism*, Durham, NC, Duke University Press

# 6

# The Drift of the National Popular Project towards 'Re-Compradorising'

The drift and the 're-compradorising' of the Arab world that is associated with it are the result of the imperialist offensive combined with the predictable running out of steam of the national popular leap forward.

The contemporary Middle East no longer has a role as a hub in the new world system, not even the one it played during the colonial system previous to the national popular upsurge. The main function awarded to the region (Arab and beyond) is that of being a major supplier of oil. As a corollary, it provides markets opened up to consumerism by the middle classes and, above all, it imports (useless) armaments (particularly by the Gulf countries that were never to use them). Of interest, too, are the investments of the financial surpluses of the Gulf: this financial market, controlled by the US, is useful to the capital of the generalised monopolies. Still more important, however, is the geographical location of the region (geography counts, after all), which makes it the prime strategic base of the Washington project for the military control of the planet.

Here I shall be dealing with the deployment of this military project and I shall end with its insignificant complement – the 'Euro-Mediterranean' project. Then I shall describe the 'responses' of the governing comprador classes in power (or aspiring to be, under the flag of political Islam) and the 'societies' that have been challenging them. These responses have, of course, been completely ineffective, as can be seen from their failure on both the Palestinian question and that of Arab unity. I shall then analyse, more specifically, some of the conflicts confronting the political forces that are now at the forefront of the stage, but also the social struggles that are clearly mounting.

The example that I have chosen to highlight – the agrarian question and the peasant movement in Egypt – shows the advantage of this method of analysis, compared with the insignificant conclusions

# The Drift of the National Popular Project

resulting from the conventional economic analyses of the World Bank and the subsequent riots. My conclusions about the different future options (and the conditions that make their implementation possible) are supported by good critical analyses of the political economy, such as those produced for Egypt by Abdel Khalek Gouda and Mahmoud Abdel Fadil, and for Morocco by the economic analysis of the Abderahim Bouahid Foundation (a document dated June 2010 entitled 'Has Morocco an economic strategy?').

The questions posed, therefore, are: will these struggles be appropriated by political Islam, or will they manage to liberate themselves from this backward-looking illusion, manipulated by the masters of the world system? Will the struggles succeed in uniting around a positive social, economic and political project that is a genuine alternative, engaging the Arab peoples in a second stage of the awakening of the South?

Clearly, these questions are in no way limited to the Arab world. They are the same that confront the other countries of the South.

In the present circumstances, no Arab country or country in the broader Middle East can aspire to become 'emergent'. Nevertheless, if the social struggles remain out of the control of political Islam, and are associated with more decisive democratic struggles, it is possible. There are even some indications that things are moving in that direction. Their final success would then create favourable conditions for 'emerging', for which at least Egypt and Algeria (also their two large neighbours, Turkey and Iran) are indisputable candidates.

## The deployment of the US military project

The Middle East, now with its extensions into Caucasia and ex-Soviet central Asia, has a particularly important position in the geopolitical strategy of imperialism and above all for the hege-monic project of the US. It owes this to three factors: it oil wealth, its geographical position at the heart of the old world and because it is now the 'soft underbelly' of the world system.

Access to oil that is relatively cheap is crucial for the economy of the dominant Triad and the best way of guaranteeing this access is, of course, to ensure political control over the region. But the region is equally important for its geographical position, at the centre of the old world, equidistant from Paris, Beijing, Singapore and Johannesburg. After the Second World War, the region, situated on the southern flank of the USSR, was thus favoured in the strategy for the military encirclement of the Soviet power. And the region has not lost its importance, despite the collapse of the Soviet adversary: by installing itself there the US could simultaneously force Europe into vassalage, because of its dependence on energy supplies, and subject Russia, China and India to various kinds of blackmail through the threat of military interventions if necessary. Control of the region would therefore extend the Monroe doctrine to the old world, which is the objective of the hegemonic project of the US. Since 1945, Washington's efforts have been constant and continual to ensure control over the region – and to exclude the British and the French – but they have not been crowned with success. We should recall its attempt to associate the region with the North Atlantic Treaty Organisation (NATO) through the 1955 Baghdad Pact (which brought together Turkey, Iran and Iraq under the umbrella of the US. It was rejected by all other Arab states and so not a great success; it disappeared with the fall of the shah), as well as, in 1979, the fall of the Shah of Iran, one of its most faithful allies. The reason for this is quite simply that the Arab (and Iranian) national popular project came into head-on collision with the aims of US hegemony. The Soviets soon understood that giving support to this project would help to defeat Washington's plans of aggression.

That page is turned, first because the national popular project of the Arab world soon exhausted its potential to bring about real change, the nationalist powers degenerating into dictatorships without any programmes. This opened up the way to political Islam and the obscurantist autocracies of the Gulf, the favourite allies of Washington. The region has become the centre of the global system, where events enable foreign intervention (including military) because existing regimes are no longer able to contain – or to discourage – them because of their lack of legitimacy among their own people.

The US operates in the Middle East in close collaboration with its two faithful allies, Turkey and Israel. The latter is, in fact, a truly unconditional ally while the former used to be so but this is no longer quite so certain. Europe has held aloof from the region, accepting the fact that the US alone defends the global vital interests of the Triad – in other words, oil supplies.

How can the US believe that it can take over control of the region? Already, a decade ago, Washington had taken the initiative of promoting the curious project of a 'Middle East common market', for which the Gulf countries would supply the capital and the other Arab countries cheap labour, reserving for Israel technological control and what intermediaries are obliged to do. The project was accepted by the Gulf countries and Egypt but came up against the refusal of Syria, Iraq and Iran. Therefore, in order to deliver the project, it was necessary to destroy these three regimes, which has been done in the case of Iraq.

The question now is what kind of political regime must be established that would be capable of supporting this project? The packaged discourse of Washington propaganda talks of 'democracy'. In fact the US is only trying to replace the out-of-date, worn-out populist autocracies with obscurantist 'Islamic' autocracies (which is made necessary by respect for the cultural specificity of the 'communities'). The renewed alliance with political Islam, which is now described as 'moderate' (that is, able to control the situation efficiently enough to prevent 'terrorism' if aimed against the US and only if so, of course) is the main line chosen by Washington, indeed the only possible one. And the alliance with the archaic autocracy of the Saudi system will be maintained at all costs.

This deployment of aggression has reduced a number of countries and nations on the frontline (Afghanistan, Iraq, Palestine, Syria, Iran) to the unusual position of destroyed countries (the first three) or threatened with destruction (the last two).

The armed diplomacy of the US intended literally to destroy Iraq well before the pretext that it gave on two occasions – Iraq's invasion of Kuwait in 1990 and then, after 11 September 2001, which was cynically used by Bush junior, lying like Goebbels ('if you repeat a lie often enough it becomes the truth'). The reason is simple. Under the soil of Iraq lies a large portion of the best oil resources of the planet. Furthermore, Iraq had succeeded in training scientific and technical cadres that were capable, because of their critical mass, of supporting a coherent national project. This 'danger' had to be eliminated by a 'preventive war' that the US assumed the right to wage, when and where it decided to do so, without the least respect for international law.

All this is quite obvious. But there are serious questions that should be examined: (1) Why has it been so easy for Washington's plan to appear as such a striking success? (2) What is the new situation that has been created for the Iraqi nation today? (3) What are the reactions of the different elements among the Iraqi people to this challenge? (4) What solutions can be promoted by democratic and progressive Iraqi, Arab and international forces?

The defeat of Saddam Hussein was foreseeable. Confronted by an enemy whose main advantage was its capability to exercise genocide by air bombing with impunity (with nuclear power awaiting in the wings), the Iraqi people had only one effective response: to resist on their invaded territory. But Saddam's regime had annihilated all means of defence accessible to his people by systematically destroying all organisations, all political parties (starting with the communist party), including the Baath Party. What is surprising in these conditions is not that the Iraqi people had allowed their country to be invaded without fighting, nor even some of their behaviour (like their apparent participation at the elections organised by the invaders) which seemed to indicate that they accepted defeat (and on which Washington had based its calculations). On the contrary, resistance on the ground is strengthening every day (despite all its serious weaknesses), which has made it impossible to establish a lackey regime capable of ensuring the appearance of order. Somehow, Washington's project has already been shown to be a failure.

This new situation has nevertheless been created by the foreign military occupation. The Iraqi nation is really threatened, if only because Washington's project cannot maintain its control over the country (and pillage its oil resources) through the intermediary of a government that seems to be national. Thus the only solution is to break up the country. Splitting it into at least three 'states' (Kurdish, Sunni Arab and Shiite Arab) was perhaps the objective of Washington, aligned with Israel, right from the beginning (the archives will tell us this in the future). The fact is that the 'threat of civil war' is the card played by Washington to legitimise its continuing occupation. Because permanent occupation was – and remains – the objective: it is the only way for Washington to guarantee its control over oil. It is certainly impossible to believe in any of the declarations about Washington's intentions, such as 'we will leave the country as soon as order is restored'. It will be remembered that the British never described their occupation of Egypt, after 1882, as anything but 'provisional' (it lasted until 1956). In the meantime, of course, the US is destroying the country, its schools, its factories, its scientific capacities, day by day, by any means, including the most criminal.

The response of the Iraqi people to this challenge does not appear – at least at present – to be commensurate with the extreme gravity of the situation. It is the least that can be said. Why is this? The dominant Western media endlessly repeat that Iraq is an 'artificial' country and that the oppressive domination of the 'Sunnite' regime of Saddam over the Shiites and the Kurds is the cause of the inevitable civil war (which only the prolongation of the foreign occupation will be capable of averting). The 'resistance' is therefore to a few Islamist pro-Saddam hard cores in the Sunni triangle. It is difficult to fall for so many counter-truths.

The Baath Party in power had evolved, as was perfectly predictable, into a dictatorship, of which the state was only half anti-imperialist, in the sense that, according to the conjunctures and the circumstances, a compromise could be accepted by the two partners (the Baathist power in Iraq and the US imperialism dominating the region). This deal encouraged the megalomaniac tendencies of the leader, who believed that Washington intended to make him its principal ally in the region. The support given by Washington to Baghdad (including the delivery of chemical arms) in the absurd and criminal war against Iran from 1980 to 1989 seemed to confirm this. But Iraq fell into the trap prepared for it: the green light was given to Saddam to annexe Kuwait (which was in fact an Iraqi province before the British imperialists had detached it in order to make it one of their oil colonies) and for a decade the country suffered sanctions the purpose of which was to bleed the country dry in order to facilitate the glorious conquest of the vacuum by the US army.

It is possible to make many accusations against the successive regimes of the Baath Party, including the last phase of its decline under the 'direction' of Saddam, but not that it stirred up the religious conflict between Sunnis and Shiites, or persecuted the Christians. Who is then responsible for the bloody clashes between the two Muslim communities and the massacre of the Christians? One day we shall surely learn how the CIA (and doubtless Mossad) organised many of these massacres. But it is also true that the political desert created by the Saddam regime and its unprincipled opportunistic methods encouraged the candidates to power of all kinds to behave in the same way, often protected by the occupiers, who were sometimes perhaps naïve to the point of believing that they could use them. The candidates in question, whether 'religious' leaders (Shiites or Sunnis), so-called notables (para-tribals) or notoriously corrupt 'businessmen' exported by the US, have never had real political influence in the country, even the religious chiefs who, although respected by their followers, did not have a political influence that would be acceptable to the Iraqi people. Without the vacuum created by Saddam we would never have even heard of their names. Given this new 'political world', fabricated by the imperialism of liberal globalisation, would the genuinely popular and national political forces, even the democratic ones, be able to reconstitute themselves?

The Kurdish question is a real issue, in Iraq as in Iran and Turkey. But we should remember that, in this context, the Western powers have always been extremely cynical in applying their double standards. In Iraq and Iran, the repression of Kurdish claims never reached the degree of permanent police, military, political and moral violence as that practised in Ankara. Neither Iran nor Iraq has ever denied the very existence of the Kurds. But all has been pardoned of Turkey, a member of NATO – an organisation of democratic nations, as the media remind us, which over the years included the eminent democrat Salazar, one of its founding members, not to mention its no less unconditional support for the democracy of the Greek colonels and the Turkish generals. The Iraqi popular fronts created around the Communist Party and the Baath Party in the best moments of their turbulent histories, whenever they had exercised responsibilities in power, always found common ground with the main Kurdish parties who, besides, had always been their allies. The 'anti-Shiite' and 'anti-Kurd' trend of the Saddam regime was certainly true: the bombing of the Bassorah region by Saddam's army after his defeat in Kuwait in 1990 and the use of gas against the Kurds. This was a response to the manoeuvres of Washington's armed diplomacy, which had mobilised sorcerers' apprentices to take advantage of the situation. It was still a criminal move, above all a stupid one, as the success of Washington's calls was very limited. But could one expect anything else from dictators of the Saddam stamp?

However, in spite of its 'weaknesses', the resistance of the Iraqi people has already routed the political, if not the military project of Washington. It is precisely this that worries the Atlanticists of the European Union, the faithful allies of the US. Its subordinate associates fear its defeat, as this would reinforce the ability of the peoples of the South to force the globalised transnational capital of the imperialist Triad to respect the interests of the nations and peoples of Asia, Africa and Latin America.

The sooner that the foreign occupation troops leave the country, the stronger will be the support given by the democratic forces in the world and in Europe to the Iraqis, and the greater the chances will be of a better future for this martyred people. The longer the occupation lasts, the bleaker the future will be when it comes to its inevitable end.

The region of the 'Great Middle East' is today at the heart of the conflict between the imperialist leader and the peoples all over the world. Defeating the project of the Washington establishment is the condition for enabling advances in any region of the world. If this does not happen, such advances will remain extremely vulnerable. But that does not mean underestimating the importance of the struggles in other regions of the world, in Europe, Latin America and elsewhere. It only means that they must form part of a global struggle that will help to defeat Washington in the region that it has chosen for its first criminal strike.

The US domination project – the extension of the Monroe doctrine to the entire planet – is overweening. For this reason I called it the 'Empire of Chaos' just after the collapse of the Soviet Union. But it will be fatally confronted by the mounting and increasing resistance of nations that will not accept submission. Then the US will be forced to behave like a 'rogue state' par excellence, replacing international law by permanent war (which has started in the Middle East but aims beyond it, to Russia and Asia), slipping down the slippery slope of fascism (the Patriot Act has already given police powers over foreigners that are unacceptable in a normal democracy).

## Terrorism and state terrorism

Terrorism, an option chosen by certain individuals organised in different degrees, is not a new phenomenon in history. It has been legitimised by certain doctrines that interpret 'anarchism' in their own way. But it is important to remember that this option is always a response to an intolerable situation and that it is often caused by the powerlessness of social actors whose disillusionment has been produced by the defeat of other means of social intervention, whether by 'revolution', the practice of populism or the electoral process.

It is therefore more important to assess state terrorism as practised systematically by capitalism in the past, particularly in the colonies. Punitive expeditions and colonial massacres fill the black pages of this history. Today, state terrorism is systematically being implemented by the US and approved by its European and Japanese allies. The American war in Vietnam illustrated Washington's cynical and cruel option, with its chemical bombardment compared with which similar crimes by Saddam Hussein were mere bagatelles. And when are we going to see the crimes against humanity, perpetrated by the highest authorities of the US, punished by hanging? Today these crimes are being committed daily in occupied Iraq, as in Guantánamo – the 'only tropical gulag', as it has been called by the Cuban government. Today, Israel is utilising, in occupied Palestine and in south Lebanon, a whole range of armaments that have been prohibited elsewhere (delayed-action and fragmentation bombs) without unduly upsetting Western public opinion. The US is, today, the veritable rogue state no. 1.

## The Euro-Mediterranean partnership

Europe and the Arab world are two regions which have maintained complex relations throughout their history on account of their geographic proximity and their common Hellenistic ancestry from which originated Christianity and Islam. However, the North–South demarcation between 'developed' Europe and the 'underdeveloped' Arab world was definitively established only belatedly, with the capitalist expansion reinforced by the colonisation of the South segment that ended only recently (the British left Egypt only in 1954 and even tried to return there in 1956 and the French did not recognise Algeria's independence until 1962).

In the post-Second World War period, the relations between Europe and the Arab world came within the dominant logic of the geopolitics and geostrategy of the US. NATO actually considered the Arab world as an opponent while the Soviet Union supported the Arab world's attempts at autonomous development. Having withdrawn from the region, Europe allowed the US to operate there alone, with the support of their loyal allies, such as Turkey, Israel and the governments of the Gulf, and thus guaranteed the vital oil supply to Europe.

Was the disappearance of the Soviet opponent going to open new prospects for genuine cooperation between the European Union and the Arab world? One would have thought so at one point when Europe took the initiative in formulating in Barcelona in 1995 a proposal on a 'Euro-Mediterranean' partnership. Today, this process is not just at a standstill; it has collapsed. The reason is that the project itself had been designed on the basis of an unacceptable and incredible principle and could therefore not be implemented, even if some of its promoters must have been well-intentioned partners.

The European partnership rallies not only the Mediterranean Europeans but all countries of the European Union. It is a right for Europeans, which, in fact, nobody can call into question (the right to think of sharing common interests and contemplating a common future). That is an indisputable right for all Europeans, even if those in each of the concerned countries also have the right to criticise (as done by some people) the European project as it stands today.

The other partner is curious; it is composed of all the riparian entities along the south and east coast of the Mediterranean. However, the majority of these riparian elements happen to be Arab countries that also belong to a distinct world: the Arab world. Whether nationalist Arab or not, this world exists and it should therefore be recognised that the Arab world could have certain common tendencies and interest and a common vision of its integration into the contemporary world. Separating the Mediterranean Arab countries from the non-Mediterranean Arab countries is actually unacceptable. What is needed is, therefore a Euro-Arab, agreement – in other words, an agreement between all the European countries and all the Arab, regardless of whether they are Mediterranean or not. The Mediterranean concept is meaningful only if it entails rallying all the riparian countries around problems concerning the common sea, for instance in the area of pollution. It is not on this narrow basis that one can contemplate the future of relations between Europe and this small portion of the South known as the Arab world.

On the other hand, the era of the Barcelona conference (1995) was also that of the Madrid and Oslo conferences, that is a period when a certain type of peace between Arabs and Israel was being promoted under the leadership of the Americans. In this way, the Europeans implemented a strategy complementary to that of the US and Israel, aimed at dictating the content of the said peace. This kind of peace imagined a basis that should have been seen in advance as being unacceptable, since it was equivalent to the establishment of a bantustan – there could not be a better term – in the occupied territories of Palestine.

It is at this moment and in this geographical context that the Euro-Mediterranean project was contemplated. It consisted of using the new international economic situation to impose on the Arabs the integration of Israel into the region. As a condition for cooperation between Europe and the Arab countries, it also posed a similar cooperation between the Arab countries themselves and Israel. It is rather as if, in the apartheid era, Europe had forced the African states to regularise their diplomatic and other relations with South Africa as a condition for the support and cooperation that the Europeans were offering them. As an apartheid country, Israel has been implementing a policy of systematic ethnic purging. It is unacceptable to put up with Israel, let alone support it. Israel should be boycotted by all civilised countries of the world.

At present, the tragedy developing in Palestine calls for strong international political intervention accompanied by effective measures for a serious boycott of Israel until this state recognises the state of Palestine. Europe intervened clamorously in Kosovo to defend a lesser cause than that of Palestine, but it tolerates the government of Israel being entrusted to a real war criminal who, has personally proclaimed his rejection of the Madrid and Oslo agreements. It is true that in the case of Yugoslavia, Europe only stood by a decision previously taken in

# The Drift of the National Popular Project

Washington. In contrast, in taking an autonomous stand on Palestine, Europe has to distance itself from the US, which is obviously difficult. It also proves that political Europe does not exist.

The so-called European proposals for Euro-Mediterranean partnership also include an economic component about which the European institutions claim to have made 'new efforts' in qualifying their proposals so that they come within the framework of 'mutual development', 'partnership' and 'joint development', in place of 'aid', the devalued term.

An analysis of these proposals shows that they are nothing of the sort. All these proposals comply completely with the exclusive logic of globalised neoliberalism (opening markets, creating 'enabling' conditions for foreign investment, deregulating and defusing protections, etc) as formulated by the US, WTO, the World Bank and IMF. Submission to the rules defined by these authorities, including the so-called structural adjustment plans, is, moreover, formulated as a pre-condition for implementation of the European proposals. Here too, the real position of Europe is no different from that of the US. In both its political and economic dimensions Europe's proposals currently form part of a dominant twofold alignment: liberal globalisation and US hegemonism. The two elements are interrelated. Accepting the exclusive logic of liberal globalisation means agreeing to give priority to the interests of dominant capital. At any rate, the interests of European dominant capital are not fundamentally different from the interests of North American dominant capital. Of course, there are conflicts, but these are common mercantile conflicts of the same kind that can crop up between the multinationals of a given country. Europe's autonomy vis-à-vis the US cannot be assumed on this basis.

Other conditions are also imposed by the European partner. Is the reference to respect for human rights as a theoretical condition of the partnership agreements desirable? Certainly, even if signed by governments that do not intend to implement its provisions, a charter can become a lever that can be utilised by victims of a system. However, this instrument will at best remain marginal because the struggle for democracy is pre-eminently the peoples' affair that must be managed in the country concerned. Internationalism in this field is very useful, but it is mainly through internal struggles and the mobilisation of democratic forces within the societies that change can be fostered.

Precisely what the external entity can do is to support and not fight the people's struggles.

However, the use that the great powers (Europe, in this case) intend to make of such interventions in the name of democracy remains dubious. The examples of double standards – which are numerous and obvious – show that this type of utilisation is absolutely cynical: the tool is mobilised against an opponent to be weakened but it is put away when faced with an ally. Moreover, the dominant concept at present is that of 'good governance', to use the jargon in fashion; in other words, the concept of acceptable governability. Alas, this is a poor concept that limits democracy to multiparty systems, formal elections and respect for a number of individual elementary rights, without recognising social, individual and collective rights, or the right to work, education, health and freedom of movement within and outside one's own country. Yet the rights constitute a whole set comprising inseparable elements. If they are not accompanied by the other rights, then political rights become instruments that can be and are manipulated and therefore undermine the cause of democracy since they destroy its credibility among the peoples themselves.

Europeans consider that Islamic governments are very likely to be set up in the whole region. Their concern is therefore that political Islam in power remains moderate, that is, that it dissociates itself from terrorist extremism. The Islamic governments (e.g. the Muslim Brotherhood) would be capable, it is believed in Europe, of controlling their frontiers and thus confining their populations within their own borders and reducing migratory flows. Also, the moderate option is considered capable of combining Islam with democracy, along the Turkish model. How realistic is this hypothesis? One could accept the 'moderate' Islam formula (we would call it 'docile' Islam), because it is in line with subordinating the economy to the requirements of globalised liberal capitalism. However, it would have to dissociate democracy (if it existed) from social progress and consequently it could not stabilise societies submitted to this formula.

Could one imagine a project of the Mediterranean Union based on an authentic partnership that allowed the countries on the northern and southern shores to negotiate the zones and various types of innovatory cooperation and thus help to revive solidarity between the

# The Drift of the National Popular Project

peoples of the Mediterranean civilisation? This page was definitively turned long ago as, with capitalism, the gap has widened between the two shores and also because the countries of the northern shore, having become imperialist, are engaged in colonial conquest of those of the southern shore. In any event, the jettisoning of the original project in favour of the Union of the Mediterranean imposed by the European Union has put an end to any specifically Mediterranean perspective.

The possible fall-out for Middle Eastern affairs from the games of the European Union and the US on the one hand and, on the other, of other powers such as China, India and Russia, should also be taken into consideration in any debate on this region.

China and India have formally declined to be actors in the settling of these questions, particularly on the issue of peace in Israel/Palestine. These two powers have stated they would limit themselves to supporting any pacific solution, without being more specific, leaving the responsibility for finding a solution only to the European and Arab actors. Russia, on the other hand, considers itself an actor which could contribute positively to the peaceful solution that is being sought. In that spirit Russia is inviting Europe (of which it considers itself to be a part) to define its own positions, independently of those of the US. It remains to be seen whether this desire to see the European Union detach itself from its Atlanticist alignment is indeed realistic.

The relationships between Europe and the Arab world are a specific part of the more general North–South relationships. At present these relationships have been characterised by the offensive of the oligopolistic capital of Triad imperialism (the so-called liberal globalisation) and the US programme for military control of the whole planet (for itself and for its subaltern allies – NATO and Japan). These relationships are therefore stamped by the aggravation of conflicts and not their reduction. Structural adjustment programmes, external debt and privatisation policies have brought about a deterioration of social conditions for the popular majorities in the countries of the South as a whole. In particular, the programmed disintegration of peasant societies has created more than 200 million 'workers on the move' (transborder migration pressures) and over 500 million if one includes internal migration within the countries concerned (from the countryside to the city shanty towns).

The immediate reactions of the popular classes concerned are not necessarily capable of finding humane solutions to this gigantic challenge. In the rich countries of the North egoistic attitudes, systematically orchestrated by the authorities and the media, are being encouraged to gain acceptance of the priority given to 'defence', so that people can secure the advantages enjoyed by the imperialist countries (particularly the exclusive access to the natural resources of the planet). Such objectives are accompanied by speeches and actions to mask violence so we continually hear about 'humanitarian' interventions, the defence of 'human rights', 'good governance' and the fight against poverty. The projects drawn up by Europe for the Arab countries all come within this framework. In the societies of the South – particularly in the Arab world – reactions are still mostly confined to illusions of backward-looking withdrawal.

In these circumstances, it is certainly difficult to respond to the challenge by organising the necessary internationalism of peoples. Nevertheless, the grounds do exist on which this internationalism could advance. It is proposed to the peoples of the West that 'our standard of living must at all costs be defended'. What model of living? Should one not respond with another question such as: 'what about the alienation of the destructive market system and illusory individualism?' The ball lies now in the court of the European left. If it dissociated itself from the European imperialist projects of unconditional support to the Israeli colonial enterprise and the military interventions of the US in the region, the peoples of Europe could certainly help the Arab world to extricate itself from the impasse of backward-looking illusions.

## The Palestinian question

Israel's colonial expansionism poses a real challenge and is not the fruit of the imaginative world of Arabs. Israel is the only country in the world that refuses to recognise any established borders (and hence should not have the right to be a member of the United Nations). Like the 19th century US, Israel thinks it has the right to conquer new areas for the expansion of its colonisation and to treat the people who have been living there for two thousand years – if not more – like 'Redskins' to be hunted or exterminated. Israel is the only country that openly declared that it did not feel bound to United Nations resolutions.

The 1967 war, which had been planned in agreement with Washington from 1965, pursued several objectives: start working for the decline of the populist nationalist regimes in the region, break up the alliance with the Soviet Union, compel them to reposition themselves and follow the footsteps of America and open up new lands for Zionist colonisation. In the territories conquered in 1967, Israel therefore instituted an apartheid system inspired by that of South Africa. Whenever it is accused of racism – which is absolutely obvious – Zionism responds, as usual, by systematically blackmailing its critics with accusations of anti-semitism and exploitation of the Holocaust, as analysed by Norman Finkelstein (2000). To carry on with its project, Israel therefore requires an Arab world weakened as much as possible at all levels.

It is here that the interests of globally dominant capital tally with those of Zionism. For one thing, the logic of carrying on with the project of actually existing capitalism has always resulted in and still contributes to polarisation on a world scale. The 'development' of any third world region – in this case, the Arab region – conflicts with the global expansion of actually existing capitalism. On the other hand, a modernised, rich and powerful Arab world would call into question the Western countries' guaranteed permit to plunder its oil resources as a necessity for the continued wastage associated with capitalist accumulation. Political authorities in the Triad countries do not want a modernised and powerful Arab world because, typically, these countries are faithful servants of dominant transnational capital.

The alliance between the Western powers and Israel is therefore built on the solid foundation of their common interests. This alliance is neither the product of a feeling of culpability on the part of the Europeans, who were responsible for anti-semitism and the crime of Nazism, nor that of the Jewish lobby's skill in exploiting this sentiment. Had the Western powers felt that Zionist colonial expansionism did not serve their interests, they would have quickly found ways to overcome their 'complex' and neutralise the Jewish lobby. I have no doubts about that, for I am not one of those who naïvely think that public opinion imposes its views on authorities in the typically democratic countries. Everybody knows that public opinion is fabricated; hence, Israel would be unable to resist for more than a couple of days if measures (even if moderate) involving a blockade were taken against it, just as the Western powers did to Yugoslavia, Iraq and Cuba. It would therefore not be difficult to bring Israel to its senses and create conditions for genuine peace, if the Western powers wanted it. But they do not.

Arab public opinion is not well equipped to understand the nature of the complementary links between the Zionist project and the general expansion of capitalism – the foundation of their convergence. In this case, Arab public opinion is the victim of the limited scope of populist nationalist thought, whose foundations it has so far been unable to criticise, let alone transcend.

After the defeat in 1967, Sadat declared that, since the US had '90 per cent of the cards' in their game (that was his actual expression), it was necessary to break with the USSR and join the Western camp and that, in doing so, Washington could be induced to exert sufficient pressure on Israel to bring the latter to its senses. Even beyond this 'strategic idea' specific to Sadat – which later developments proved to be flimsy – Arab public opinion remained altogether unable to understand the global process of capitalist expansion, let alone to identify its real contradictions and weaknesses. Is it not alleged and repeated that the Westerners will finally realise that their actual interest lies in maintaining sound relations with the two hundred million Arabs – their immediate neighbours – and not in sacrificing such relations for the unconditional support of Israel? This thinking suggests that the Westerners concerned (that is to say dominant capital) want a modernised and developed Arab world; it also reveals a lack of awareness that the Westerners, who rather want to make the Arab world powerless, consider it expedient to support Israel.

The option chosen by the Arab governments – apart from Syria and Lebanon – to subscribe to the American plan for the so-called lasting peace through the Madrid and Oslo negotiations (1993), could not have produced any results other than those that it generated: a green flag for Israel to carry on with its expansionist project. By today openly rejecting the terms of the Oslo agreement, Ariel Sharon is displaying what should have been understood much earlier: the agreement had nothing to do with a lasting peace but was rather aimed at opening up a new phase for Zionist colonial expansion.

## The Drift of the National Popular Project

The permanent state of war imposed on the region by Israel and the Western powers supporting its project in turn constitutes a powerful motive for the perpetuation of the autocratic regimes of the Arab countries. This blocking of a possible democratic evolution weakens the opportunities for revival in the Arab world, thereby paving the way for the deployment of dominant capital and the hegemonic strategy of the US. They have come full circle, for the alliance between Israel and America serves the interests of the two partners.

The fight for democracy and social progress in the Arab world is therefore not contingent on the so-called peace plans, which are something else. On the contrary, the effective conduct of this battle is contingent on unveiling the real objectives of these projects to discredit them. I think it is necessary to establish the line of arguments that made me draw this personal conclusion.

The Palestinian people's intifada is a struggle for national liberation, probably the major struggle of this kind in our era. It simply expresses the people's desire not to submit to the racist apartheid system in the Zionist fashion. It will end only if Israel recognises the right of Palestinians to their state, which will not be tomorrow, or if the powers in the developed capitalist countries undergo profound changes in kind (to the extent of forcing dominant capital to renounce its strategy of systematically weakening the position of the peripheral peoples – in this case, Arabs – in the global system); this will not be realised in a hurry either.

The Israeli authority in the territories occupied since 1967 (Gaza, the West Bank, the Golan) is pursuing the plan to expand Zionist colonisation, thereby recognising only the rights of Jews (I emphasise Jews because in the state of Israel itself, the non-Jews are not accorded the same rights, neither collective nor individual), and this constitutes the definition of the apartheid racist state. The set of measures taken to this effect include expropriating lands for new settlers, plundering water resources and jeopardising any form of elementary economic life for Palestinians.

Initially, this system gave the impression of being capable of achieving its ends, as the Palestinian people appeared to have accepted the timid management of daily activities in the occupied territories by notables and the trading bourgeoisie. The Palestine Liberation

Organisation (PLO), which was driven away from the region after the invasion of Lebanon by the Israeli army (1982), appeared to no longer possess the means to oppose the Zionist annexation from its exile in Tunis.

The first intifada took place in December 1987. An apparently spontaneous explosion, the intifada expressed the outburst of the working classes, and particularly of the most wretched social groups, confined in refugee camps. The intifada boycotted the Israeli authority by organising systematic acts of civil disobedience. Israel reacted with the colonial brutality that defines its nature but was unable to re-establish its police force nor to bolster the timid Palestinian middle classes which were acting as a buffer. The intifada advocated a mass return of the political forces in exile, the establishment of new forms of local organisation, and the middle classes' patronage of the sustained liberation struggle. The intifada was an affair for young people – Chebab al intifada – who were initially not organised in the formal PLO networks. The four components of the PLO (Fatah, loyal to its chief, Yasser Arafat; the Democratic Front for the Liberation of Palestine – DFLP; the Popular Front for the Liberation of Palestine – PFLP; and the Communist Party) immediately joined the intifada and thus won the sympathy of many of these Chebab. Overtaken because of their slackness in the previous years, despite a couple of actions credited to the Islamic Jihad that reappeared in 1980, the Muslim Brotherhood made way for a new form of struggle embodied in Hamas, which was established in 1988.

Although after two years of expansion this first intifada appeared to lose impetus, on account of its violent suppression by Israeli armed forces and authorities (who used firearms to fight Palestinian children, closed the 'green line' to Palestinian workers, the sole breadwinners of their families, and so on), the stage was set for a US-sponsored 'negotiation' that was crowned with the Madrid meeting (1991) and subsequently with the so-called Oslo Peace Accords (1993) that allowed for the return of the PLO to the occupied territories and its transformation into a Palestinian Authority (1994).

The Oslo Accords had imagined the transformation of the occupied territories into one or more bantustans to be definitively integrated into Israeli territory. Without showing much imagination, the Zionists and their American and European sponsors replicated in detail the entire

# The Drift of the National Popular Project

apartheid system of racist South Africa. At any rate, Israel had been a faithful friend of the apartheid regime, which shared with Israel the same fundamentally racist vision of humanity. In this context, the Palestinian Authority was to crystallise into nothing other than a false state – like those of the bantustans – indeed, to be the channel for transmitting Zionist order.

Back in Palestine, the PLO-turned-authority managed to establish its order but not without some ambiguity. The authority absorbed into its new structures most of the Chebab who had co-ordinated the intifada. It acquired legitimacy through the 1996 elections in which the Palestinians participated massively (80 per cent) and an overwhelming majority elected Arafat president of this Authority. All the components of the Palestinian political spectrum (Fatah, DFLP, PFLP, Communist Party and Hamas) showed a great sense of political maturity by refusing to be polemical during the campaign and transferred the choice of the electorate to individuals who had been loyal and efficient in the struggle, regardless of their partisan sympathies. However, the authority had to contend with acute financial problems as Israel controls the entire economy of the territories, which, moreover, cannot maintain direct relations with the outside world. On the other hand, the Gulf states virtually stopped offering financial assistance to the authority, using the pretext of Palestine's sympathy for Iraq during the invasion of Kuwait in 1990. For their part, the Europeans, who had made pleasant promises, released funds for Palestine in droplets and even agreed to subject their financial transactions to Israeli control. To cope with the situation, the authority acquired a (de facto) monopoly of commercial transactions by eliminating the unreliable local bourgeoisie and thus managed to realise resources for the survival of its embryonic state machinery.

At this juncture, I will avoid entering into facile arguments 'for' or 'against' the authority because, in my opinion, the Palestinian Authority is in an ambiguous situation: will it agree to fulfil the functions assigned to it by Israel, the US and Europe – 'governing a bantustan' – or side with the Palestinian people who refuse to be subjugated?

According to the partisans of the bantustan project, the overstaffed police force (some 50,000 agents or more) allegedly does not carry out the functions expected of the service – cracking down on the Palestinian people to compel them to accept their fate. At any rate, it could also be asserted that this force is not excessive, considering the level of violence perpetrated by the Israeli armed forces whom they sometimes have to face, especially if members of the Palestinian police force refuse to suppress their people.

The financial and commercial monopolies held by the Palestinian Authority offered a propitious opportunity for distributing stipends and facilitating the creation of a new class of nouveaux riches wholly dependent on representatives of the authority. Alas, it is true that the Palestinian leaders concerned could be reproached for not behaving like exemplary militants, administering public property without deriving the least profit for personal use – but then could the authority survive without such monopolies?

It is actually because the Palestinian people are opposed to the bantustan project that Israel decided to denounce the Oslo Accords – despite having dictated their terms – with a view to solely substituting the use of military violence for the accords. War criminal Ariel Sharon's provocation on the Esplanade of the Mosques in 1998 (but with the support of the then Labour Party government, which provided him with tanks), the triumphant election of this same criminal as head of the Israeli government (and the collaboration of doves like Shimon Peres in the cabinet) are therefore the root causes of the second intifada which is currently in progress.

Will this second intifada liberate the Palestinian people from the prospect of their planned submission to the Zionist system of apartheid?

In any case, the Palestinian people now have a real national liberation movement with specific characteristics. It is not based on the single party model; it appears to be united and homogenous, but is not actually so. It is composed of members who maintain their personality, their visions for the future, their ideologies, their militants and even their clients, but are able to agree to pursue the struggle together. An amorphous group of organisations, associations and NGOs provides for the operational means of this movement. Certainly, this group is a real melting pot with certain NGOs that might merely be serving as screens for speculative corruption or for the penetration of Israeli and American intelligence agencies. But it is this same nebulous group that guarantees daily survival under the dreadful conditions due to the military aggression of the enemy. These organisations help the schools and health centres to operate in addition to supplying and distributing basic commodities. Should this positive role be spurned?

## Arab unity: the Arab world frozen in its powerlessness

Pan-Arabism is both a reality and a positive phenomenon. Given the cultural destruction and other effects of the globalisation process, if the French-speaking community, the Portuguese-speaking community and the spirit of the Latin-American family are frameworks for legitimate resistance (and they are, in my opinion), then what is the basis for sniggering at Pan-Africanism or Pan-Arabism? Why should the familiarity between peoples occupying a territory stretching from the Atlantic to the Gulf and using the same language (despite the local variants) be devoid of significance and interest?

Yet, saying that there is 'only one Arab nation' divided up against its will entails an assumption that should be avoided. It is because this national question remains infinitely more complex than implied by the ideology of 'Arab nationalism' (*qawmi*, as opposed to *qutri*, concerning the frameworks defined by the borders of the Arab states). The national reality of the Arab peoples is expressed in terms of the overlapping stages of a pyramid. The Pan-Arab dimension (*qawmi*) is a reality. But the local dimensions (*qutri*) are no less a reality. In fact, if it is true that the demarcation of historical Syria (the present-day territories of Syria, Lebanon, Palestine and Jordan) is recent (1919), artificial and actually the outcome of an imperialist partition, like that of the fertile Crescent (historical Syria and Iraq), it would be ridiculous to claim that Egypt, Morocco and Yemen are artificial and recent fabrications. Whether ancient or new, the expression 'local nation' (*qutri*) is based on the interests and real perceptions of their specific characteristics.

The national liberation movements and the populist nationalisms they generated were necessarily deployed on the basis of such realities in the states as they are. The development strategies they wanted to establish on self-centred foundations – so as to modernise their societies, transform them progressively and assert their autonomy vis-à-vis imperialism – could be nothing other than what they were: designed and implemented in the states (*qutri*).

The Pan-Arab dimension could have called for implementation of complementary strategies aimed at strengthening each partner's self-centred structures and not those to be substituted for such structures. That was not the case, because the representatives of the populist nationalisms were not equipped to efficiently design such complementarity, their perception of the real nature of the modern capitalist challenge being what it used to be – insufficient, to say the least. That is why all that the 'technocrats' in their service could conceive of was nothing other than 'common markets' which, to be precise, is a capitalist strategy that is absolutely inappropriate.

At the political level, the same limitations of both populism and the autocratic state accounted for the failures. The Baath, which presented itself as the promoter of Arabness (*ourouba*), was unable to go beyond incantation and the analogy with experiences of the German and Italian unity created by conquest of the German and Italian states by one of them (Prussia and Piedmont), which were caricatured without the least awareness of the fact that the conditions on the periphery of the system in the 20th century were not those of 19th century Europe.

The official Pan-Arabism of the populist authorities was overtaken leftwards for a while by the *qawmiyin* movement, a group of young revolutionaries imbued with Marxism, Maoism and Guevarism, who initiated the formation of the radical parties of Palestine (Naief Hawatmeh's Democratic Front and George Habache's Popular Front), the popular revolution in South Yemen and the War of Dhofar. In comparison with most of the analyses proposed, which are almost always too ideological (obsessed with identifying errors and 'deviations'), Sanallah Ibrahim's novel *Warda* provides a better insight into the slow death of this movement, its profound aspirations for social, collective and individual liberation (with particular regard to women), and the illusion that the Kalashnikov – over-popularised in this era of modern Arab history – could become an effective substitute for the popular classes' inertia. This Arab version of focalism (*foquism*, Che Guevara's theory of revolutionary warfare) faded away like the original one in Latin America.

The official Pan-Arabism promoted the blossoming of organisations operating within the whole Arab entity. In particular each of the middle-class professions was identified with a sometimes active Pan-Arab organisation (Arab lawyers, Arab engineers, Arab doctors, Arab writers, etc), just as there is, at least on paper, a confederation of trade unions (Arab Workers Union). In the 1970s and 1980s, the intensification of intra-Arab migrations (towards the oil-rich countries) certainly helped to popularise the mutual knowledge of the Arab peoples. But it did so in a general atmosphere of depoliticisation and in an environment dominated by the super-reactionary practices of the Gulf states. Its effects are therefore very ambiguous. Inverse capital flows were no less ambiguous in their effects, mainly benefiting the coffers of Islamist businessmen.

Autocratic Pan-Arabism is dead. To be convinced of that, it suffices to have attended (as the writer did) some of its (funeral) 'services', which each year assemble the cohort of its 'historic leaders' – tie-wearing men currently over 70 years old on average, and closed to women and younger people – who still feel no more than nostalgia for the populist era. Its overtures to the Islamic current have certainly not endowed it with new life. On the contrary, it contributes to its dilution in the new shallow illusion – that of the Islamic nation (*al umma al islamiya*).

This page of history has turned. The Arab world no longer has its own project, neither in the local states nor in the entire Pan-Arab entity. That is the reason why the projects thought up for it by external agents (the US and Europe) seem to impose their programme.

Nonetheless, in the Arab world, the popular feeling of belonging to the same cultural community, if not to the same 'nation' in the strict sense of the term, is a reality that, over the past decades, has become very strong. One might have hoped that this shared sentiment would have generated serious cooperation between the Arab states, even compelled them to start building a political unity of some sort (confederal, federal, unitary). It has not happened.

The Arab League, the full name of which is the League of Arab States, was conceived along the lines of the United Nations as an inter-state organisation whose members conserve all their sovereignty, without renouncing it, even if only partially, on behalf of super-national powers. In that sense the league resembles the African Union and the Organisation of American States, rather than the European Union.

The creation of the league must also be seen as an insipid substitute for Pan-Arabism. It has created a series of specialised Arab inter-state organisations based on the model of the United Nations family. Their balance sheet remains modest: many studies, reports and projects, some of them of good quality, but few concrete achievements.

Integration efforts in the region have therefore taken other paths. At first, when triumphant Pan-Arabism was at its height in the middle of the 1950s, when the Algerian liberation war got under way, and up until the defeat of the third Israel–Arab war in 1967, there were efforts to accomplish this unity – even if it was only partial at the start – through the mobilisation of powerful political forces, of which the Egypt–Syria unification, which joined together in the United Arab Republic (1957–61), was the culminating point. The failure of this form of Arab unification certainly sounded the knell of this Nasserite–Baathist strategy and led to the exacerbation of animosities, if not conflicts, between the governments of their immediate neighbours (Algeria–Morocco, Syria–Iraq, Saudi Arabia–Yemen, Iraq–Kuwait).

Simultaneously, from 1973 onwards, the oil manna seemed to take over from the radical political desires of Pan-Arab populism. This manna was accompanied by a huge movement of internal migration, with people leaving the poor countries (Tunisia, Egypt, Sudan, Palestine, Lebanon, Syria and Yemen) for the rich ones (Libya, the Gulf countries). However, feeling threatened by this 'invasion', the Gulf countries reacted, as we know, by gradually replacing Arab migrants with immigrant Asian labour, coming from Pakistan, India and the Philippines. The oil manna also financed considerable public transfers. But these, far from being seen as the condition for integrating projects, have on the whole been wasted in the private consumption of the governing classes and the public consumption of subsidised states. All this was completely foreseeable, the ultra-conservative powers of the Gulf countries acting as conveyor belts for the requirements of liberal globalisation and the hegemonism of the US, which they never thought of challenging.

The parallel financial support to the dominant currents of political Islam to which they profess allegiance completes the negative image of the effects of the oil manna, as political Islam refuses to be interested in Arab unity, replacing it by the call for the Muslim *umma*. Here there is a play on words in Arabic, which is unfortunately untranslatable: manna (*al fawra*) has taken the place of revolution (*al thawra*). The oil manna has also been able to finance, here and there, certain private investments. But these too fit perfectly into the policies of reinforcing parasitical comprador bourgeoisies who do not envisage any future other than liberal globalisation. Thus the regionalisation/integration of the Arab world has not been able to make any progress worthy of the name over the last three decades.

The Arab world possesses only subordinate positions in the world system. Its considerable oil exports are not a real substitute for an effective industrialisation, capable of meeting internal needs and intervening in shaping world markets. There are a few marginalised rich people in the Arab world, like the Gulf countries, as elsewhere, like Gabon, just as there are many marginalised poor ones. Neither have the means to impose themselves as active participants in shaping the world system. They remain passive actors, forced unilaterally to adapt, even though the supply of oil by the region is vital for Western consumers.

The Arab world is going through a stage in its history that is marked by the absence of any of its own projects. It is not surprising that it is others who have taken the initiative to make the proposals that are imposed on their Arab partners. Thus the US, which considers the Middle East as a priority region under its exclusive authority (the Europeans having only been invited to support their presence in the region since the defunct Soviet Union was turfed out) has, with their two allies Israel and Turkey (and the unconditional support of the Gulf regimes) concocted the project of a Middle East common market.

The Europeans, for their part, made proposals for what they called a Euro-Mediterranean partnership, which fits into the same logic. However, although this project has already failed it has helped to deepen the Maghreb/Mashreq rupture. The countries of the Maghreb, through their association agreements with the European Union, have become more integrated into the European productive system (to which they furnish goods produced by subcontracted, badly paid labour) than those of the Mashreq. The 'sharing' of the burden, as the US calls it, turns out to be a division of labour that gives the US the Middle East and its oil resources while the Europeans get the Maghreb and its emigrants.

## The backward-looking impasse

The image that the Arab and Islamic region has of itself today is that of societies in which Islam is at the forefront in all fields of social and political life. This is taken to such an extreme that it seems incongruous to imagine that it could be otherwise. Most of the foreign 'observers' (political and media representatives) conclude that modernity, if not democracy, is accommodating to this heavy presence of Islam, which de facto prohibits secularism.

Pictures of masses of prostrate bearded men and armies of veiled women lead to conclusions that are rather premature about the intensity of the religious adhesion of individuals. The social pressures that are being exercised to obtain this result are rarely mentioned: women have not chosen the veil, they have had it imposed upon them, also with violence, and if they absent themselves from prayers it can cost them their work, sometimes their lives. Western 'culturalist' friends, who call for respect of the diversity of convictions, do not often investigate what has been done to transmit the image convenient for those in power. It is true that there are the 'mad God people'. However, are they proportionately more numerous than the Catholics of Spain who participate in the Easter processions? Or the uncountable numbers of people in the US who listen to the telepreachers?

In fact, the region does not always convey this image of itself. Apart from the differences from country to country, it is possible to identify a large region that stretches from Morocco to Afghanistan, integrating all the Arab peoples (except those in the Arab peninsula), the Turks, the Iranians, the Afghans and the peoples of ex-Soviet central Asia, in which the potential for the development of secularism is far from negligible. The situation is different for other neighbouring peoples, the Arabs of the peninsula and the Pakistanis.

In this large region the political traditions have been strongly influenced by radical currents of modernity: the Enlightenment, the French Revolution, the Russian Revolution and the communism of the Third International have influenced people much more than the parliamentarism of Westminster. They have inspired the main models of political transformation that the governing classes have implemented and in some aspects they can be described as 'enlightened despotism'.

This is certainly the case of the Egypt of Mohamed Ali and Khedive Ismail. Kemalism in Turkey and modernisation in Iran used similar methods. The national populism of more recent times belong to the same family of 'modernist' political projects. There have been numerous varieties of the model (the Algerian FLN, Tunisian Bourguibism, Egyptian Nasserism, the Baathism of Syria and Iraq) but the direction of the movement has been analogous. And what appeared to be extreme experiences, the so-called communist regimes in Afghanistan and South Yemen, were in fact hardly different. All these regimes had many achievements to their credit and they therefore received wide popular support. This is why, although they have not been really democratic, they opened the way to a possible evolution in that direction. In certain circumstances – as in Egypt from 1920 to 1950 – electoral democracy was attempted, supported by the moderate anti-imperialist centre (the Wafd), but it was combatted by the dominant imperialist power (Great Britain) and its local allies (the monarchy and the Muslim Brothers). Secularism – to be sure, implemented in very moderate versions – was not 'refused' by the peoples. On the contrary it was the clerics who seemed obscurantists in the general opinion of the public, which was true of the great majority.

Modernist experiences – from enlightened despotism to radical national populism – did not occur by chance. They were imposed by strong political movements, dominant in the middle classes, who thus expressed their will to impose themselves as full partners in modern globalisation, with all their rights. These projects, which one could call 'national bourgeois', were modernist, secularising and with the potential for evolving towards democracy. But this is precisely why they came into conflict with the interests of dominant imperialism, which fought them without respite and, to do this, systematically mobilised the declining obscurantist forces.

The history of the Muslim Brothers is well known. It was literally created in the 1920s in Egypt by the British and the monarchy to bar the way for the democratic and secular Wafd. It is also well known that, after the death of Nasser, they returned to Egypt in strength from their Saudi asylum, organised by the CIA and Sadat. Familiar, too, is the history of the Taliban, trained by the CIA in Pakistan to fight the 'communists' who had opened schools to all boys and girls. It is even known that the Israelis first supported Hamas to weaken the secular and democratic currents of the Palestinian resistance.

There is no doubt that Saudi Arabian society had never even begun to leave tradition behind when the ocean of oil lying under its soil was discovered. The alliance between imperialism and the archaic governing class, which was immediately sealed, was good business for both partners and breathed new life into Wahhabite political Islam. As for the British, they were able to break up Indian unity, convincing the Muslim leaders to create their own state of Pakistan, which has been locked up in political Islam since its very birth. It is interesting to note that the 'theory' according to which this was legitimised – attributed to Mawdudi – was originally entirely drafted by English orientalists at the service of his majesty. But political Islam would have had great difficulties in crossing the frontiers of Saudi Arabia and Pakistan without the permanent and powerful support of the US.

It is now clear that the US took the initiative to break the united front of the Asian and African states, which had been established in Bandung in 1955, by creating an 'Islamic Conference' which was immediately promoted by Saudi Arabia and Pakistan from 1957 onwards. This was the means by which political Islam penetrated the region. The very least that could be concluded from these observations is that political Islam was not spontaneously affirmed by the peoples concerned because of the strength of their religious conviction. Political Islam has been built up systematically by imperialism and, of course, by reactionary obscurantist forces and subservient comprador classes. There is no doubt of the responsibility of the left, not seeing what was happening and therefore being unable to deal with the challenge.

Stressing the false contrast between modernity and authenticity was a major plank in the obscurantist offensive that swallowed up political Islam. It was a false contrast in the sense that the content of criticised modernity was left vague (was it the principle that proclaims that human beings make their own history or vulgar manifestations of capitalist modernity?), while authenticity only invoked eulogies of the past. Thus we heard King Hassan II of Morocco trumpeting about *isala* (authenticity) as opposed to *hadatha* (modernity) in sermons during the month of Ramadan. Mobutu made similar discourses in Zaire. Both of them, among the most odious political figures of our

# The Drift of the National Popular Project

times, combined a mixture of the most vulgar consumerism of the new rich with an 'anti-Western' discourse. This offensive of obscurantism, preached by post-modernism, is inseparable from neoliberalism and its imperialist extension.

## Economic and social drift: the example of Egypt

### A dislocated economy

The absence of any articulation between the different sectors of production in the contemporary Egyptian economy is today so serious that one can hardly talk about a 'national production system'.

And yet such a system was very much in existence in the old globalised capitalism (1880–1950), based on the monoculture of cotton, on which were grafted financial and commercial activities and some light industries that were expanded in parallel with the cotton exports. The growth of the system, managed by a hegemonic social alliance of the large agrarian landowners with foreign capital, was based on the consumption of a minority. Agriculture both supplied the main exports and covered the essential food needs at a price that made it possible to pay low wages. The state had no function at all beyond the strict maintenance of order. It was a form of peripheral capitalism, dependent of course, but it was fully coherent.

The national populism of the Nasser phase proposed replacing it with a different coherence based on industrialisation. The role of agriculture was then seen as having to contribute to the financing of industry, while the relative stagnation in the standard of living of the peasantry which that would involve would be compensated for by a reduction of inequalities in the rural world (the objective of the agrarian reform). Maintaining the ability of agriculture to cover the food needs of the country, even to the detriment of the former growth in cotton exports – to be compensated for by manufactured products – was an objective that was coherent with the logic of the whole project. The state had become an active agent in this transformation, through its social expenditure (for the education and health necessary for modernisation and industrialisation), its interventions in redistributing income (control of prices and subsidies) and its role in the planning of the economy (facilitated by the dominance of public ownership).

This model did not function successfully for more than a short period: a decade, from the Suez War in 1956 to that of 1967. Its rapid erosion, which was well understood at the time by Mohamed Dowidar and Mohamed Mahmoud El Imam, was the result of its own deficiencies combined with the aggressive strategies implemented by imperialism and its regional tool, Israel.

What followed, with the 'liberalism' of three decades, the 1970s, 1980s and 1990s, was a dismantling of the 1960s model without replacing it with any other really coherent alternative model. The economy of Egypt now constitutes a series of 'activities', juxtaposed side by side. Their different logics of reproduction are more conflictual than complementary, while the state has been made to 'disengage' itself, to give way to a 'market' with the mythical function of ensuring the coherence of growth. The disarticulation of the system has been made evident by the distortions that have gradually assumed monumental proportions.

For example, overall growth was increasingly ensured by tertiary activities at the expense of the material base (agricultural and industrial production). Also the Nasserite project had proposed reinforcing inter-industrial complementarities to establish the autonomy of the national productive system vis-à-vis the world economy, in order to give it negotiating strength over the conditions of insertion into that economy. But this was abandoned in favour of the immediate profitability of the companies considered separately one from another (the view that normally accompanies privatisation). These two series of distortions in turn produced a growing deficit in the commercial balance of payments. Contrary to the flimsy discourse of conventional economics, uncontrolled 'opening up' and liberalism do not produce a 'spontaneous' equilibrium in foreign trade. Instead, they deepen the permanent deficit of the weaker partners, involving a continual process of devaluations that, in turn, facilitates the pillage of resources by dominant imperialist capital.

In 2000, imports rose to 48.6 billion Egyptian pounds as against exports that did not exceed 16.2 billion. The Egyptian economy is no longer just one of a dependent peripheral capitalism (as it has always been): it has reached a stage of extreme vulnerability. It is no longer

# The Drift of the National Popular Project 199

possible to see how its 'development' will turn out. The Egyptian ship is sailing without any compass. Its captain does not know where he wants to go and is not concerned to know where the currents are steering his ship. In fact the direction taken depends entirely on the global 'conjunctures' that occur one after the other and to which the Egyptian economy is forced to 'adjust', day by day, with all the precariousness that these adjustments bring with them. Thus it is, for example, that the commercial deficit is covered only by random resources – financial transfers from emigrants, tourist income, the indebtedness of foreign aid – that depend exclusively on decision-making centres outside the country. The entry of Egypt into the oil production club has certainly lightened the external balance by reducing imports (Egypt covers its internal oil consumption from its own production) and there is a positive balance in the exports of oil products. This limited and perhaps temporary advantage has facilitated the establishment of a political power that follows the logic of permanent precariousness.

## An agriculture in difficulty

Agriculture has always formed an important part of the economy of Egypt, half of whose population is still rural (the great majority are still peasants). The contribution of agriculture to GNP has, however, gradually diminished from 33 per cent in 1960 to 17 per cent in 2000. Also, agricultural labour was only 29 per cent of the employed work force in 2000, as opposed to 49 per cent in 1960. Reading between the statistics, therefore, one can see that in the rural world there is a large number of unemployed and/or under-employed, whose growth is indisputable and which is assuming alarming proportions. The increase in the 'value' of agricultural production during the last three decades of liberalism must itself be questioned. Official statistics put it at 2.9 per cent annually for the 15 years 1982–97, a higher rate than the growth in population (2 per cent). But this growth is almost exclusively due to a transfer of production that had been traditional until 1970 (cotton and cereals) towards more profitable speculations (vegetables and fruit, animal products). The price to pay has been a huge loss in the food autonomy of the country. In the 1990s the production of Egyptian agriculture did not cover more than 50 per cent of the consumption of wheat and 85 per cent of that of maize, 57 per cent of that of vegetable oils, 67 per cent of that of sugar, 75 per cent of that of fish, 80 per cent of red meat. It is, however, true that rice production profited from an export balance of 362 million Egyptian pounds in the year 2000.

For the production of food crops, there has unquestionably been a tendency to decline over the last three decades of the 20th century. The imports of food products to compensate for this growing deficit ended the role that agriculture had fulfilled: being the main supplier of the means to pay for the imports required by industrial development. The bill for food imports in 2000 was 9.1 billion Egyptian pounds, compared with exports reduced to 1.3 billion (of which only 673 million pounds were for cotton, which previously had been the main source of foreign currency). The agricultural balance was thus a third of Egypt's overall commercial trade balance.

Reducing the food deficit is not only a political requirement, which is to lessen the country's vulnerability to the political manoeuvres of imperialism (above all of the US) and to the economic strategies of the collective imperialism of the Triad (which continue, both through the WTO and the agricultural export policies of Europe and the US, to pursue the objective of 'opening up' the countries of the South to their food exports). It has become an essential condition for Egypt in pursuing any industrial development, as the capacity to cover the importations necessary for such industrialisation has been reduced because the agricultural trade balance is in deficit due to increasing food dependency.

## Growing tensions among the peasantry

The agrarian reforms of the Nasserite era certainly had some impact, but it was limited. They made it possible to transfer the property of the large landowners to middle peasants, but they ignored those without land and the overwhelming majority of smallholders (units of less than a *feddan*, which is half a hectare). These reforms had one essential political objective: to break the strength of the large landowning class, which was the backbone of the Egyptian upper bourgeoisie, and to reinforce that of the middle and wealthy peasants so that they supported the regime. The reforms also had positive economic effects, enabling a modest, but nevertheless real growth in basic food production (and somehow maintaining a certain food autonomy for Egypt). These positive effects in turn reinforced the differentiations within the middle strata of the peasantry to the benefit of the richer ones who had greater access to modernisation facilities (credits and equipment).

Cooperatives were set up and the peasants were forced to join them (the cooperatives managed credits and marketing, while allowing private ownership and land use). They had different objectives: to siphon off from agriculture the finance needed for industry (through price control) and perhaps to lessen the tensions between the different middle and rich peasants. But on this last point the results are dubious. The cooperatives, in spite of their bureaucratic nature, like that of the workers' unions, constituted power centres within the regime in the sense that state power had to recognise their legitimacy and thus to negotiate the terms of its policies with them.

There was an essential component in the reforms: the creation of ceilings for renting agricultural land. This was practically a blockage, what with inflation and the de facto deterioration in land rents of the owners to the benefit of the users. As for the rural proletariat (the landless) and the poor peasants, they had to be satisfied with modest improvements, made possible by the setting of a minimum rural wage.

The agrarian reform was gradually called into question over the last three decades of the 20th century and this trend was reinforced, at the social level, by a revival of polarising trends. Official statistics show that the proportion of poor peasants (those with less than one *feddan*) rose from 26 per cent in 1960 to 58 per cent in 2000. To these should be added the landless, who were excluded by definition from the records of the agricultural holdings. Whatever the exact numbers of the landless, there is no doubt that the overwhelming majority of the rural peasant population of Egypt today – some two-thirds – consists of proletarians and poor peasants who are virtually excluded from access to land. This population has practically no rights. In 2000, the middle category of peasants (units of 1–10 *feddans*) were exploiting 50 per cent of the agricultural land, as against 60 per cent in 1960. And while their proportion in the peasant population has diminished – due to the increase in the number of the poor – the number of families and that of the units concerned (like the total surface they occupy) has remained almost unchanged.

The rich peasants and the agrarian capitalists (including the enterprises managed by agribusiness) – of which the holdings exceed 10 *feddans* – now control more than a third of all the agricultural land.

Information about the share in the value of agricultural production of each social group is hard to come by and, in the absence of credible income declarations, of uncertain validity. However, there are indications that the distribution of agricultural production and revenue is more unequal than that of the area covered by the holdings and therefore the rich peasants have been almost the exclusive beneficiaries of the liberalisation measures. A large majority of these rich peasants have more than 10 *feddans*, although there are some smaller but more intensively cultivated units, specialised and advantageously located, which have also benefited from recent developments. The middle peasants have been vociferous in claiming that a minority of rich peasants have been the only beneficiaries of the policies that have been implemented by the state in line with the proposals of the US (USAID) and the World Bank.

Between the ambitions of the rich peasants and the capitalists who are hurrying to grab more land on the one hand and, on the other, the poor peasants whose plight is dramatic, the middle peasants fear falling into the situation of the latter, although they constitute the main body of the peasantry that has been visibly reviving since the 1990s. Since 1971 the dominant political power in Egypt has been engaged in liberalisation policies, but it has refused the 'shock therapies' as it is aware of the violent opposition that they would certainly provoke in Egyptian conditions.

It is worthwhile recalling the series of measures that have been taken over the last 30 years:

1971 Decree of President Sadat indemnifying the 'victims' of the agrarian reforms. It was to strike a moral blow at the principle of the reform and to prepare the ground for legitimising the reconstitution of agrarian capitalism
1975 A law authorising share-cropping contracts (which had been abolished under Nasserism in favour of tenant farming, with a rent fixed by law) at free and negotiated rates
1976 The cooperatives were dissolved and responsibility for agricultural credit transferred to banks

1978 The legally regulated tenant farming rents were raised
1980 The legally regulated tenant farming rents were raised again
1981 The maximum agricultural holding allowed was raised to 2,000 *feddans* for an individual, 3,000 for a family and 10,000 for a company
1992 A law decisively abolished the intervention of the state in fixing land rents, leaving them to rise in accordance with the 'market'.

It was this last measure that brought about the revival of the mass protests of the middle peasantry.

Egypt had an important peasant movement that developed in the 1940s and 1950s, while the role of the old cotton/monarchical system was being reduced in the wider economic system. Influenced by the communists, the slogan 'the land belongs to those who work it' became widespread in the countryside and started a movement bringing together for the first time the landless peasants and poor middle peasants, which led to a well-known series of bloody events (Behietam, Koufour Negm).

The 1952 reform had thus occurred just in time to prevent the breaking out of civil war. But the reform, while it satisfied the middle peasants, left the poor peasants to their fate, as I have mentioned. They reacted and demanded the radicalisation of the reform, as could be seen from the violence that broke out in the village of Kamsheesh, which is also well known. The repression by the powers at that time was very severe and the withdrawal by the communists of their support for the regime as from 1955–56 closed the door to any thought of radicalisation.

The movement that has revived since then is that of the middle peasants: the rural proletarians and the poor peasantry hardly participate in it. Also, it has to be said that this movement of the middle peasantry was very slow in reacting to the liberalisation measures: for example, to the law of 1992 which for the first time treated agricultural production and the land as 'ordinary goods'. Its recent demands were very moderate, adopting the discourses of the American experts based in Cairo and of the WTO. They only called on the government to 'amend' the law – nothing more. There are several reasons for this. First, the skill of the state apparatus (including the justice system) in only putting new laws into effect gradually, to avoid clashes. Thus only a small number among the 1,600,000 tenancy contracts that were in principle subject to revision were examined by the competent authorities. The landowners were also called upon to calm their ambitions, with the reminder that the 'ancient' traditions of recourse to private violence were 'out of date'. The other reason was the effects of massive emigration towards the oil countries as from 1973. Egyptian migration involved millions and, as it was rotated, it benefited almost all families, particularly the rural ones, as two-thirds of the emigrants were middle or poor peasants from the villages.

The middle peasants were thus able to finance the modernisation not only of their living conditions, such as housing, but also of their agricultural land. Water pumps everywhere were mechanised, with oil replacing animal traction and waterwheels almost disappearing from the landscape. They also sometimes broadened their activities to include new, non-agricultural rural enterprises in the fields of transport and trade in particular. But this was in no way comparable to the extent and efficacy of the non-agricultural rural enterprises of China. The more fortunate of these middle peasants joined the rich peasant class. As for the poor peasants and the rural proletariat, they also benefited in their way from the migration, by going in for modest activities such as the purchase of a taxi or a van, covering their survival needs by the savings they had made while working abroad. They also benefited from the emigration en masse in that the casual seasonal labour necessary at certain times of the production cycle became rare and there was a considerable increase in waged seasonal labour. There is little doubt that the massive migration largely contributed to delaying collective struggles, both in the countryside and in the town, and it was responsible for weakening trade union militarism. But it seems that this migration is coming to an end.

The organised political parties have obviously reacted and responded in their own way to the revival of the peasant movement. The two left-wing parties (the Tagammu and the Nasserite Party) have openly and formally supported the gatherings of tens of thousands of peasants throughout the country, in all the prefectures and sub-prefectures from north to south. They were particularly numerous in the second half of the 1990s. But the parties have not 'organised' them

# The Drift of the National Popular Project

and they have not dared to try and offer them a framework of a unified national representation. Extremely nervous, they have preached restraint and calmed the agitation of the demonstrators. The Islamist parties, strangely, have kept their distance. In parliament, as in their press, they have unconditionally supported the liberalisation measures as the 'right interpretation' of Islam, always expressing their hatred of socialism. Their credit has accordingly suffered a lot. And while the middle strata of the peasantry (but much less than the poor) remains attached to religion, it is with a conservative and non-politicised interpretation (private property is 'sacred').

The peasant movement itself is thus very fragmented, which enables the left-wing parties to speak in its name through the weak coordination committees that they have set up for this purpose. The proposals of these committees are moderate and come under three headings:

1 Amending the law on the tenancy contracts and a return to legal ceilings to rents. This is not for even a minimal agrarian reform, but only for agrarian legislation that excludes foreign agribusiness companies from having property rights.
2 Supporting the reconstruction of cooperatives that are independent of political power, managed democratically and freely by their members. The objective is to compensate for market uncertainties (prices of inputs, sales of production and credit) in favour of the peasants.
3 Restoring to the state its responsibilities, particularly its duty, traditional in Egypt, to decide the crops allowed on the agricultural units. The objective is to protect the food autonomy of the country.

It is possible that this programme is acceptable and credible in the short term and that it can also become more efficient, thus contributing to a widespread rallying of the middle peasants and the sympathy of the whole nation for their demands. However, this programme ignores the principle of the equal right to land of all peasants, including the poor and landless, which had been a major theme in the programme of the Egyptian communists up until the 1950s. Thus the present programme, put forward in the name of the peasant movement, continues to exclude the poor, who represent two-thirds of the peasant rural population. However, in the long term, the fundamental problems of the country and an effective strategy cannot be resolved only in terms of the demands, however legitimate, of the middle strata, threatened by unbridled liberalism. Egypt suffers, in common with only three other countries (China, Vietnam and Bangladesh), from a terrible scarcity of arable land in proportion to its peasant population. Whereas there are unfavourable ratios of land to peasants in certain regions, it is only with these four countries that it applies to a whole nation.

China and Vietnam have made radical revolutions based on the principle of equal access to land for all peasants, particularly the poor and landless. It is by implementing this principle, however bureaucratic its mode of operation, that these two countries have managed to maintain their food autonomy. China feeds 22 per cent of the population of the planet reasonably well with 6 per cent of its cultivated land. Vietnam is in a similar position: it decently feeds its people with very scarce land. Both countries have managed to ensure a minimum of inequality found nowhere else in the world. China has also managed to implement an agricultural and rural development programme that is linked to a strategy of efficient and accelerated industrialisation and modernisation. It is true that the very principle of equality of access to land, and still more, its effective implementation, are eventually threatened by what has been happening these last 20 years. But that is another problem.

The authorities in Bangladesh and Egypt never adopted the principles of equal access to land, even at the height of Nasserite radicalisation in Egypt. Apart from the appalling social inequalities caused by this refusal, it renders a society, the nation and its economy extremely vulnerable. Hence, aligning with the principles of globalised liberalism has, in record time, caused devastating damage to the social and national fabric. As for Egypt, this alignment has already been reinforced by dramatic food dependency, the acceleration of social inequalities and the dislocation of the economic system.

This comparison destroys the validity of the dominant conventional discourse which, in the case of Egypt and Bangladesh, attributes the failure of their rural development and their overall poverty to their 'natural' conditions and their demography.

## Political conflicts and social struggles

In the region at present, the political conflicts are between three forces: those who hark back to the nationalist past (but who are in fact only the degenerate and corrupt heirs of the bureaucracies of the national populist era); those who demand political Islam; and those who are trying to emerge with a 'democratic' demand that is compatible with a liberal economic management. These three 'tendencies' express the interests of the comprador classes that are affiliated with the existing imperialist system. In fact, US diplomacy is using the conflicts between these three forces for its own exclusive benefit. None of these forces is acceptable to a left concerned with the interests of the popular classes and with those of the nation. Efforts to enter into the conflicts through alliances with one or other of these forces (preferring the existing regimes to avoid the worst – political Islam – or, on the contrary, trying to ally with the latter to get rid of the regime) will lead nowhere. The left must affirm itself by supporting the struggles on the ground where they have their natural place: the defence of the economic and social interests of the popular classes, of democracy and of national sovereignty, that are seen as being inseparable.

A quick look at the global situation today easily reveals that nothing has changed: the Mameluke power is still in existence. The first striking similarity with the past consists in the supreme authority exercised by the military in Algeria, Egypt, Syria and Iraq; in some areas, the institution is disciplined and strictly subjected to a respected hierarchy (Egypt) while elsewhere, it is parcelled up between many generals permanently engaged in muffled or open contentious rivalry (Algeria). Indeed, it is probably true that the military is not the firm guarantor of stability that it appears to be. At least, even if the military is partly influenced by political Islam, and is by no means immunised against the centrifugal forces that can be fanned by ethnic or religious diversity, the fact remains that this institution was the sole inheritor of the era of populist nationalism that spanned the 1950s, 1960s and 1970s. It therefore preserves a nationalist tradition that has not quite disappeared. As nobody took the farcical elections seriously, and in particular the uninterested working classes, one president succeeded another peacefully, or through a 'coup', as happened in the time of the sultans, pashas and Mamelukes, who were always under the threat of assassination by their peers.

No doubt, in Morocco, Saudi Arabia and the Gulf Emirates, it is the monarchical institution, which is itself merged with the Moroccan and Wahhabite type of religious institution, that directly sees to the transfer of supreme power.

The second striking similarity with the Mameluke autocracy lies in the inter-penetration of the business world and the world of power. It is because, truly speaking, there is no genuine 'private sector' and not many autonomous capitalists managing their businesses are assured of the ownership of their enterprises. The Egyptian language coined another term for the new millionaires of the 'open economy' (*infitah*) involved in the new liberal globalisation. It distinguishes between the 'private' sector (*khas*) – in other words, normal and authentic capitalist business – and the 'personal' sector (*firdani*), that is, business existing through the complicity of the powers that be. Whenever the private sector exists, it is composed of medium-scale enterprises somewhat jostled by the economic situation and liberal globalisation. On the other hand, the 'personal' sector is the one whose turnover increases annually but is at the same time fraught with the scandal of unequal distribution of income. A well-known example can be found in a famous Egyptian firm run by a multibillionaire, which snaps up all the state contracts to subsequently subcontract them, regardless of the laws against this practice. Most of the profits accruing from the so-called private economy in the Arab world of the last 20 years therefore appear as a real political rent.

The third similarity consists of the exploitation of traditional, conservative religious legitimacy. It is noticeable that the more the Mameluke-comprador power is compromised by its concrete submission to dominant imperialist interests, the more it aligns itself with the exigencies of liberal globalisation and the more it tries to compensate for the loss of national legitimacy brought about by such submission. This stiffens its so-called religious discourse, thereby generating competition with the rival Islamist movement. That was exactly what the Ottoman and Mameluke ancestors did as they yielded to the imperialist diktats of previous centuries.

# The Drift of the National Popular Project

Certainly, the reader will point out that the phenomena described above are not specific to the Arab world. Indonesia provides a striking analogy of a dictatorship of the military-mercantile complex associated with religious rhetoric. Would one therefore be tempted to see in it the impact of an 'Islamic culture'? But then why is it that yesterday's China of the warlords and Kuo Ming Tang and today's Philippines present similar examples in several essential respects? It would therefore be wiser to see the religious, cultural, conservative, military–mercantile autocratic model (Mameluke–comprador/rent-holders) as the product of 'underdevelopment', to understand it not as a 'time lag', a 'stage' of development, but as the other side of the polarising global expansion of capital. The latter produces not modernisation (and the subsequent potential for democracy) but rather the opposite – the modernisation of both autocracy and poverty. Authentic modernisation and democratisation are brought under control by taking a stand against the dominant forces of the global system, not by following in their wake.

In any case, in the Arab world, this contemporary resurrection of Mameluke autocracy would not have been imagined a century or even 50 years ago. On the contrary, the page seemed to have been turned for good.

In the first phase, the Arab world – at least its Egyptian and Syrian centres – appeared to have embarked on an authentic bourgeois modernisation process. Mohamed Ali and then the Nahda of the 19th century seemed to have prepared for that. The Egyptian revolution of 1919 was the first strong expression of that process. It was not by chance that this revolution took place under the banner closest to secularism known in the history of the Arab world, with the proclamation of 'Religion is for God, the fatherland for all', and the choice of a flag with both crescent and cross. In the Ottoman empire, the Tanzimat initiated a parallel evolution inherited by the Arab provinces and which they continued to develop after the empire's decline. Constitutions, civil codes, 'liberal' bourgeois parties and parliamentary elections inspired the hope that the society was moving in the right direction despite all its inherent weaknesses and inadequacies. In terms of real economic and social development – which easily found expression in the weakness of the local bourgeoisie vis-à-vis the then imperialists and their local reactionary allies, and the aggravation of the social crisis for that matter – the meagre results ultimately ended this first period of ineffective modernisation of the Arab world.

The second phase was, therefore, the populist nationalism of the 1950s, 1960s and 1970s. The triumphant Nasserism and Baathism and the Algerian revolution seemed capable of stemming the social crisis through the deployment of a more determined anti-imperialist policy (promoted with Soviet support) and active economic and social development policies. That possibility is no more, for reasons that are not analysed here, which include the system's internal contradictions and restrictions and the reversal of the global economic and political situations.

At this time the pre-modern autocratic state resurfaced while the society was no longer comparable in any way to the one that existed a century or even half-century ago.

The social crisis today is incomparably more acute than it used to be a century or half-century ago. It is not that the society is 'poorer' on the whole. On the contrary, the progression is indisputable in terms of average real incomes. It is not that wealth in this entity is distributed more inequitably than it used to be. On the other hand, the key change in this area is the expansion of the middle classes in Egypt over 50 years: from 5 per cent to 15 per cent for the country's upper class population and 10 per cent to 30 per cent for all the constituent social groups (according to Galal Amin 2001). At any rate, the modernisation that has taken place has also been that of poverty.

The intensity of the crisis is commensurate with the urbanisation of the Arab world, which constitutes its key indicator. More than half of the Arab population is now urbanised. However, this massive transfer is not the outcome of a two-sided agricultural and industrial revolution, more or less similar to the one that built the developed capitalist West or the Soviet world and which contemporary China has embraced for half a century. It is, rather, the result of the absence of both agricultural and industrial revolution. The growing rural misery is simply transferred to urban areas that modern industries and activities cannot absorb. The structure of social classes and categories in which this crisis found expression no longer has anything to do with that of the Arab world a century or 50 years ago.

With the period of populist nationalism over, the discredited single party system gave way to the explosion of the multiparty system, which the world media hastened to acknowledge as the beginning of a democratic development which was naturally and obviously promoted by the opening up to markets as envisaged by fashionable parlance.

The paradox here is that this explosion of the multiparty system was accompanied by a prodigious regression to the Mameluke type of autocracy.

Nasserism had purportedly nationalised politics (actually placed politics under state control) in Egypt; that is, it had used violent repression to suppress the two poles between which the active political forces and public opinion were divided – the bourgeois liberal pole and the communist pole. By this means too was created an ideological vacuum that Islam had to fill gradually in the Nasserian era, and violently as from 1970. The influence of the religious institution encouraged by Nasser's modernisation of Al Azhar did penetrate the expanding middle classes, key beneficiaries of the populism that dawned with improved education and employment. Apparently domesticated, Al Azhar did not manifest any disturbing signs to the regime; that was the time when its fatwa justified socialism. The Muslim Brothers, who sometimes thought of imposing their presence in the regime, opposed a repression that always proved to be wavering in their regard, as many Free Officers had been closely associated with them. Whereas they were formally dissolved, they continued to be tolerated through the 'religious associations' that progressively infiltrated the state machinery, particularly the education, legal and media sectors.

When Sadat decided to turn to the right after Nasser's death in 1970, the stage was set to place political Islam abruptly in the limelight with the support of Gulf oil money and the open support of American diplomacy. The price lay in the 'opening' (*infitah*) initiated by Nasser after the 1967 military defeat that prepared the ground for reintegration into the global capitalist system, the break with the Soviet alliance and finally, the trip to Jerusalem (1977) and subsequently, the Madrid–Oslo process (1993).

All the same, it still took ten years for the law to grant (in 1979) a controlled multiparty system, which was initially limited to the three 'tribunes' of the defunct so-called Socialist Union of the left, centre and right. The unchanged constitution vests the president with powers that place him above the legislature, the executive and the judiciary. The newly granted and controlled democracy ('elections' must guarantee the perpetuation of the power of the president approved by the military), was negotiated with the US, which gave the president its blessing (as per the 1991 agreement between the government of Egypt and USAID), thereby making it possible for Washington to issue a certificate of democracy to the Egyptian government.

One cannot therefore have many illusions about the 'political parties' that arose from these political calculations. The Democratic National Union does not have a greater presence than the Socialist Union, which it inherited. The latter did not even enjoy the historic legitimacy of the communist party models (of USSR, China or Vietnam) of which it constituted a caricature. Before enduring the deteriorating effect of their solitary exercise of power, the Communist Parties in question organised real revolutions. In contrast, the Egyptian Socialist Union was never more than a mere collection of opportunists without much conviction, which was convenient for the enlightened despot. The self-dissolution of the Egyptian communist organisation in 1965, which happened not without reluctance on the part of many militants, did not bring about any considerable improvement in the system since the government had taken rigorous measures to forestall the materialisation of this 'threat' to it.

Among the new political parties, Tagammu, which tried to rally the Nasserian leftists, and inheritors of the Egyptian communism, suffered the defection of the Nasserians. Nostalgic for the past, and apparently lacking the capacity to understand the nature of the new challenges, the old Nasserians contented themselves with the rhetoric of the Arab nationalist discourse (*qawmi*) and therefore initiated a process of reconciliation with the Islamists, who were also very fond of simple rhetoric. At any rate, Tagammu will remain a hope for the revival of a political debate worthy of its name, provided it succeeds in mobilising the militant traditions it has so far been trying to benumb.

The Labour Party organised by Adel Hussein (who died in 2001 and was succeeded by a member of his family) had to mobilise the Islamist discourse with greater apprehension, while its leader presented himself as the rival to the traditional leaders of the Muslim Brotherhoods.

Up until this point, the Egyptian parties' political democracy therefore did not go beyond a limited campaign. Renouncing any form of action – which the regime formally prohibited – and contenting themselves with discourses, these parties did not present themselves as a real alternative to the ruling power. They did not develop credible alternative programmes but rather took to intermittently criticising government action.

The resultant drift occasioned by this political vacuum contributed to the reaffirmation of the Mameluke autocratic tradition. The most disturbing demonstration of this drift unexpectedly found expression during the 1999 parliamentary elections: a crowd of so-called 'independent' candidates exploited the possibilities that this situation offered to them. They were not opponents, or even disguised as such, but rather candidates for that class of entrepreneurs – receiving funding from the state (typical of the Mameluke system) – who often managed to form a group of lobbyists strong enough to 'win' the election amidst the indifference of the majority of the population. The term *baltagui*, which the Egyptian people immediately gave them, aptly caught what they were – since the term means 'loutish band leaders', with all that implies. The liberal 'academics' – Americans among others – who hailed the 'birth of a bourgeoisie of entrepreneurs' probably mislead ignorant external opinion but not the Egyptian people.

Under these circumstances, the sole force that presents itself as an alternative to the real power – that of the military – is the Muslim Brotherhood. However, the latter have no project other than autocratic power of the same nature, in which the religious institution would take the place of the military. In that context, the Muslim Brotherhood is not similar to Christian-Democrat parties, even though people sometimes try to make them appear as such. As for the rest – adhering to globalised liberalism and the local money-oriented comprador economy – there is no difference. That is the reason why the diplomacy of Washington actually sees in the Muslim Brotherhood an alternative solution, if necessary.

Nasser's rule was the planned project of an enlightened despot. The regime's socio-economic project was a real one that was implemented with determination. That is why, in spite of its dictatorial behaviour, backed-up by the police, the regime had to take – and did take – into account the social forces which expressed themselves through workers' unions, student movements, professional associations, rural cooperatives, the media and intellectuals. Nasser had a name for these agencies – *marakez quwa* (power centres) – and his use of this political language testifies to his acknowledgement of their significance.

In Egypt, there were 25,000 union committees (which still exist) integrated into 23 unions that formed a single confederation of trade unions (the General Workers' Union of Egypt) during Nasser's regime. This body rallied between three and four million real members (probably small, in comparison with the 15 to 17 million wage earners, but still considerable, as the number included almost all those salaried employees working in the modern enterprises). Nasserism had given them real powers, not to participate in the running of enterprises (these powers were a mere façade) but rather to manage the workforce (tenure, etc) and living conditions (housing, consumer cooperatives, etc). Having renounced 'class struggles', the working class was compensated with improved material living conditions. However, the militant spirit and communist influence continued to exist at the grassroots (in the 25,000 local committees) even though the regime took steps to gain effective control over the unions by appointing loyal agents to managerial positions at national level. This explains the low permeability of the working class that hitherto clamoured for political Islam.

What is the situation today? The emigration openly promoted from 1970 onwards certainly weakened the militant force. Why fight to obtain at best a meagre salary increase if one could achieve more by working for a few months in the Gulf States, in Libya or in Iraq? As usual, emigration encouraged the search for individual solutions and weakened the collective fight. Now that emigration is stemmed, are there any signs of a possible recourse to the Egyptian tradition of collective solutions? The new laws deregulating the labour market in turn weakened the unions, thereby paving the way for wholesale unemployment. This policy, which generated poverty that people were allegedly willing to fight, has so far not appealed to the champions of democracy among the leaders of the globalised system.

Many indexes indicate a resumption of the struggles. The actions, often violent, can henceforth be counted in thousands rather than hundreds, but these will always be scattered. In 1998, 70 strike actions took place in the country's largest enterprises. The forceful intervention by the special security forces in each of these strikes was difficult to conceal. Some modest victories were recorded here and there. Very little is said about such events. The political parties are silent on this subject. Nobody – of course not even the Islamists – wants to take the risk of being associated with such struggles. The working class struggles remain isolated but are neither unknown nor unpopular.

In the rural areas, Nasserism operated through some 15,000 input-purchasing and consumer cooperatives. Although dependent on sections of the middle peasantry and mostly influenced by those who were richer, these cooperatives were not chambers for recording decisions taken by the minister of agriculture, as too often assumed, but rather partners whose views were taken into account. This made it possible to avoid conflicts and marginalise the resistance of the poor classes among the peasantry.

The new liberal policy – the suppression of subsidies, credit liberalisation and the increase of interest rates from 5 per cent to 14 per cent, the threefold increase in the rates of ground rent and, finally, the liberalisation of relations between landowners and tenants (the rights of tenants had been guaranteed until then by the renewal of leases) – broke up the cooperative movement, and enabled the rich peasantry to get richer while the middle classes became more impoverished. The frequent but isolated acts of violence that accompanied this change of direction did not prevent the implementation of the liberalisation process. In 1993, Tagammu did attempt to establish a new peasants union. However, it retracted after harassment by the administrative authorities. That did not prevent the protest movement of the majority of tenants from growing fast in 1998. Nevertheless, the government moved skilfully, granted concessions to some parties at the expense of others and with these tactics neutralised the movement (perhaps provisionally?).

In taking a stand openly in favour of owners in the name of the sacrosanct right to property, did the Muslim Brotherhood miss the opportunity to mobilise in their favour this rural community perpetually sensitive to the religious discourse? In fact, the Muslim Brotherhood knew what they were doing. They deliberately aligned themselves with the rural rich, just as they did with the urban compradors, since they were primarily concerned about preserving their image as the valid intermediary for dominant capital and American diplomacy. Their discourse appealed to only the middle classes (as will be seen through the efforts they made in the professional associations), because they assigned 'radical' Islamic organisations (Islamic Jihad and others) to recruit their henchmen among the poor middle classes and the lumpen proletariat. In avoiding attempts to defend or condemn these organisations, the Muslim Brotherhood showed they knew that the state destabilisation operations conducted by these organisations objectively strengthened them in their capacity as candidates for the 'changeover'. The Muslim Brotherhood continues to convince their interlocutors that they alone – in power – would be able to put an end to the 'terrorist' transgressions.

The discourse and actions of political Islam therefore target the middle classes as a matter of priority. This class's expansion enhanced the organisations' exceptional influence in the political life of the country. There are 23 big professional associations (lawyers, doctors, journalists, engineers, pharmacists, teachers, etc) with hundreds of thousands of members and a large number of networks of local agencies. Nasserism controlled without much difficulty these entities, which pre-eminently constitute the mass of principal beneficiaries of the populist socio-economic growth.

The social crisis fomented by the liberal economic policies offered political Islam the opportunity to assume leadership of many of these associations on account of the lack of general debate among the parties. In 1993, the state reacted with legislative provisions that enabled it to bring the hostile associations under control again. To some extent demagogic, the official discourse accurately reveals how 'politicised' the associations have become at the expense of their defending the real interests of the professions. It remains to be seen whether the defence of these interests did not in turn conflict with the liberal policies of the state. That could be the starting point for a promising militant action in favour of the Egyptian leftists.

The outburst of community life, which will be discussed later, offered the opportunity for the formation of new associations of 'businessmen'. The ancient Industrial and Commercial Society having been dispersed by Nasser, and the chambers of commerce having lost their functions during the planning period, the new business associations filled a real gap. There is much talk about them and they are presented as proof of the vitality of capitalism. The reality is very

## The Drift of the National Popular Project

different, for the new associations include only a clique of political rent seekers. However, their impact in real life is far from negligible. They are regarded as sages and sometimes they even succeeded in having their points of view adopted (policies that guarantee their private income) against some recalcitrant ministers.

The student movement had traditionally played a leading role in Egypt, in the Arab world as well as in the third world as a whole. It was the forum for a dominant communist influence for decades. Even during the glorious period of Nasserism, when this system was accorded prestige and respect, the Nasserian students themselves were identified with the left wing of the regime. They belonged to those who were mobilised after the 1967 defeat to advocate radicalisation of the regime while Nasser himself chose, in contrast, to make concessions to the right by initiating the *infitah*.

There is no longer any student movement – at least not until now (the on-going 'revolution' may change this). The reasons for this evolution, certainly witnessed over nearly all the contemporary Third World, are complex and have not been adequately examined to date. The tremendous expansion of the middle classes, which is the outcome of the wave of post-war national liberation struggles, as well as the population and number of universities, all take their share of responsibility for this depoliticisation process. However, this process was often aided by the authorities' use of systematic repression. That is the case with Egypt. Before and after Nasser, the government deliberately supported the establishment of the Muslim Brotherhood in the university through substantial external funding (from sources in the Gulf states) so as to prevent communism. Moreover, Nasser's 'modernisation' of the Azhar University opened it up to the teachings of obscurantists, who have their share of responsibility for the drift. The fact remains that the university still plunges into a state of unrest from time to time, but exclusively over matters concerning the Palestinian question (in support of the two successive intifadas), and there is no longer any mobilisation around criticism of the liberal economic and social policies. The aggravation of the social crisis, the worsening situation of the middle classes and the decline of outlets for graduates have reinforced the instinct for survival, all the more so as the deteriorating quality of education compromises the analytic potential that the youths previously had. The penetration of Islam is the outcome rather than the cause of this drift.

The worlds of the press, intellectuals, artists (especially film-makers) and writers (poets and novelists) have always been present and active on the Egyptian political scene. In the Nasserian era, Al Ahram, the institution then headed by Hassanein Heykal, was considered to be one of the power centres that enjoyed a certain dose of tolerance from the enlightened despot. In spite of the high quality maintained by Al Ahram, its newspaper (a 125-year old daily comparable to the world's leading newspapers in terms of quality) and its think tanks, these media currently have insignificant influence in Egyptian society. The mass media – especially the television organisations – vie for monopoly of the empty official discourse and an equally mediocre and obscurantist Islamist propaganda. The few 'independent' television channels (Nile TV) operate a self-censorship that annihilates their potential scope – those of all the Arab countries are no better, with the exception of Lebanon's copious network of political television channels. Qatar's new television outfit (Al Khaleej) owes its success to its hosting of lively debates, even though this medium's channels are carefully closed to any leftist radical criticism. Al Khaleej has now shown its real face, supporting NATO's interventions and Wahhabi reactionary plans. Egypt still boasts a quality film industry, even if large-scale commercial production often obscures its existence. Literature – Egypt is a country of novelists, most of them being of considerable merit – also has substantial cultural and political influence. Cinema and novels constitute the mainstay of Egypt's surviving analytical political culture.

The lack of democratic management reflected in virtually all kinds of political and social organisations – parties, workers' unions, professional organisations (and in the new developing community life, as will be seen later) – is a major negative feature of Egypt, and perhaps of other Arab countries. These institutions are led by more or less irremovable 'historic heads' rather than militants.

To complete this picture of struggles, it is worth pointing to the increasing emergence of new forms of struggles by the poorest classes that are barely noticeable because isolated from the visible organisations. The world of street vendors, car park attendants and squatters is no longer an unorganised informal sector. Initially attacked for infringing formal rules and regulations, the poor social classes finally asserted themselves – through collective actions – and made their claims heard to such an extent that the state renounced the initially scheduled destruction of shanty towns in Cairo, which it replaced with development projects (water supply, road works, etc).

This picture of politics and social struggles in Egypt cannot be generalised to cover the entire Arab world without considering the actual conditions and historical origins, which vary from country to country even though a few similar trends can generally be identified.

Egypt, Syria, Iraq and Algeria share in common the fact that, in the course of the 1950s, 1960s and 1970s, they carried out a set of populist and nationalist experiments very similar to one another in their essential structures.

In Syria and Iraq, the Baathist Party initiated these experiments. Unlike Egypt, whose evolution in this regard was triggered by the Free Officers' military coup d'état, without any partisan preparation, the Baath remained the central pole for the political organisation of Syria and Iraq (whereas the Socialist Union of Egypt never really existed). The military nature of the Syrian and Iraqi regimes led to an infiltration of their armies by the Baath (or its segments). In Egypt, Nasser gradually imposed the populist option against the will of the majority of leaders from among the Free Officers – who were rather reactionary – but these conflicts at the top were not replicated at any time in the ranks of the army, which remained disciplined. There is only one pharaoh in Egypt, just as there is only one emperor in China. Thus, the system prevailing in the Baathist model is rather like a Baathist-military-mercantile autocratic complex in which the rhetoric of Baathism (Arabism initially) fulfilled functions similar to that of the religious discourse elsewhere. The conflict between this model of autocratic power and political Islam therefore assumed more violent dimensions whereas in Egypt the inter-penetration of the two forces at play in the post-Nasserian system operated differently.

Since the Baathist model, initially at least, had a genuine partisan base, it consequently became 'more efficient' in its dictatorial practices: bringing to heel the dissident political organisations (just as was done to at least some of the Syrian and Iraqi communists), destroying opponents (bourgeois liberals, non-compliant communists, Muslim

Brothers), absolutely subjugating the social organisations (by suppressing all activities at grassroots level, in the workers' unions for instance), whereas in Egypt, the regime had to make do with them. The system's weaknesses are attributed to other equally objective factors, particularly specific regional characteristics and the ethnic and religious diversity of the two countries. This diversity was managed in a dubious if not unskilful manner, to say the least, which in any case did not give a single thought to the principles of democracy. The supreme leaders' personal qualities and flaws therefore became a determining factor. A typical example was Hafez El Assad, a patient, diplomatic and intelligent leader in Syria, who incidentally had direct experience of confrontation with Israeli expansionism, the strategic ambitions of which he managed to contain through firm resistance without falling for the illusion of 'negotiated solutions' under the guidance of American diplomacy. As regards Iraq, a series of murderous military officers – from Abdel Salam Aref to Saddam Hussein – led their country to the tragic impasse in which it finds itself today.

The initial populism has faded away, but may reappear in the frame of the on-going 'revolutions'. The military–mercantile complex has embarked on an *infitah*, unconfirmed but visible in the eyes of public opinion, and worthy of recognition in one way or another. The legitimacy and credibility of the original vision of society and of the attendant Pan-Arab discourse are therefore considerably eroded. The political and social struggles are resurfacing actively. The fact that a thousand Syrian intellectuals signed a petition pressing for democracy, without facing repression (a novelty), probably foreshadows the starting point.

Algeria had a different history. Here, the national liberation struggle assumed another dimension under the leadership of the National Liberation Front (FLN), an authentic and powerful party comparable, at this level, to the communist parties of China or Vietnam, even if it was distinguished by its ideology (actually limited to the national claim), its vision of society (or rather the absence of the latter) and therefore by the social content of the resultant power. Similarly, it can be said that, national awareness in Algeria has been the result of this struggle and that the Algerian nation and FLN have therefore become synonymous.

The tragedy stemmed from the rapid substitution of the ALN (the army, a border unit that had not been the mainspring of the FLN struggle) for the FLN right from July 1962, or probably earlier, and subsequently at the time of Boumediene. Hoisted to the summit of power, and the exclusive centre for final decisions, the army destroyed the legitimacy and credibility of the FLN. Algerian populism did not outlive Boumediene. In choosing Chadli to succeed Boumediene, the army ceased to be unified and disciplined, as each of its generals grabbed a segment of the military–mercantile powers – the Mameluke way. Algeria entered into a period of turbulence, serious political conflict and repeated social struggles that simultaneously produced the worst (the reality to date) but also the best possible results (without that being the outcome of a fake and groundless optimism).

This is because the Algerian people aspire to political and social democracy probably more than any other Arab people. This aspiration certainly dates back to the colonial era, to the ambiguity of its discourse and to the forms of resistance it generated. Not even the FLN populism of the glorious era of Boumediene's short reign could really curtail such an aspiration. The Algerian Charter of 1964 (a true copy of the Nasserian model, promulgated in 1961), which was revised in 1976, asserted a few major principles aimed at merging social interests, which were not being granted recognition because of their allegedly conflicting nature.

In reality, therefore, other 'power centres' had to be recognised (in the Egyptian fashion). The first comprised workers' unions, which were important, active and demanding (at least at the grassroots level), with rebellious militants in the bureaucratically imposed departments. Improperly subjected to the FLN, they have become active during the last few years: now, thousands of strike actions and 'incidents' are recorded each year. On the other hand, the peasantry, brutalised and altogether destroyed by colonisation and the liberation war, could not assert itself as an autonomous force, in spite of the hopes initially placed in the 'self-management' of domains recovered from colonisation in the 1960s. That is why the 'agrarian revolution' proclaimed by Boumediene was a binding official order that did not depend on the support of any peasant movement. It was later smashed silently, in the same way as it was 'made'. Otherwise, the peasant question found expression in ethnic diversity – through perpetuation of the Berber phenomenon. But here too, the deplorable management of this real diversity as part of a poorly designed Arabisation policy, and the constant negation of the problem in the tradition of autocratic powers, produced no results other than making the problem explode through many crises.

Another explosion that foreshadowed crisis took place in 1988 in the form of an action taken by the low-class urban population, and particularly its marginalised youths, who had no future and whose more than deplorable conditions worsened as the new liberal policies abolished the vestiges of social populism. It was therefore not a revolt of the 'working class', neither a 'peasant rebellion' nor a movement of the middle classes and intellectuals demanding political democracy, but actually an explosion of new categories of the victims of contemporary capitalism, people without any tradition of organisation and without any ideological culture.

It is therefore understandable that this outburst, which resulted in the recourse to elections in 1992, ended in deadlock. For one thing, patrons of the 'Islamist movement' were intelligent enough to understand that the process gave them all the chances they needed. A furious electorate chose to say 'no' to the ruling authority, by saying 'yes' to the Islamists, who therefore presented themselves as the sole visible alternative. This was fortunate, since the ruling authority opted to fight back but proved incapable of re-forming or had no intention of doing so. Therefore Algeria landed in the infernal cycle created by two opposing accomplices who wanted to ensure that the sole option left for the people would be either 'them' or 'us'. There is no need to say more about the assassinations for which the Islamists claimed responsibility, particularly those perpetrated against journalists, teachers and democratic artists – personalities who could constitute the third and sole valid choice. There is no need to recall that the massacre of villagers in Mitidja enabled agribusiness speculators to buy up the best lands of the country at zero prices. Unlike the writings of several foreign analysts, it is Yasmina Khadra's novels that give a better insight into the nature of the logic dictating the option for political Islam.

However, the 1988 explosion created a shock such that right from 1989, the law authorised reforms in the country's political life. Fifty political parties and 55,000 associations were registered. What is looming on the horizon, beyond the figures that astonish observers, lies in both range of aspirations to political and social democracy and the objective possibility of their crystallising around a 'third force' that is potentially the most powerful. That phenomenon has not materialised to date for reasons that are difficult to accept – personal conflict between resurrected 'historic leaders'. The proliferation of associations actually engaged in the fight for democracy and social reforms – in defence of human rights, against torture and deliberate killings, for revision of the family law, for cultural rights of the Berber people, etc, do not constitute an alternative to the fundamental shortage of leaders, no more than did the increasing working class struggles pointed out earlier on.

Unfortunately, what is lacking is a unified popular leadership from which an alternative could be developed in all of its dimensions: defining an authentic economic and social development policy (that will not be pure rhetoric or the expression of a populist nostalgia); defining a new citizenship, a specific code of democratic rights; defining a modern nationality, at the same time Arab and respectful of the Berber reality; defining the terms of compromise between the conflicting interests of the social classes and groups; and defining the role of the state and linkages with the global system. That is a lot to do.

For its part, Sudan presents two major contradictions, which have not found a solution – and will not find any – through the acts of violence perpetrated for half a century. Political Islam – in power here – has proved in turn that it was incapable of finding a solution.

The first of these contradictions opposes the rural world of the Arab-Islamic North to its urban counterpart. Sudan's rural areas are closely managed by two brotherhoods – the Ansar and the Khatmia – based on a model dominant in the African Sahel from Senegal to the Red Sea.

The two major political parties (Mahdists and the National Democratic Party), which are closely linked to frontiers of the brotherhoods (and constitute the historical Islam actually existing in Sudan) are therefore assured of their victory in any election, even though they obviously have no programme apart from the one aimed at managing the society as it is. In contrast, the urban sector is surprisingly developed: there are powerful workers' unions (particularly in the railways sector, which is vital to this vast country), a vanguard students' union, professional organisations comprising active and democratic middle classes (an exception or almost unique in the Arab world), blossoming community life involving women's movements and the strong ideological influence of the communist party.

This conflict is insoluble, for it dictates the changeover from military dictatorships, behind which are rallied the two brotherhoods, amidst popular democratic demonstrations which have the potential to terminate the existing system.

The second conflict in Sudan opposes 30 million inhabitants of the Arab-Muslim north to the religiously different south (with between a quarter and one-third of the population). Sudanese governments are unable to consider managing this contradiction other than through constant war, whereas it is not difficult to think up a solution based on democracy, local autonomy and recognition of diversity. At any rate, this solution is advocated by all the democratic forces of the north, particularly, the communist party, and is even implemented by these forces for very short periods (never exceeding a few months) in places where they wield power, only to be called into question by reactionary forces which are ever ready to use violence to topple the former group. This solution is also recommended by political forces of the south, whose army – under John Garang – is designated as the Sudan Peoples Liberation Army (without reference to secession), not by chance. This page has been turned with the independence of South Sudan.

The successful intrusion of political Islam has been the outcome of weariness due to repeated failures, the massive injection of Saudi financial resources (channelled through a powerful mercantile class that is itself affiliated to the brotherhoods), and the tactical genius of a very ambitious power-hungry religious fanatic, Hassan Tourabi. In concluding an alliance directly with the military dictatorship (of Nimeiry, and subsequently al-Bashir) while short-circuiting the brotherhoods, Tourabi dreamt (or, while seeking in reality to entrench his power, pretended to be dreaming) about 'purging' and 'Wahhabising' the country's political Islam (hence, the support enlisted from Saudi Arabia).

The resources used by the military–Islamic dictatorship were therefore meant to be 'modern' and to put an end to the 'toleration' of the historic brotherhood Islam. This explains the series of harsh laws prohibiting free union activity (1992), subjugating community life

# The Drift of the National Popular Project

(especially the blossoming of associations in charge of humanitarian relief operations in this country plagued with war and famine – the law of 1995), gagging the press (law of 1996) etc. The fact remains that all the attempts made to substitute a network of new 'modern' institutions – controlled by Tourabi's personal power – for the prohibited democratic organisations produced no result, strictly speaking. The few 'NGOs' that appeared to survive the massacre have been wholly reabsorbed by the brotherhoods.

Obviously, the regime's economic and social actions could only end in disaster: totally subjected as it is to the logic of globalised liberalism – to the extent of caricaturing the political racketeering of the military–Islamic–mercantile clans – the political Islam in power in Sudan could only gruesomely aggravate all of the problems.

The regime adopted a casual attitude towards this drift by allowing the war in the south to peter out, by allowing all the western provinces (Kordofan, Darfur) – mainly Muslim – and the eastern provinces (Kassala) to be governed by way of semi-secession. The regime's main concern has been to keep up appearances by remaining masters of the street in the capital and in the immediate neighbourhoods. Its principal achievement therefore consisted of creating the so-called people's defence and student security networks, recruited from among the *lumpen*, to do no more than terrorise people, in the Iranian Pasdaran fashion.

The Achilles heel of the system is its total lack of any kind of legitimacy, which does not allow for political succession. Any Islamic power in Sudan other than the brotherhoods will have much difficulty taking root in Sudan, unlike Iran, where the *wilaya al faqih* is supported by a real national church (Shiite in this case) established as an institution dominating the state, in contrast to Saudi Arabia, whose monarchy links tribal legitimacy with the Wahabite version of Islam (or Morocco, whose monarchy is both national and religious in character).

The democratic opposition is not dead. It has survived all the brutalities of political Islam. However, virtually all of its leadership has been compelled to go into exile in Egypt, which hosts the National Democratic Alliance of Sudan, created in Asmara in 1995 from the merger of all the parties and organisations prohibited in Sudan. Egypt, which has never thought of treating Sudanese nationals as aliens, has therefore received an indefinite number of emigrants estimated at at least two million (the majority being ordinary workers obviously fleeing their country's declining economic life). At any rate, the potentially powerful front has no programme to enable it to co-ordinate struggles – which remain isolated, but frequent in the country – and strengthen their capacity to crystallise into an alternative.

Based on a twofold national and religious legitimacy, the Moroccan monarchy encouraged democratic reforms so long as they pleased the king. Moreover, such initiatives have the advantage of not threatening the local dominant classes or the global system. However, it must not be forgotten that the growing contradiction between the hopes nurtured by these positive developments on the one hand and, on the other, the symptoms of social crisis – which this kind of democracy makes it impossible to alleviate – may cause a violent explosion one day.

Whereas elsewhere – in Egypt, Tunisia and Iraq for example – national liberation struggles were compelled to distance themselves from, or even to oppose, the local monarchies, in Morocco things were different. Istiqlal – the movement's conservative wing – which dominated the political scene for a long time and never became negligible, intended to do nothing more than restore Morocco's sovereignty and monarchy. The modernist wing itself was compelled to silence its views on the monarchy. At any rate, this modernist wing had many bases in the country. These included powerful workers' unions that remained so, despite the erosive effects of economic liberalisation and unemployment. The unions even managed to safeguard their autonomy not only vis-à-vis the state (which never sought to subjugate them – since it was not a populist state) but also vis-à-vis their political allies and defenders (UNFP, which became USFP, and the communist party, now PPS), the growing middle class itself, which aspires to attain portions of the power monopolised by the Maghzen (the court) and the peripheral business bourgeoisie groups, which were themselves excluded from the Maghzen.

The phases through which the monarchy made gradual concessions to these forces are well known: from the first parliamentary elections of 1963 to the constitutional amendments of 1962 and 1996, from the first 'democratic' experiences (that is, in accepting that the government emerged from relatively fair elections) to the one that brought USFP and its leader, Abdel Rahman Youssofi, into the government in 1998, it is said that the system was developing into a parliamentary monarchy, which would preserve its religious aura. After all, is not the queen of England the head of the Anglican church?

The Moroccan authority therefore has no serious political problems. The Moroccan middle classes have no 'problem of identity', unlike in neighbouring Algeria. By the way, the Moroccan system has managed its cultural-ethnic diversity without provoking cleavages in the nation, according to the traditional principle of duality between the Maghzen (urban areas and neighbouring countryside) and the Bled Siba (distant countryside, the majority being of the Berber stock), while the king renews tribal allegiance without ever touching the autonomy of the local chieftainships. In taking the initiative to promote the Amazigi culture and language, the Moroccan system never considered that there could be a contradiction between Arabness, Islam and the Berber reality. Political Islam, which is trying to make a breakthrough here, just as it did elsewhere, is confronted with a Maghzen religious legitimacy, which to date it has been unable to call into question. On the other hand, however, the ruling power is confronted with social problems that are assuming increasingly serious dimensions, as none of the country's successive governments, not even those that can rightly boast about democratic legitimacy, ever tried to get out of the rut of globalised liberalism. It is therefore not by chance if here too, the repeated explosions are the work of the urban poor, the new class of victims of modern capitalism – explosions contained or repressed by violence amidst the silence of the leading democratic forces. But for how much longer?

Of all the contemporary Arab politicians, Bourguiba in Tunisia was the one who had the greatest secular convictions – although not democratic ones. His successor, Ben Ali, continued in this path, while maintaining an odious police dictatorship (on the pretext of fighting Islamist infiltration) and a frenzied attempt to seize all the wealth of the country for those nearest to him and for his family.

According to the criteria of the World Bank, Tunisia and Morocco have had a certain 'economic success'. But according to the analyses of political economy critics in these two countries, this success is very vulnerable, as it is based mainly on tourism. Two safety valves have encouraged pursuit of this model: the delocalisation of some parts of European industry, such as ready-made garments, and emigration. These taps have now been turned off and violence could no longer be avoided. It enabled the Tunisian people to chase Ben Ali out of the country.

## Bibliography

Amin, Galal (2001) *What Happened to Egypt* (in Arabic), Cairo, Dar Al Shorouk

Finkelstein, Norman (2000) *The Holocaust Industry: Reflections on the Exploitation of Jewish Suffering*, London, Verso

Fondation Abderrahim Bouabid (2010) *Le Maroc a-t-il une Strategie de Développement Économique?*, Rapport 2010, Rabat

Gouda, Khalek, writings in Arabic magazines and journals

Abdel-Fadil, Mahmoud, writings in Arabic magazines and journals

# Conclusion: A Formidable Challenge

Most of this book (chapters 2 to 5) had been written before the explosion of 2011, the importance of which convinced me to analyse it in the first chapter.

Chapter 5 had already analysed the conflicts and struggles in the Arab world, from which it could be understood by us, if not by all the 'foreign observers', that the explosion would happen. The analysis also stressed the confusions and impasses in which these struggles remain embedded. From the start I posed the questions in Chapter 5: Will these struggles be 'appropriated' by political Islam or will they manage to liberate themselves from that backward-looking illusion? Will the struggles succeed in uniting around a positive, social, economic and political project that is a genuine alternative?

The explosion of 2011 makes it possible to imagine an effective alternative response to the challenge. But the challenge is formidable and it is not impossible that the movement will become bogged down, or fail. This would be because periods of decline, such as those of the last 40 years, delay the crystallisation of coherent alternatives. In such periods critical thought also suffers from the decline of society. The confusions of the Nahda, which were at the origin of the national and popular response it evoked, are an example of the tragic insufficiency of Nasserism and the other expressions of national populism at the forefront of the Arab stage between 1950 and 1980, which I also analysed in Chapter 5. Is there going to be, then, a repetition of this tragic aborting, because the movements suffer from the insufficiencies and confusions of critical thinking of the last four decades?

It is a formidable challenge and not only for the Arab and Islamic world. It is for all the radical left, in both the South and the North. This is because the transient triumph of the capital of generalised and globalised monopolies has inoculated people with the 'liberal virus' (the title of one of my works, 2004) all over the world. This virus convinces its victims of the false thesis of 'capitalism as the end of history' at the very time that the system has run its course. It has become a synonym for many of the invasions of barbarism and it no longer has the necessary legitimacy to ensure the stability of its reproduction. The submission that accepts the requirements of this chaotic reproduction thus finds its necessary compensation in support for obscurantism, formulated in religious, ethnic or communitarian terms, according to the circumstances. The general adhesion to 'moneytheism', with the US setting the example, is thus accompanied by a retreat into obscurantist forms. In this context I refer to my article 'L'internationale de l'obscurantisme' (2011a). In the Arab and Islamic world, this association of complementary alienations, mercantile and religious, which is reflected in support for both submission to the 'market' and the project for the theocratic state (the 'Islamisation of politics and society') is a mortal threat to all progress towards the democratisation of society, social progress and the adoption of the necessary anti-imperialist positions.

The decline of senile capitalism – that is, 'the autumn of capitalism' – does not automatically bring about advances towards a better alternative perspective – 'the spring of the people'. These two realities could become two sides of the same coin – or not. But there could be no coincidence unless, and to the extent that, the struggles of the peoples in the South and in the North succeed in building their convergences into a universal and pluralistic socialist perspective (respecting diversity in the invention of the future). Only in this way can they put to rout capital's responses to its decline, which, in their turn, can only lead to generalised barbarism. History is not written before it has been lived.

As for the countries of the region there are several possible candidates for 'emerging': Egypt, Turkey, Iran and Algeria. But this emergence cannot be soundly based in the long term unless alternative systems, built up through the present struggles, move beyond the simple adoption of rhetorical, anti-imperialist postures and effectively delink themselves from imperialist globalisation, working for social progress and the democratisation of society. This formidable challenge, thus defined, may evolve in different ways, favourable or unfavourable, for the emergence of the peoples and nations concerned.

The democratic question cannot be reduced to the formula of representative electoral democracy, which is itself in crisis. Its alternative – the democratisation of society in all its dimensions – is not only 'difficult'. Response to the challenge does not exclude possible formulas such as 'enlightened despotism' (as opposed to obscurantist

## Conclusion: A Formidable Challenge

despotism, or police despotism, in short). These 'solutions' have flourished in the distant and recent past and they have not lost their potential for renewal. But so can democratisation, especially when it is associated with social progress and forms part of the construction of an authentic multipolar world.

The adversary, globalised monopoly capitalism, has various formulas for the peripheries (the South) but they do not differ greatly: police dictatorship without a project (the dominant model over the last 40 years) or conservative theocratic (or ethnocratic) dictatorships (Washington's current project) – at best, given the appearance of powerless electoral democracy.

Western opinion (if that term has any meaning) all too easily believes that there is no alternative to political Islam for the countries concerned. Fear of falling into the trap of Islamophobia makes it all too easy to accept this sad alternative – when it is not one. A number of works published in Great Britain and in the United States (see for example, Rostami-Povey 2010) put forward the argument that 'the Islamisation of power and of society' – in this case, Iran – is not incompatible with 'progress'. It is constantly repeated that in Islamic Iran, the marriage age of girls has been raised, as has the number of women at work, illiteracy has been reduced as well as infant mortality, while the number of students has increased, etc. However, these statistics, certainly not without importance, also apply almost everywhere (Egypt, for example) and they only mean that no society can completely escape from certain minimum requirements of the 'evolution of the modern world'. But they do not mean that there has been a general systemic evolution that is equal to the challenge.

The failure of Iran to impose itself as an 'emerging' power, is not unrelated to the Islamist ideology that cannot imagine an economic system other than that of the existing market – an insignificant version of the 'bazaar', as pointed out by Saeed Rahnema (2010) and as I myself have written with reference to Somalia (2011b). It is not very different with the Muslim Brothers in Egypt. This 'market economy, miserable and dependent' is perfectly compatible with an equally lamentable interpretation of the sharia, reduced to implementing brutal forms of forced submission on women and the application of penal law. The battle for secularism conditions, in the Muslim world as elsewhere, the possibilities of social and democratic advances, which are themselves the condition for a sustainable emergence of the nations and peoples concerned.

In this book I have tried to convince the reader that the events under way will have no meaning, in the sense of being able to confront the challenge, unless a long-term view is taken of their implications. As always, the past can enlighten the present. But, inversely and complementarily, decrypting present events helps to give meaning to a reading of the past.

## Bibliography

Amin, Samir (2004) *The Liberal Virus: Permanent War and the Americanization of the World*, New York, Monthly Review Press

Amin, Samir (2011a) 'L'internationale de l'obscurantisme', Pambazuka News, 18 July

Amin, Samir (2011b) 'Is there a solution to the problems of Somalia?', Pambazuka News, 17 February

Amin, Samir (2010) *From Capitalism to Civilisation: Reconstructing the Socialist Perspective*, New Delhi, Tulika Books

Rahnema, Saeed (2010) 'Ahmadinejad: anti-imperialist or deceptive populist?', paper delivered at an Iranian Human Rights Society debate, York University, Toronto, 25 November

Rostami-Povey, Elaheh (2010) *Iran's Influence: A Religious-Political State and Society in its Region*, London, Zed Books

# Index

Abdeljelil, Mustafa Muhammad, 40
Abderahim Bouahid Foundation, 169
Aboud (general), 154–55
Achcar, Gilbert, 130
Afghanistan: in ancient trade system, 91; communist party in, 150–53, 163; political Islam in, 139; Soviet intervention in, 156; US aid to Taliban in, 33
Africa: liberation movements in, 146; as periphery, 114; US military bases in, 40
agrarian reform, 28, 201–3
agriculture: in Egypt, 199–200; peasantry in, 200–206
Al Ahram, 218
Alexander (the Great; king, Macedon), 85–86, 96, 112, 117
Algeria, 220–23; internal reforms in, 10–12; revolution in, 74–76
Ali, Ben, 48, 73, 227, 228
Allende, Salvador, 50
Alliance of Socialist Forces (Egypt), 28
al Qaida, in Yemen, 7
America, 116; colonisation of, 106
Amin, Kassem, 130
Andréani, Jacques, 164
Arab League (League of Arab States), 191–92
Arab Mashreq, 85
Arab nationalism, 189
Arab spring, 6–7, 18, 38–42; future of, 70–76
Arab Workers Union, 191
Arab world, 18, 95–96; ancient Middle Eastern civilizations and, 85–86; current Europe and, 177–78; current status of, 168; education in, 54; historic European hostility toward, 120; Nahda in, 129–30; national popular project of, 170; Pan-Arabism in, 189–93; radical nationalism in, 146–47; tributary form of, 104–5

Aref, Abdel Salem, 157, 220
Arrighi, Giovanni, 104
al-Assad, Bashar, 79–80
El Assad, Hafez, 12, 220
Atlantic Alliance, 164, 165
autocratic states, 132–34
Al Azhar University, 30, 211, 217–18

Baathist parties and regimes, 219–20; in Iraq, 154, 157, 172–74; Pan-Arabism of, 190; in Syria, 12, 40–41
Baghdad Pact (1955), 170
Bahrain, 41
*baltagui*, 213
Bandung Conference (1955), 24, 69, 143
Bandung era of non-alignment, 6, 71, 142–45; end of, 145–46; socialism and, 160
Bangladesh, 206
banks and banking, 149
Banna, Hassan el, 37
barbarians, 103, 121
Barcelona conference (1995), 177, 178
Bardo Museum (Tunis), 72, 74
Beblawi, 67
Behrain, 7
Belalloufi, Hocine, 11
Belhadj, 76
Ben Ali, Zine El Abidine, 9
ben Laden, Osama, 58
Berbers (people), 223, 227
Boikov, 40
Boumediene, Houari, 221
bourgeoisies: in Egypt, during 1950s, 68; in Egypt, in reactionary bloc, 29; revolutions by, 108
Bourguiba, Habib, 9, 39, 73, 227
Bourguibism, 8
Bremer, Paul, 79
BRICS (Brazil, Russia, India, China and South Africa), 71, 80, 81
Buddhism, 91, 92; in China, 112

Bush, George W., 25, 171
business associations, 216–17
Byzantine empire, 85, 112

capitalism, 229–31; during Bandung era, 144–45; beginnings of, 109–10; decline of, 42; democracy associated with, 161; in Egypt, under Sadat, 64; European development of, 95, 105–8, 120; in Japan, 114; as "market economies," 164–65; in Middle East, 97–98; modernity and, 128, 130; political Islam and, 139
Carter, Jimmy, 165
central Asia, 95
Central Intelligence Agency (CIA), 50; in creation of Muslim Brotherhood, 195; in Egypt, 26, 27, 48, 49; in Iraq, 174; in Syria, 41
Chadli Benjedid, 221
*Charlie Hebdo* (magazine), 72
Chebab al intifada, 186, 187
China: as adversary of US, 77–78; ancient, trade of, 86–95; ancient civilization in, 84; communist party in, 166; Confucian-Chinese tributary system in, 98; links between Japan and, 115–16; Middle East and, 177; peasants in, 206; post-Mao, 145; revolution in, 162–63; tributary mode in, 104, 111–12; tributary society in, 122–23
Christianity and Christians, 111; in Iraq, 174; under Roman empire, 113
Clinton, Hillary, 25, 27, 34
Comintern (Communist International), 145
communist parties, 151–58; in China, 162–63; as democratic forces, 163; in Egypt, 205–6, 212; in Iraq, 172, 174
communists, 68
comprador bourgeoisie: in Egypt, 10–11, 29, 32, 75; oil mania and, 193
Conference on Security and Cooperation in Europe (CSCE), 164

Confucianism–Taoism: in China, 98, 112; in Japan, 114
cooperatives, agricultural, 201, 202, 205, 215
Copts, 22, 25, 33; excluded from Egyptian political life, 35; Muslim Brotherhood and, 36
corruption, 38
cotton, 197
Council of the Gulf States, 67–68
Council of Ulemas (Egypt), 57
Courmont, Barthélémy, 77
Crusades (Frankish wars), 125
Cuba, 166

Daesh, *see* Islamic State
Darraj, Fayçal, 104
democracy, 13–16, 62–63, 73, 164–67; after Arab spring, 8; democratisation process toward, 72; depoliticisation and decline of, 61; in Islamic governments, 180; political Islam and, 59–61, 136; socialism and, 160–63
democratic movements: in Egypt, 26–28; reactionary block opposition to, 29–31
Democratic National Union (Egypt), 212
democratic socialism, 161
depoliticisation: decline of democracy and, 61; Islam and, 13–14, 60; Nasserism and, 59
Dowidar, Mohamed, 198

Eastern Europe, 42
education, 54; Al Azhar University, 30, 211, 217–18
Egypt: after 1967 war, 184; agriculture in, 199–200; ancient, 88; under British control, 23, 141–42; British invasion of (1882), 173; chronology of events in, 45–47; comprador bourgeoisie in, 10–11; debates of 1950s in, 68–70;

Index

democratic movement in, 26–28; depoliticisation in, 60; economy of, 197–99; elections in, 56–58; emergence of, 21–22, 63; limits of Nasserism in, 147–49; lumpen development in, 64–67; media on, 47–48; Napoleon's conquest of, 125; under Nasser, 23–24; after Nasser, 12; neoliberalism in, 53; peasantry in, 200–206; political Islam in, 7–9, 31–34; political parties in, 212–13; reactionary bloc in, 29–31; revolution in, 74–76, 209; under Sadat and Mubarak, 24–25; tributary society in, 123; US polices toward, 34–38, 81–82
elections: in Algeria, 222; depoliticisation and, 60; in Egypt, 38, 46–48, 56–58, 212, 213; in Lebanon, 132; in Morocco, 227; in Palestine, 187
Engels, Friedrich, 121
Ennahda (Tunisia), 8
Erdoğan, 79, 81
Ethiopia, 23
Eurocentrism, 128; political Islam and, 131, 134
Europe: crystallisation of capitalism in, 120; development of capitalism in, 95, 110; in Euro-Mediterranean partnership, 176–82, 193; mercantalist transition in, 105–8; modernity in, 119; Renaissance in, 128, 129; sea transport used by, 116; take-off of, 93–94; trade between rest of ancient world and, 85, 89; tributary systems in, 113
European Union: Arab world and, 177, 193; Turkey in, 81; Union of the Mediterranean proposal of, 181
evolution: on humans, 99–100; social, 108–10

Fabius, Laurent, 50
Fadil, Mahmoud Abdel, 169
Federation of Egyptian Industries, 69
feudalism, 106–7, 113, 121
film, in Egypt, 218
Finkelstein, Norman, 183
FIS (*Front Islamique du Salut*; Islamic Salvation Front; Algeria), 76
Frank, Andre Gunder, 104; on lumpen development, 14, 53; on permanent world system, 99, 101; Pirenne and, 118–21
Free Officers (Egypt), 69, 147, 211, 219
French Revolution, 162
fundamentalisms, 72

Gaddafi, Muammar, 39, 40, 50; South Yemen and, 157; Sudan intervention by, 155
Garang, John, 224
General Workers' Union of Egypt, 214
Genghis Khan (Mongol ruler), 92, 94, 103, 114, 116
Georgia, 166
Germany, 42
globalisation, 6
Gorbachev, Mikhail, 156, 165
Gouda, Abdel Khalek, 169
Gramsci, Antonio, 147
Great Britain: Egypt invaded by (1882), 173; Egypt under control of, 23, 36, 125, 141–42; Muslim Brotherhood created by, 195
Guevara, Che, 190
Gulf Arab states: migrations to, 192; Muslim Brotherhood supported by, 52; Syria and, 13; as US ally, 78
Gupta state (India), 113, 118

Habache, George, 190
el Hafez, Yassine, 104
Hamas, 186, 196
Han dynasty, 118
Hassan II (king, Morocco), 196
Hawatmeh, Naief, 190
Hellenism, 112, 124–25
Helsinki agreement (1975), 164

Heykal, Hassanein, 218
Hinduism, 113, 114
humankind, 99–100
human rights, 179
Hussein, Adel, 212
Hussein, Saddam, 14, 62, 157, 220; defeat of, 172; Iraq under, 174–75; Kuwait invaded by Iraq under, 173

Ibrahim, Sanallah, 190
Imam, Mohamed Mahmoud El, 198
imperialism, 13–16, 105; during Bandung era of, 144
India: ancient civilization in, 84, 86, 87; ancient trade of, 91, 95; Middle East and, 177; tributary society in, 122–23; tributary system in, 113, 116
Indonesia, 114, 209
International Criminal Court (ICC), 79
intifada, 186–88
Iran, 79; ancient, 85; in Baghdad Pact, 170; depoliticisation in, 14; goals of US in, 15; Islamic revolution in, 55, 60, 158–64; Islamisation of, 231; nuclear program of, 80; political Islam in, 139; Turkish–Mongolian invasions of, 88; war between Iraq and, 173
Iraq, 150–52, 154, 157, 220; Baathist Party in, 219; in Baghdad Pact, 170; destruction of, 171–72; education system in, 54; after Hussein, 14–15; under Hussein, 62, 174–75; permanent US occupation of, 172–73; Turkish–Mongolian invasions of, 88; US interventions in, 78–79
Islam: in ancient world, 85; in central Asia, 114; depoliticisation and, 14, 60; in Kazakhstan and Russia, 92–93; Mamelukes and, 126–27; modern, 54; in Morocco, 12; Muslim caliphate of, 112; replacing local religions, 115; secularism versus, 194; spread of, 117; Sufism in, 33–34; *see also* political Islam

Islamic Renaissance, 135–36
Islamic State (ISIL; ISIS; Daesh), 79, 81
Islamophobia, 231
Israel, 62; in 1967 war, 24; allied with US and Saudi Arabia, 34, 51; armaments of, 176; Egypt and, 8, 54; in Euro-Mediterranean partnership, 178; Iran and, 80; Lebanon invaded by, 158; Palestine and, 182–89; Syria and, 13; as US ally, 78, 170
Istiqlal (Morocco), 226
Italy, 93; development of capitalism in, 120; mercantalist capitalism im, 106

Japan: links between China and, 115–16; as peripheral tributary, 113–14; in triad with US and Europe, 63, 77
Jews, 185

Kassem, Abdel Karim, 154
Kawakibi, Abd al-Rahman, 130
Kazakhstan, 91–93
Kefaya (organization), 7, 25, 48
Kerry, John, 79–80
Khadra, Yasmina, 222
Al Khaleej (television network), 218
Khmer empire, 114
Korea, 112
Kurds, 174
Kushāna empire (India), 113, 114
Kuwait, 157, 173

Labour Party (Egypt), 212
Latin America, 160
Lausanne Agreement, 80
League of Arab States (Arab League), 191–92
Lebanon, 132, 158
Lenin, V. I., 105
liberation theology, 135
Libya, 12, 78; Arab spring in, 39–40; revolts in, 50
Lin Chun, 162
literature, in Egypt, 218
lumpen development, 64–67

# Index

Maghreb, 193
Mahdists (party, Sudan), 223
Maistre, Joseph de, 136
Malaysia, 114
Mameluke state and autocracy, 105, 126–28, 211; in current Middle East, 207–9
Mansour, Fawzy, 96, 104
Mao Tse Tung, 38
Marx, Karl, 101, 109; on capitalist production, 104; on stages of civilisation, 121; on universal suffrage, 161
Mashreq region, 85, 193
Al Mawdudi, Abul Ala, 136
media, 218
mercantalism, 105–8, 117
Mesopotamia, 88
middle classes, 195; development of, 120; in Egypt, 26, 210; political Islam and, 216
Middle East: ancient civilizations of, 84–88; Arab conquest of, 124; Arab-Islamic civilization in, 95–96; as central region for trade, 116–17; in Euro-Mediterranean partnership, 176–82; proto-capitalism in, 97–98; stagnation of, 95; trade between ancient China and, 88–89; tributary society in, 123; tributary system in, 112
Middle East common market, 171, 193
migrations and migrants: within Arab world, 192; from Egypt to oil-producing countries, 204, 214; from Sudan to Egypt, 226
military power: in Algeria, 221; in Middle East countries, 207; of US, 169–75
Mitterand, François, 165
Mobutu, Sese Seko, 196
modernity, 128–30; in Arab world, 195; in Egypt, 36; limits and contradictions of, 130–31; Salafis opposed to, 10; secularism and, 194

modes of production, 100–101; mercantalist, 105–8
Mohamed (Prophet), on Chinese science, 87
Mohamed Ali, 11, 125, 127, 209
monarchies, 107, 113, 133; in Morocco, 226–27
Mongol empire, 116
Mongolia, 91–92, 94
Monroe doctrine, 170, 175
Morcos, Elias, 104
Morishima, Michio, 114
Morocco, 169; economy of, 227–28; monarchy in, 133, 226–27; possibilities of democratic evolution in, 12
Morsi, Mohammed, 46–48, 55, 67; in election of 2011, 56; in election of 2014, 68; opposition to, 69
Mouassassa Iqtisadia (Egyptian firm), 148
Mubarak, Hosni Said, 24, 27, 30; abdication of, 45; arrest of, 38; demonstrations against, 48, 69; Muslim Brotherhood and, 31
Mughal empire (India), 113
Muslim Brotherhood (Egypt): agrarian reform and peasantry opposed by, 28, 215–16; creation of, 23, 195; in current Egypt, 213; demands of, 37; on demands of protests, 45; democratic movement and, 26, 27; Egyptian constitution proposed by, 57; Egyptian government of, 46–48, 67; in election of 2012, 7; Free Officers and, 211; in Iraq, 157; during Mubarak rule, 24; Party of Freedom and Justice of, 35–36; political Islam of, 31–34, 76; in reactionary bloc, 29–31; Salafism and, 9, 10, 61; sharia under, 35; in Sudan, 155, 156; in Syria, 13, 41; triumph of, 51–55; in Tunisia, 73–74; US support for, 49, 81–82
Muslim caliphate, 85, 112, 124–25

Mussolini, Benito, 23

Nahda (organization), 128–30, 209; in Egypt, 36, 51; Salafism and, 61; in Tunisia, 73–74
Napoleon Bonaparte (emperor, France), 125
Nasser, Gamal Abd al-, 12, 69, 217; Egypt under, 213–14; Kuwait independence and, 157; peasantry under, 29–30; takes power, 23
Nasserism, 11, 22–24, 68–69, 75, 211; depoliticisation under, 59; Egyptian economy under, 198; in Iraq, 157; limits of, 147–49; lumpen development under, 64–67; professional associations controlled by, 216
Nasserite Party (Egypt), 204–5
National Council (Egypt), 28
National Democratic Alliance of Sudan, 225
National Democratic Party (Egypt), 29–31
National Democratic Party (Sudan), 223
Nationalist Party (Egypt), 141
National Liberation Front (FLN; Algeria), 220–21
national liberation movements, 6
National Transition Council (Libya), 40
NATO (North Atlantic Treaty Organization), 164, 165; Arab world and, 177; Baghdad Pact and, 170; intervention in Syria by, 50–51
neoliberalism, 6–7, 53, 179
Nimeiry, Jaafar, 155, 157
Non-Aligned Movement, 146; *see also* Bandung era of non-alignment
North Yemen, 157
nuclear weapons, 159

Obama, Barack: Egypt and, 25, 27, 34, 38; Muslim Brotherhood and, 10
oil (petroleum): in Iraq, 171; in Middle East, 146–47, 168, 169; political Islam and, 192–93

Organisation for Solidarity with the Peoples of Asia and Africa, 146
Oslo Peace Accords (1993), 184, 186–88
Ottoman empire, 85, 97, 125, 127

Pakistan, 34, 166
Palestine, 182–89; Europe and, 178–79; radical parties in, 190
Palestine Liberation Organisation (PLO), 185–87
Palestinian Authority, 186–88
Pan-Arabism, 189–93
Paris Commune, 162
Party of Freedom and Justice (Egypt), 35–36
patriarchy, 133
Patterson, Anne, 46
peasantry: in Algeria, 221–22; in Egypt, 29–30, 199–206, 215
Peres, Shimon, 188
peripheries: decline of capitalism in, 42; democracy in, 16, 60–61; repression of nationalism in, 53; trade between centres and, 115; in tributary systems, 110–11
Philippines, 41
Pirenne, Jacques, 109, 118–21
political Islam, 15–16, 134–40; in Algeria, 11, 76; Arab unity and, 192–93; democracy and, 59–61; depoliticisation leading to, 13–14; in Egypt, 7–9, 25, 30–34, 76; Eurocentrism and, 131; in Iran, 158; Islamic governments and, 180; in Morocco, 227; in Sudan, 224; in Tunisia, 7–9; US allied with, 78, 171
Pomeranz, Kenneth, 104
post-modernism, 133–34
Powell, Colin, 79
privatization of Egyptian economy, 64
professional associations, 191, 216
proletariat, rural, 201, 204
Putin, Vladimir, 166

Qatar, 218

# Index

Qing dynasty (China), 92

Rahnema, Saeed, 231
Raimbaud, Michel, 49, 51
Razek, Ali Abdel, 130
reactionary bloc, in Egypt, 29–31
Reagan, Ronald, 145
Reda, Rachid, 37; Achcar on, 130; Salafism and, 9, 23, 61; Wahhabite Islam and, 34
religions: in ancient civilizations, 89, 91; Buddhism, 92; cultural areas tied to, 102; in divisions of power, 208–9; incubation periods for, 112; Islam replacing local religions, 115; of Mamelukes, 127; modernity versus, 128; secularism and, 129; spread of, 103; state religions, 111; in tributary societies, 122; *see also* Christianity and Christians; Islam; political Islam
Renaissance, 128, 129
Roman empire, 113, 118
Russia, 15; invasions of, 88; Islam in, 92–93; Middle East and, 177; under Putin, 166; *see also* Soviet Union
Russian Revolution, 162

Saad, Ahmad Sadek, 96, 104
Sabbahi, Hamdeen, 46, 56, 68
Sadat, Anwar, 24, 30; after 1967 war, 184; on agrarian reform, 202; Egyptian constitution changed under, 35; Muslim Brotherhood and, 31; privatization of Egyptian economy under, 64; turn to right by, 211
Saladin (Salah El Dine), 125, 126
Salafism, 9–10, 30, 52, 61–62; in current Islam, 58; political Islam and, 33; in Saudi Arabia, 81
Saleh, Ali Abdullah, 80
Sassanid empire, 112
Saudi Arabia, 166; allied with US and Israel, 34, 35, 51; political Islam in, 58; Sudan and, 224; Yemen and, 80–81

SCAF (Supreme Council of the Armed Forces; Egypt), 55, 57
sciences: in China, 87; in Europe, 107
secularism, 129, 194, 195, 231–32; in Egypt, 209
Sedki Pasha, 23
September 11th terrorist attacks, 171
Shafiq, 46, 56
Sharaby, Hashem, 132–33
sharia (Islamic law), 35; in Egypt, 37, 57, 67; liberation theology and, 135
Sharif, Amir, 49
Sharon, Ariel, 184, 188
el-Shater, Khairat, 46
Shiites, in Iraq, 173–74
Sisi, Abdel Fattah el, 46, 57, 67–70
slavery, 121–22
socialism, 160–63; as "centrally planned economies," 164–65
socialist parties (Egypt), 28
Socialist Union (Egypt), 211, 212, 219
Somalia, 60, 78
South Africa, 187
South America, 41
South East Asia, 114
South Sudan, 224
South Yemen, 150–54, 157
Soviet Union: Arab world and, 177; collapse of, 156; Helsinki agreement and, 164; after World War II, 143; Zhdanov Doctrine of, 145; *see also* Russia
Stalin, Josef, 145
state: absolute monarchies as, 107, 113; autocratic, 132–34; religions of, 111
state terrorism, 176
strikes, 214–15
student movement, 217
Sudan, 78, 150–52, 154–58, 163, 223–26
Sudan Peoples Liberation Army, 224
Suez Canal, 23
Sufism, 33–34
Sunnis, in Iraq, 173–74
Syria: Arab spring in, 40–41; under Assad, 220; Baathist Party in, 219;

changing borders of, 189; current status of, 12–13; NATO intervention in, 50–51; US policy in, 79–81

Tagammu (party, Egypt), 28, 204–5, 212, 215
Taha, Mahmoud, 135
Taliban (Afghanistan), 33, 140, 195–96
Tantawi (Marshal), 46
taxation, 65, 66
technology: of China, 116; transfers of, 102–3
television, 218
terrorism, 72–73, 176
Tibet, 92
Tourabi, Hassan, 224, 225
Toynbee, Arnold, 108–9
tributary systems: development of, 98–104; diversity of, 104–5; mercantalism and, 105–8; world systems and, 110–23
Tunisia: Arab spring in, 39, 73–74; economy of, 227–28; political Islam in, 7–9
Turkestan (Uighuristan), 89, 90
Turkey: in Baghdad Pact, 170; Kurds in, 174; Syria and, 13, 50, 81; as US ally, 78; US support for, 34

Umma Party (Egypt), 141
Union of the Mediterranean, 181
unions: Arab Workers Union, 191; in Egypt, 214
United Arab Emirates, 154
United Arab Republic, 192
United Nations, 164–65; Arab League and, 191–92; Israel and, 183
United States: Africom military headquarters of, 40; allied with Saudi Arabia and Israel, 51; armed interventions by, 146–47; Egypt and, 8, 25, 32; Egypt policy of, 34–38, 54; geostrategy of, 77–82; Islamic Conference created by, 196; Israel and, 183–85; Middle Eastern policies of, 62–63; military aid to Egypt from, 30; military power of, 169–75; Muslim Brotherhood supported by, 49, 52; political Islam as ally of, 33, 139; under Reagan, 145; state terrorism by, 176; Syria and, 12, 13; after World War II, 143
urbanisation, 210

Vietnam, 112, 206
Vietnam War, 176

Wafd, 22, 23
Wahhabi Islam, 58; in Egypt, 33–35; Reda and, 58
women: in Afghanistan, 33; in Egypt, 35; under Islam, 194; Nahda and, 129; in Tunisia, 73
working classes, in Egypt, 214–15
World Bank, 14, 30, 65
world systems, ancient, 110–23

Yemen, 80–81; al Qaida in, 7; South Yemen and North Yemen merge, 157; *see also* South Yemen
Youssofi, Abdel Rahman, 227

Zaghoul, Saad, 141
Zaire, 196
Zennadi, Samia, 76
Zhdanov Doctrine (Soviet Union), 145
Zionism, 51, 183–84
Zirrik, Constantin, 104